About the Author

STEPHEN J. KRAUS IS AN author, speaker, and expert on the psychology of success. In his writings and speeches, he teaches the science of success, synthesizes decades of research on personal achievement, and explores the "greatest hits" of psychology's most fascinating research. At the same time, he de-bunks self-help snake oil and unmasks self-improvement urban legends. This unique combination – a rigorous scientist who empowers people with psychological tools for success – has even led some to call him a combination of Tony Robbins and Mr. Spock. He is Founder and President of Next Level Sciences Inc., a peak performance consultancy, and has consulted for many Fortune 500 corporations, as well as for the U.S. armed forces in their efforts to improve the recruiting, retention and performance of America's military personnel.

Steve is a featured speaker at business and scientific conferences throughout the world. He has appeared on television, and his insights are regularly quoted in the media. Steve's articles have appeared in outlets as diverse as *BrandWeek*, the *San Francisco Chronicle*, *Contemporary Psychology*, and a variety of scientific psychology journals. His article on the relationship between attitudes and behavior is one of the most widely referenced works on the topic in the psychological literature, and is cited in major textbooks.

Steve received his Ph.D. in social psychology from Harvard University at age 25, and twice won Harvard's award for excellence in teaching. Steve taught psychology at the University of Florida, where he was a campus favorite thanks to his teaching style of busting popular myths, illustrating psychological principles with vivid demonstrations, and translating scientific research findings into practical learning.

PSYCHOLOGICAL FOUNDATIONS OF SUCCESS

A Harvard-Trained Scientist

Separates the

Science of Success

from

Self-Help Snake Oil

To Bryce,
Best wishes for
great success!
Steve Kraus

PSYCHOLOGICAL FOUNDATIONS OF SUCCESS

A Harvard-Trained Scientist
Separates the
Science of Success
from
Self-Help Snake Oil

Stephen Kraus, Ph.D.

ChangePlanet Press
San Francisco, California

ChangePlanet Press (www.ChangePlanet.com)

ISBN 0-9725540-1-7
Library of Congress Control Number: 2002095452

PUBLISHER'S NOTE
This book is designed to provide accurate and authoritative information about the subject matter covered. It is sold with the understanding that the publisher is not rendering psychological, financial, or other professional services. If expert assistance or counseling is needed, the services of a competent professional should be sought.

Names and identifying characteristics of people in the book have been changed to protect their anonymity.

Book & cover design: Roz Abraham, Regent Press.

Bulk purchase discounts are available for sales promotions, premiums, fund raising or educational use. For information, please visit *www.NextLevelSciences.com*

Acknowledgements

IT IS DIFFICULT FOR A WRITER TO ADMIT that words are inadequate for describing some thoughts and emotions. But that is precisely the prospect I face as I thank those who helped make this book a reality. My family – Dad, Linda and Mark – have provided support in limitless ways: financial, emotional, intellectual, professional. The same can be said for my beautiful and brilliant fiancée, Simone. For my Dream Team of these four, there are no words to express my gratitude.

Others deserve thanks as well. My editor Lisa Alpine gave the manuscript a thorough reading, and guided me through the publication process. My friend Greg Crabb walked with me on the path toward greater achievement, giving me a fresh perspective on the process, and serving as a relentless role model of honor and integrity. Many others deserve thanks, not so much for their direct contributions to this book, but rather for their broader role in my intellectual development – I no doubt overlook many by limiting this list to Barry Schlenker, Gene Thursby, Robert Cialdini, Ellen Langer, Bob Rosenthal, Ralph Rosnow, and Amy Schafrann. Three additional role models deserve note, but sadly they are posthumous – Carl Sagan, Stephen Jay Gould, and Roger Brown each inspired me to synthesize and popularize science. Which brings me to my final, and perhaps greatest, debt – the one I owe to the scientists and scholars on whose work this book is based. This book synthesizes decades of research, but I would have nothing to synthesize were it not for the hard work of these men and women. I hope I have treated their work with the respect it so richly deserves.

Contents

Why

WRITING A BOOK is a massive undertaking, equal parts rewarding act of creation and self-inflicted torture. So for any book, I think "Why?" is a fair question. Why did I write this book? The answer was perhaps best captured by a friend of mine who once half-jokingly referred to me as a combination of Tony Robbins and Mr. Spock, and I have to confess there is a kernel of truth in that otherwise overly colorful description. Tony Robbins, famous for his firewalk seminars and slick infomercials, empowers people with psychological tools for success, and brings a fun, flamboyant style to self-improvement. For people of my generation, Spock was a Vulcan, not a pediatrician; *Star Trek's* Mr. Spock, a childhood hero of mine, was logical, rational, thorough and scientific. Moreover, Spock was a master of synthesizing information; Captain Kirk turned to him not for a delineation of isolated facts or research findings, but rather for a coherent plan of action based on the best available information, tempered by Spock's practical experience.

When those two influences are combined, the answer to the question "Why?" begins to come into focus. Serious scholars have learned a tremendous amount about success; psychologists, sociologists, and other social scientists have explored the differences between more successful and less successful people in many different domains through well-designed, carefully-controlled research. In getting a Ph.D. in social psychology from Harvard University, I began my career in that world of scientific research, and I knew the depth and power of the information there. Unfortunately, far too little of this research finds its way into mainstream success (i.e., self-help) books. The market for self-improvement is massive; success-oriented books regularly top best-seller lists, and millions more are spent annually on audiotapes, seminars, personal coaches, and the like. Although some of these products are excellent, it is equally clear that the strong demand for success tools has not always been met with quality offerings. Too often, these books and products are just success snake oil: naïve, repetitive, simplistic, ineffective, and sometimes just simply wrong. Frequently they are based purely on personal experience and often-repeated anecdotes, overlooking volumes of relevant, soundly-conducted research.

My objective in writing this book is to explore the art and science of success. I've integrated decades of research on human change and peak performance into a straightforward, empowering, empirically-based system for enhanced success and happiness that anyone can understand and use. Developing these scientifically-based tools has become my passion, and that answers the question of "Why?".

. . .

Lots of Footnotes: What's Up with That?

A book of science has some different requirements from most in the self-help genre. One is footnotes. Flipping through the pages of this book, you will notice a lot of footnotes. If your initial impression is that they are daunting or might be intrusive to the reading experience, then fear not. Reading the footnotes is optional, and skipping them will not substantially detract from the value that you will derive from the book. The footnotes are there for three main reasons:

• First, they help distinguish assertions based on scientific research from my own intuition and insights. This book is about the art and science of success, and footnotes generally document scientific findings, whereas the lack of footnotes generally implies my assertions about the art of success.

• Second, in some cases, footnotes contain information that may be less relevant to the casual reader, but still of interest to those who want to dig deeper on complex topics. These footnotes include more detailed research findings, esoteric philosophical arguments, methodological issues, and other relevant-but-tangential information. Footnotes containing this kind of substantive information are marked with an underlined number (for example, 4) much like a hyper-link on the Internet.

• Finally, the bulk of the footnotes are simply citations – that is, they give credit where credit is due. These document where the original studies or other sources can be found, enabling interested readers to find the original articles for more detailed information. Citations are a key part of the scientific process, preventing the perpetuation of "self-help urban legends," but they are also a courteous acknowledgement of the hard work and insights of others. Sadly, when today's success books do build on scientific research, they too often do so without attributing findings to the original sources or acknowledging the scholars who have devoted their careers to their research.

• • •

A Word About Science Writing and Success

In describing scientific studies on success, I focus on the bottom line: the key findings, and the implications for people seeking to achieve more. But you should know that the studies themselves are often far more sophisticated than I describe. Many use complex methodologies and statistical analyses to rule out plausible alternative hypotheses, demonstrate true cause-and-effect relationships, make precise comparisons versus control groups, and so on. To explain fully the methodology of each study would require a book many times this size. And more importantly, that book would have many fewer readers, because such methodological details, although crucial to the advancement of science, are less-than-scintillating tangents of little interest to most readers. Still, you should rest assured that the findings I describe are based on soundly-conducted, well-documented, sophisticated research. The vast majority of the studies I cite are published in "peer-reviewed journals" – meaning they are reviewed and approved for publication by experts who ensure the research is well-conducted and the conclusions are sound.

The bottom line conclusions that I draw are usually based not on a single study, but rather on a collection of studies using a variety of methodologies. Sometimes these studies yield conflicting results, or at the very least a range of results; when appropriate, I have used judgment and experience to synthesize conflicting findings into a coherent, actionable point of view. But that process also requires some simplification, as describing every bit of reasoning used in reconciling conflicting findings could easily add a thousand pages to this book. In particularly controversial fields, I detail my reasoning in the footnotes. More often, I provide citations for these studies so that interested readers can examine the original sources for more information, to explore the methodological details, or examine conflicting findings to reach their own conclusions. To help that effort, when possible, instead of citing detailed technical articles in academic journals, I cite more accessible books and review articles that will be of greater value to most readers. Interested readers can first turn to these sources for more detail on a given topic; those sources in turn cite many (often highly technical) journal articles for the hardy few who want to read the original sources.

Chapter One

Three Expectations
You Should Have
About This Book

Expectation #1:
Enjoy Yourself

ALTHOUGH THE WORDS "science" and "excitement" may not naturally go together in your mind, many people would agree that psychologists and other scientists have conducted some fascinating research on various aspects of human behavior. That compelling research makes my job as a writer much easier, but it should also raise your expectations – you have every right to expect this book to be fun and interesting reading. The fundamental insights into success that comprise this book, in and of themselves, should be enjoyable reading for anyone interested in the topic (and everyone should be). But we live in what is, in many ways, an entertainment-driven society, and I have tried to make this book entertaining as well. I have tried to balance scientific rigor with a sense of humor, and to present interesting ideas in creative ways. Moreover, the book answers a number of compelling (dare I say, "sexy") questions that help make it enjoyable reading, including...

• What separates the history's greatest artists, scientists and businesspeople from those who are merely good in their fields?
• What techniques do psychologists use with elite athletes to bring

about peak performance?

- What attitudes and actions are common among America's wealthiest people?
- Who successfully kicks habits like tobacco, alcohol and other drugs?
- Who loses weight and keeps it off?
- Who recovers from mental illness?
- How successful are people at identifying the drivers of success and happiness in their own lives?
- Does goal setting really enhance performance? And if so, what are the characteristics of effective goals?
- Do subliminal self-help tapes work?
- Why do some societies incorporate psychedelic drugs into cultural traditions like vision quests?
- Why do some self-help seminars involve walking barefoot on hot coals, and others involve verbal abuse?
- What scientifically-supported insight into happiness is a key element in the mythology of many cultures?

· · ·

Expectation #2:
Learn a Lot

An entire chapter of this book explores the emphasis that successful people put on learning, and certainly learning is a key objective of this book. Scientists have learned a tremendous amount about the nature of personal change and the keys to happiness. These *success basics* should be learned by everyone – they should be taught in our schools and our homes – but such life skills are too rarely taught explicitly. For some reason, no institution in our educational system routinely offers courses on "How to figure out what you want out of life, and how to get it." This book is a potential textbook for such courses, and is just one step in a larger effort to encourage people to take greater control of their lives. Just as important as learning these strategies for success is learning *why* they are effective. There is tremendous power in knowing why something works. It builds a sense of confidence and mastery; moreover, on a practical level, it enables you to better customize techniques to your needs, and better "adjust-on-the-fly" to changes in circumstance.

. . .

Expectation #3:
Improve the Quality and Trajectory of Your Life

The most crucial expectation you should have of this book is that it will improve the quality and trajectory of your life. We increasingly live in a bottom-line world, and the bottom line in evaluating a book is whether or not it adds value to your life. As a result, my objective is to have everyone who reads this book look back upon the experience as not only being fun and educational, but one which prompted some significant changes in their lives and an overall quickening in the rate of their personal progress. To use a term popular among business consultants, this book is designed to be *highly actionable*. At the very least, I hope that every reader takes away at least one actionable idea or technique that will be put to use in his or her life.

Encouraging change and growth is no small task, particularly because this book is read by many different types of people, each at different points in life and with different needs. Many of the people who read this book are already highly successful achievers, and they are looking for an extra edge to take them even further, or to achieve the often-elusive goal of balance. Some are seeking to reinvent themselves, and disprove F. Scott Fitzgerald's often-quoted but absolutely wrong remark that "there are no second acts in American lives." Still others are students using this book as a text in classes on life skills or "positive psychology." Many who read this book are entrepreneurs striving to build empires from nothing, or are driven salespeople seeking to rise to the top of their potentially lucrative profession. For others, their drive for achievement is manifests itself, not in career ambitions, but in a desire to build stronger families and communities. Some who read this book are struggling, at least in some aspect of their lives. Some are in therapy, and are looking for complementary tools and techniques to facilitate the process of therapeutic change. Others are struggling alone, perhaps with destructive patterns of eating, drinking, smoking or gambling. Some are unable to stop grieving for a loved one. Others question their ability to succeed. The list is endless. In each case, this book can help.

This book provides potent strategies and tools for success, and it potentially boosts the motivation to use them, but it cannot do the work for anyone. Change and success, as we shall learn, take work. The promise of easy change is tempting, and is a favorite promise of marketers, but it is generally too good to be true. We all want the quick fix – diet pills over sensible eating and exercise, for example – but they rarely work in the long-term. Simply put, this book involves work; not just reading it, but actively thinking about how it applies to your life and putting its principles into action. No book can provide direct answers to a specific individual's problems, but it can provide tools that the reader can customize and apply to his or her life. Consider, for example, the underachiever who wanders aimlessly through life, without the sense of vision or purpose common among highly successful people; this book does not provide a generic, pre-fabricated sense of purpose, but it does contain insights and techniques for helping people clarify their own vision and life objectives. Applying these tools requires thought and effort, without which this book – indeed, no book – can change the trajectory of one's life.

Chapter Two

Separating the Science
of Success From
Self-Help Snake Oil

How do we know what really works?

I MUST CONFESS that I am fascinated with late-night television. Particularly infomercials. From low-fat grills plugged by overweight boxers to knives that can cut through tin cans and shoes (for all my shoe-slicing needs), infomercials offer an intriguing window into the extremes of our sometimes hyper-commercialized culture. Most interesting to me are the infomercials that combine savvy marketing with a hucksterism that would make P. T. Barnum blush to sell psychologically-oriented products and services. A credit card seems to be the only prerequisite for acquiring a photographic memory through home-study courses, revolutionizing one's life instantly with audiotapes, or my personal favorite, achieving psychological breakthroughs at seminars that feature walking on red-hot coals. Despite a Ph.D. in social psychology from Harvard and a stint as a psychology professor at the University of Florida, I had never learned anything about these techniques, and certainly never came across anything in mainstream psychology that offered such dramatic results or a money-back guarantee. Still, scientists must be open-minded, and a decade as a business consultant taught me that there is considerable psychological wisdom outside the ivory towers of academia. So I set out to evaluate all the psychological tools for success and personal growth available, from those published in scientific journals to those sold on infomercials. I read the books, listened to the audiotapes, attended the seminars, and interviewed others who have done the same. I have even walked barefoot on red-hot coals and jumped off the top of a telephone pole – all at seminars devoted to success. Throughout it all, I have tried to answer the question: "What really works?"

· · ·

"Triangulating" on the Truth

There are two primary ways to figure out what really works. The first is to "triangulate" on the truth, which simply means looking at many different sources of information about success, and focusing on the conclusions about which there is agreement and consensus. Obviously we can be more confident in a conclusion if it is based on different sources that collected their information in different ways. Scientists call this idea *methodological pluralism*. Instead of drawing conclusions from just one study, scientists prefer to draw conclusions based on several studies conducted by different researchers using different methods. All sources of information have unique strengths, and all have weaknesses or limitations. In looking to multiple sources of information, the methodological weaknesses of one are cancelled out by the strengths of another, and we can begin to "triangulate" or "zero in" on the truth. In terms of understanding the nature of success, there are a half-dozen or so major sources of information to which we can turn.

Great thinkers. People have been thinking about success and well-being for thousands of years, so it comes as no surprise that many fundamental truths about these topics have come from philosophers and writers throughout the ages. In many cases, the insights of these great thinkers have anticipated the findings of scientific research by centuries; as Freud once said, "Everywhere I go, poets have been there before me." Unfortunately, despite their brilliance, the great thinkers of history have been notoriously unable to agree with each other about much of anything, so we can not rely on them alone to understand the true drivers of success and happiness.

Case studies. Perhaps the oldest strategy for achieving success is to observe highly successful people and simply do what they do. This process, known formally as modeling, leads us to conduct case studies of history's most successful people to see what can be learned from their lives. This book includes insights derived from case studies of scientists like Albert Einstein, inventors like Thomas Edison, composers such as Johann Sebastian Bach, religious leaders such as Mohandas Gandhi, business leaders such as Bill Gates, and many more. Conversely, we will examine case studies of underachievers so that we can avoid modeling the attitudes and behavioral patterns that keep them from reaching their potential.

Successful companies. Businesses obviously have a vested interest in understanding success. At a corporate level, much is known about what distinguishes highly successful companies from less successful ones, and many of these insights can be applied to individual success. We can, in a sense, run our lives the way successful executives run their companies. Businesses have also learned a great deal about individual success, having invested billions of dollars in understanding effective leadership and peak performance in the workplace. In sales, for example, much is known about the psychological factors that distinguish those who consistently surpass their quotas from those who burn out and leave the profession.

Societal wisdom. Businesses are just one of many organizations with a vested interest in understanding and communicating the keys to success. Society as a whole, and the social institutions that make up society, have implicit and explicit ideas about success, and convey these ideas in many ways. One is "popular wisdom" – sayings and cliches that become so woven into our everyday lexicon that we often cease to notice them or appreciate some of the subtle and profound messages they convey. Another is mythology – ancient stories that often contain timeless and universal truths that remain relevant even today. The modern equivalents of mythology – media outlets like movies, television, books, and even children's stories – also perpetuate ideas about success and well-being across generations.

Psychotherapy. Therapists such as psychiatrists and clinical psychologists are on the front lines of human change. Of these, Sigmund Freud is best known, but time and empirical research have not been kind to many of Freud's ideas, so you won't be reading about the Oedipus complex or anal-retentive personalities in the pages of this book. Freud's ideas dominated psychology for decades, but over time new approaches to psychotherapy emerged that focused less on childhood traumas and more on the cognitive and behavioral patterns of individuals as they are now. These therapeutic techniques, honed through decades of clinical use and tested in hundreds of studies, have been adapted for individuals to use themselves and incorporated into this book (of course, no book can substitute for sessions with a trained therapist). One challenge here is that therapy, like psychology as a whole, has traditionally focused on people with "deficits" in functioning or emotional well-being (over the past century or so, there have been over 70,000 scientific articles on depression and 57,000 on anxiety, but fewer than 3,000 on happiness and 6,000 on life satisfaction[1]). As a result, I've further modified some therapeutic techniques to help people already functioning at "normal" levels achieve even greater success; after all, this book is about the science of success and well-being, not the science of normalcy.

Success writers. The great philosophers from history were generalists, writing on a wide-ranging variety of topics, of which success and happiness were but two. Over time, a new breed of writers emerged who focused specifically on success. You may not be familiar with the term "success writer," but you probably are familiar with these individuals, as they write the""self-help" books that so regularly populate best seller lists. I prefer "success writer" because the term "self-help" comes with a bit baggage, and to some people has connotations of being simplistic, naïve, or too "touchy-feely." Other common terms have baggage as well. To call an individual a "self-help guru," for example, is overly dismissive, but calling some-one a "peak performance expert" (as they might bill themselves) is a bit presumptive and risks becoming an unwitting arm of their mar-keting efforts. "Self-improvement" and""personal growth" may be relatively accurate descriptors of this field, but both terms have ac-quired baggage as well. "Motivational" and""inspirational" have a different type of baggage, and imply simply an emotional pump-up without practical tools or techniques. Amid this linguistic minefield, I think the term "success writer" strikes the right balance.

. . .

The Science of Success

From ancient philosophers to modern therapists, from mythology to success writers on *Oprah*, insights into success come from many sources, and our first strategy for understanding "what really works" involves exploring all of these sources, seeing which conclusions they share, and "triangulating" on the truth. Our second strategy focuses on one source of information in particular: scientific research. The core elements of science are familiar: observation, measure-ment, testing hypotheses in an objective way, and publishing re-search so that others can evaluate the conclusions and attempt to replicate the findings. The essence of science can be summed up in one phrase, and it's not Jerry McGuire's catchphrase "Show me the money" (as any number of poor scientists will attest).[2] Instead, it is show me the evidence. Real evidence.

If you are trying to convince me that something as simple as re-peating incantations such as "I like myself" can improve my self-esteem (a claim made in many popular success books), then show me some convincing evidence. Convincing evidence is *not* a story about how it must be effective because you heard it worked for a guy who once sat next to your cousin's girlfriend's ex-roommate on a plane. Evidence that involves telling stories is called *anecdotal evidence*, and it is rarely convincing by itself, particularly when the story is undocumented. Convincing evidence would be a carefully-conducted study in which a group of volunteers have their self-esteem measured in a reliable manner, and then half are randomly assigned to repeat the affirmations, while the other half does not repeat affirmations and serves as a control group; after the first group repeats the affirmations, everyone's self-esteem should be measured again. If the results show that repeating affirmations does lead to enhanced self-esteem, and the findings are confirmed by other studies that vary minor aspects of the research (such as how self-esteem is measured or which affirmations are repeated), then we can begin to have some confidence in the conclusions. This process may not be as easy to explain as the story of the guy who sat next to your cousin's girlfriend's ex-roommate on a plane, but it's obviously much more convincing. It's real evidence.

Astronomer and debunker of pseudo-science Carl Sagan wrote that extraordinary claims require extraordinary evidence. So if someone is trying to convince you that he was abducted by aliens or was Napoleon in a past life or is able to talk to the dead, then he better have, as a young friend of mine says, "some really freaking terrific evidence." And if someone is trying to sell you a product that offers effortless success in life for only three easy payments of $69.95, then they'd better have some really freaking terrific evidence as well. The bottom line is that if we want to be in a position to evaluate the claims made by marketers, and to really understand how we can achieve more success and happiness in life, then we'll need to look at the evidence. Real evidence. Scientific evidence. In a sense, scientific evidence is just one of many sources of information about success, but it deserves special attention for one crucial reason: *science has an unparalleled track record for uncovering the truth.*

Science has reshaped how we view the world around us and our place in it. Science has enabled everything from electricity to telephones to Internet technology, giving us the modern conveniences and control over our environment without which modern life would be unthinkable. Science stands at the heart of modern medicine, which has fueled the dramatic increase in life expectancy seen over the past century. The list goes on and on. Of course, like any tool, science has been used for less admirable purposes like creating gunpowder and nuclear weapons. Still, if given a choice, most of us would choose life today with all its complexities over life a thousand years ago. Science is not a panacea, but it is the single best tool for understanding and reshaping the world around us. As Einstein put it, "All our science, measured against reality, is primitive and childlike – and yet it is the most precious thing we have."

Although many of the advancements enabled by science are quite familiar, perhaps less well-known are the advancements made by psychology and other social sciences. For example, recent decades have seen dramatic improvements in our ability to treat mental illness (which is particularly fortunate given that rates of depression and anxiety have risen to epidemic levels). But psychology is much more than the treatment of disorders. Researchers have also made significant inroads into understanding how the brain works, how memory functions, how personality traits develop, how children mature, and so on. And, most importantly for our purposes, scientists have examined the nature of success and well-being. We now know a tremendous amount about what separates successful people from less successful people in many aspects of life. When it comes to success and well-being, scientific research is the single best tool we have for understanding "what really works," and for evaluating claims made by success writers who hope to profit by selling us their books and other products.

. . .

Success Snake Oil

Let's consider an example that highlights the importance of using science to understand what really works. Would you take a prescription drug that had not been scientifically studied? Hopefully not (although that's essentially what you're doing if you take most herbal supplements, but that's another story). When your doctor prescribes a drug, you probably don't personally head to the library and review the scientific research yourself. But you probably do assume that the manufacturer conducted careful scientific research showing the drug to be safe and effective, and that the government has overseen the research and approved the drug. Before the 20th century, no research on drugs was required – practically anyone could sell any form of medicine and make any claims about its effectiveness. Salespeople traveled the country peddling various "snake oils" touted as having any number of medical benefits. Despite slick sales pitches, most snake oils did not deliver the medical benefits they promised. Interestingly, many snake oils did actually make people feel better, as they contained a mixture of alcohol and opium known as laudanum. It pretty much doesn't matter what's wrong with you – taking alcohol and opium will make you feel better. It's an important lesson: snake oil might make you momentarily feel better, but that doesn't mean it is safe, effective or does what marketers claim.

Snake oils are rare today, thanks to government regulation. Unfortunately, in the world of success books and products, we still live in a largely unregulated era of snake oil. Wild, unsubstantiated claims abound. Let's consider an example of success snake oil: subliminal self-help tapes. These tapes are a multi-million dollar business, and it is easy to see why. Their promise of easy, effortless change is a marketer's dream. Simply listen to the tapes, we are told, and although the subliminal messages in them can't be heard audibly, they tap the power of the subconscious mind to bring about massive change and success. If you want to lose weight, for example, there's no need for the inconvenience of exercise or the sacrifices involved with healthy eating – simply listen to the tapes and pounds will melt away. And losing weight is just one example – other tapes promise to boost self-esteem, improve memory, increase worker productivity, and even aid in the recovery from sexual abuse. There's only one problem: they don't work.[3] If it sounds too good to be true, then it probably is – and effortless change via subliminal tapes is indeed too good to be true. Every independent scientific study has reached the same conclusion – these tapes are a waste of money.

In fact, only one reliable effect of subliminal tapes has ever been demonstrated, and it is not the effect that marketers of these tapes promise. It is an effect that psychologist Anthony Pratkanis, an expert on subliminal phenomena, and his colleagues have called the *illusory placebo effect*. To understand this effect, let's consider one of the studies conducted by Pratkanis and his colleagues. They recruited people interested in subliminal techniques, and before the study began, each participant was given several tests of self-esteem and memory. Participants were then given subliminal tapes designed to improve either self-esteem or memory, but with a twist. Half of the participants received tapes that were correctly labeled, but the other half were given mislabeled tapes – some received self-esteem enhancers that were labeled as memory improvers, while others received memory improvement tapes that were labeled as self-esteem enhancers. Everyone was given instructions on how to use the tapes, and each participant was called weekly with encouragement to continue listening to the tapes. Five weeks later, the self-esteem and memory of all participants were measured again.

Consistent with other studies, these tapes did not deliver the benefits their manufacturers had promised, as there was no significant improvement in self-esteem or memory. Although the tapes themselves had no effect, the *labels* did. Those who listened to tapes labeled as self-esteem enhancers believed their self-esteem had improved (in fact, self-esteem remained stable); similarly, those who listened to tapes labeled as memory enhancers believed their memory had improved (in fact, their memories had not improved). This is the illusory placebo effect. Like a placebo, the tapes had an effect only because the users expected them to have an effect, but the effect was illusory, not real. Just as 19th century snake oils containing laudanum made people feel better without providing the promised medical benefits, so do today's subliminal success tapes.

Despite numerous studies demonstrating that subliminal tapes are worthless, people continue buying them in large numbers. The problem is that manufacturers of these products have become experts at deceptive marketing, and they conveniently ignore the carefully-conducted studies demonstrating the ineffectiveness of the tapes. As Anthony Pratkanis put it, "Tape company representatives are likely to provide you with a rather lengthy list of 'studies' demonstrating their claims. Don't be fooled. The studies on these lists fall into two camps – those done by the tape companies and for which full writeups are often not available, and those that have titles that sound as if they apply to subliminal influence, but really don't."

These deceptive marketers often point to one study in particular, known to many as the "Eat Popcorn/Drink Coke" study. Conducted in the late 1950s, this study flashed the messages "Eat Popcorn" and "Drink Coke" briefly on a movie screen. Thousands of moviegoers were supposedly exposed to these messages over the course of six weeks, and the result was reportedly an increase in Coke sales of 18% and in popcorn sales of nearly 58%. Reports of the study fueled international outrage – several countries outlawed subliminal advertising, and the Federal Communications Commission threatened to strip the broadcast license of anyone using subliminal advertising. Amidst this well-publicized furor, a much quieter development was unfolding. Researchers throughout the world were trying – and failing – to replicate the dramatic findings of the Eat Popcorn/Drink Coke study. A Canadian television show, for example, flashed the subliminal message "Phone Now" during its regular airing. Not only was there no increase in phone calls, but when viewers were asked to guess what the message had been, none of the 500 who guessed did so correctly (interestingly, nearly half reported feeling hungry or thirsty, demonstrating not the power of subliminal persuasion, but rather the power of suggestion – those familiar with the Eat Popcorn/Drink Coke study experienced what they expected to experience).

This and other failures to replicate the original never got the widespread publicity of the initial study. The media sells stories, and the story that marketers are manipulating our unconscious minds sells well, whereas a story of carefully-conducted research failing to confirm the initial results is decidedly less sexy.

Here's another fact that didn't get much publicity: James Vicary, the author of the initial study, admitted in 1962 that he had simply made up the results to attract customers for his failing marketing business. Regardless, this "study" and others like it, fueled by a growing distrust of advertisers, became ingrained in American popular culture. By the early 1980s, more than four-in-five Americans had heard of subliminal advertising, and of those, two-in-three believed it could be effective in selling products. By the 1990s, $50 million a year or more were being spent annually on subliminal success products, despite a total lack of compelling evidence that they work.

. . .

Success Urban Legends

The popularity of success snake oil like ineffective subliminal products highlights the importance of looking to scientific research as a source of information about success. Research answers the question "What really works?" and subliminal tapes clearly do not. Let's consider one more example that underscores the need for scientific rigor in the study of success: the Yale Study of Goals. This study has become a staple in the repertoire of motivational speakers and modern success writers. It has even been described in more than one best-selling book.[4] As typically described, there are three elements to the study:

• The 1953 graduating class at Yale was interviewed.
• 3% had written specific goals for their futures.
• 20 years later, that 3% was found to be worth more financially than the other 97% combined.

This study would indeed be a dramatic illustration of the power of goal setting, except for one minor point – it was never conducted. This "study" is what I call a success urban legend. Urban legends are false stories passed from one person to the next, evolving with repeated retelling, until they are eventually accepted as true. The story of an escaped murderer with a hook instead of a hand is perhaps the most famous urban legend, and although the Yale Study of Goals is clearly a less gruesome tale, it follows the same pattern of being passed uncritically via word-of-mouth until it is accepted as truth. The Consulting Debunking Unit of *Fast Company* magazine deserves credit for unmasking this urban legend.[5] When they approached Tony Robbins for documentation, a spokesperson explained that the background material for Robbins' 1986 best-seller *Unlimited Power* (which cites the study) "met a disastrous end," and suggested that success writer Brian Tracy might know more. Tracy learned of the study from success writer and sales expert Zig Ziglar. Ziglar, who frequently refers to the study, was unable to locate it, suggesting "try Tony Robbins." The circle was complete.

There are literally hundreds of published studies on goals. I have read virtually all of them, and although I have read about the Yale Study of Goals in several popular success books, I have never seen a single reference to it in the research literature. But the most compelling evidence that this study is in fact a success urban legend comes from Yale University itself. Yale gets numerous requests for information about this study, and despite extensive research, has never found any evidence that it was ever conducted. As one Yale spokesperson put it, "We are quite confident that the 'study' did not take place. We suspect it is a myth."

In recounting the success urban legend of the Yale Study of Goals, I do not mean to belittle today's success writers. In fact, throughout this book, I will examine many of their ideas that do stand up to scientific scrutiny. Nor do I mean to suggest that setting goals is ineffective, as many studies (reviewed in the Strategy chapter) have documented the performance-enhancing power of properly-set goals. But I do mean to underscore the importance of scientific rigor in the study of success. Scientists recognize that often-repeated stories are not necessarily true, and therefore emphasize documenting sources and publishing research so that everyone can review and confirm the results. Again, if we want to know what really works, and avoid falling prey to snake oil and urban legends, scientific research must be one of our most important sources of information.

. . .

Resources

It is often difficult to distinguish scientifically-valid ideas from snake oil because many success writers label their ideas as "scientific" when such a label is far from warranted. In *I'm Dysfunctional, You're Dysfunctional*, Wendy Kaminer suggested that writing a popular success book is a simple, two-step process: "Promote the prevailing preoccupation of the time – the acquisition of wealth or health – as the primary moral imperative. Package platitudes about positive thinking, prayer or affirmation therapy as sure-fire, scientific techniques." To help you separate the science of success from self-help snake oil labeled as scientific, here are four resources that you might find helpful…

- *www.csicop.com*. This is the web site of the Committee for the Scientific Investigation of Claims of the Paranormal. One of the best debunking sites on the Internet, it offers a level-headed perspective on snake oil like subliminal tapes, as well as scientific looks at paranormal phenomenon like ESP, psychics, UFOs and haunted houses.
- *www.skepdic.com*. The Skeptic's Dictionary is another excellent debunking site. Among other things, this dictionary has encyclopedia-like "entries" about popular success writers, and an excellent section on urban legends.
- *www.NextLevelSciences.com*. In the interest of full disclosure, I should start by pointing out that this is my web site. In addition to articles and a free email newsletter, it contains links to the best self-improvement and psychology-related sites on the Internet.

I've tried to weed out snake oil sites, and unlike many major search engines, I don't allow sites to buy their way on to the list.

- *A Top Six list.* Concerned that someone is trying to sell you self-help snake oil? Try checking their claims against this David Letterman-style Top Six list…

Top Six Signs a Marketer Is Trying To Sell You Self-Help Snake Oil

6. They refer to studies or statistics without documenting their sources. Nobody enjoys footnotes, but they play a vital role in science. Footnotes are like studies proving the effectiveness and safety of prescription drugs – you don't necessarily need to read them yourself, but you should be sure they exist.

5. They promise instant change. Although the decision to change can happen in an instant, lasting change is a process with ups and downs, and almost always involves setbacks to be overcome.

4. They promise effortless change. Lasting change requires thought and effort. If it sounds too good to be true, it probably is.

3. They promise to "tap the power of the subconscious mind." That's how marketers of success snake oil talk, not psychologists.

2. They promise to eliminate fear forever. This isn't possible. And even if it were possible, you wouldn't want to. Fear is an important call to action. If you're about to be run over by a bus, fear is a good thing.

1. They tell you people only use 10% of their brains. This is one of the oldest urban legends in psychology, and is patently false. Trust me – if someone removed 90% of your brain, you'd notice the difference. Well, actually, you wouldn't notice the difference, because you'd be dead. But those around you hopefully would…

Chapter Three

The Single Biggest
Barrier to Success

What holds people back?

DICTIONARIES DEFINE SUCCESS as getting what you want. Success is aspiring to something and then achieving it. Success is desiring something and then accomplishing it. That's what this book is about – how to best figure out what you really want, and how best to achieve it (of course, getting what you want and wanting something good for you are two different things, as we'll discuss later). But in daily life, too often success remains elusive. Let's consider a few examples...

- *Weight loss.* Losing weight is the most commonly set goal, yet it is quite possibly the least commonly accomplished. And even when people do lose weight in the short-term, they rarely keep it off in the long-term. When the National Institute of Health reviewed decades of research on weight loss, they concluded that "Weight loss at the end of relatively short-term programs can exceed 10% of individual body weight: however, there is a strong tendency to regain weight, with as much as two-thirds of the weight loss regained within 1 year of completing the program and almost all by 5 years."[6]
- *Smoking cessation.* Mark Twain once joked, "To cease smoking is the easiest thing I ever did; I ought to know because I've done it a

thousand times." Millions of Americans would agree. Seventy per-
cent of smokers want to quit, and nearly half try each year.[7] But
success is elusive. If you followed a group of people trying to quit
smoking, 80-90% would be smoking a year later, and over 95%
would have smoked at some point in the previous 12 months.[8]
Even formal treatment programs rarely have success rates over
25%.[9] And those who do kick the habit typically struggle in doing
so. Successful quitters generally go through a cycle – trying to
quit, failing to do so, and trying to quit again – several times before quitting for good.[10]

- *Entrepreneurship.* Starting a business has always been a key element
  of the American Dream. Too bad it isn't easier. Over a half million
  businesses close each year.[11] Only half of new "employer businesses"
  (those with employees) survive four years, and the failure rate is
  likely much higher among businesses without employees.

In these three areas, and in many more domains of life as well, the
pattern is clear: a few people truly succeed, but most do not. Certainly
some people lose weight, or stop smoking, or build successful businesses, but they are far outnumbered by those who fail in these endeavors. The question is: Why? What holds people back? What separates the "lucky" few who truly succeed from the many who do not?

In fact, "luck" has relatively little to do with it. Success is rarely
an accident. There are consistent patterns of attitudes and actions
that differentiate more successful people from their less successful
counterparts. These differences appear in study after study, and stand
out when we explore the lives of successful people. True achievers
think about their lives differently, and use different techniques for
bringing about life changes. The biggest barrier to success, then,
lies in the process of how people try to bring about success. *True
success in life isn't rare because people are weak or lazy or lack willpower. True success in life is rare because too often people use flawed
strategies for success.*

The most frequently used strategies for personal change and success generally leave much to be desired. Again, let's consider a few examples:

- *Willpower.* Perhaps the most commonly used strategies for change involve what we might call "willpower." Unfortunately, despite its popularity, willpower is rarely a powerful recipe for change. For example, when a team of psychologists and health professionals[12] held a "stop smoking contest," they found that the two most commonly used strategies both centered on "willpower" – 81% of the participants repeatedly told themselves "I don't need cigarettes" and 80% reminded themselves of the commitment they had made. Unfortunately, neither of these willpower-based strategies proved effective, as those using them were no more likely to "kick the habit" than those who did not.

- *New Year's resolutions.* Over 4,000 years ago, Babylonians tried to start the new year "fresh" by repaying debts and returning borrowed items.[13] Two thousand years ago, Romans ended the year by reviewing the one before, resolving to achieve more, and paying homage to Janus, the god of doorways and beginnings (and namesake of the month January). Today, as the season rolls around, about 40% of adult Americans intend to make a New Year's resolution. And the trend is growing. Polls from 1939 and 1940 found that only about one-in-four intended to make a resolution in prewar America.[14] But as with willpower, the popularity of a strategy does not necessarily imply the effectiveness of that strategy. Roughly half of those who made resolutions the previous year report keeping them, but these retrospective, self-reported success rates are probably overstated.[15] Other studies suggest that 20% is a more likely figure,[16] but when asked about specific resolutions, a still different and likely more accurate pattern of results emerges. For example, at some point in their lives, nearly half of Americans have made a New Year's resolution to lose weight or change their eating habits; of those, 20% broke their resolution within a week, 68% broke it within three months, and only 15% kept their resolution for a year or longer.[17]

• *Affirmations.* Many popular success books advocate the use of "incantations" or "affirmations." Simply repeat phrases such as "I like myself" over and over again, we are told, and soon we will experience an enhanced self-image and boosted self-esteem. This idea is not new. In the 1920s, French pharmacist Emile Coue created a national fad of "autosuggestion" by encouraging everyone to repeat the mantra: "Day by day, in every way, I am getting better and better." Repeating it aloud 20 times each morning and evening was supposed to result in health, wealth and pretty much whatever else one wanted (it does, after all, specify improvement "in every way"). This technique supposedly influenced the "unconscious mind" (yes, marketers of success snake oil were using that line even 80 years ago), and struck a chord amidst the growing popularization of Freudian psychology. Unfortunately, this simplistic technique was no more effective in the 1920s than it is today. As any experienced mental health professional will attest, helping individuals change their self-concepts is not so easy.

• *Cold turkey.* In the "stop smoking" contest described above, 91% of the participants tried to stop immediately. Although there is some debate about this even among health experts, the research suggests gradually reducing nicotine consumption over a two- or three-week period probably leads to the best long-term success rates.[18]

. . .

Two More Effectiveness "Tests"

Clearly, research casts doubt the effectiveness of the more common strategies for personal change. But there are two other "tests" that are helpful in evaluating techniques for success. The first is what I call the "pay for it" test. Suppose you were struggling to make a change in a particular area of your life, and you decided to pay a psychologist or other professional therapist to help you. Now suppose that your therapist told you to "make a resolution, change cold turkey, use a lot of willpower, and say 'I like myself' 50 times a day." You would probably feel that you weren't getting the most powerful psychological tools known to science, and you would be right. And you would probably feel that you hadn't gotten your money's worth. In other words, these techniques fail the "would you pay for it?" test.

The most common strategies for success also fail the "thought and effort" test. Marketers may try to persuade us that their products enable effortless change, and although I wish change was that easy, the evidence is quite clear that success in life requires thought and effort. In different areas of life, from weight loss to smoking cessation, from academic success to dating, those who are more successful are those who use multiple techniques for change; moreover, they use those techniques more frequently, more consistently, over longer periods of time, and thoughtfully apply different techniques to different kinds of problems.[19] These findings are echoed in the practical experience of therapists, virtually all of whom would agree that change requires thought and effort. All forms of effective psychotherapy are premised on the notion that clients need to be thoughtful about their situations, and to do significant "homework" between sessions.

. . .

The Most Powerful Success Strategies Known To Science

If the most common strategies for success aren't supported by research, and fail common sense tests as well, then the question obviously becomes: What works? What effective strategies for change can replace the flawed, "naturally-occurring" ones that are more commonly used? That's precisely what the remainder of this book presents – a straightforward, five-step process that encompasses the most powerful tools for change and success known to science. One chapter is devoted to each step: Vision, Strategy, Belief, Persistence and Learning. Each chapter begins with the basics or *Common Knowledge* – given that success and well-being are ancient topics, it should come as no surprise that the fundamental importance of each step is already well-known. We then explore *Uncommon Knowledge*, providing a depth of understanding made possible by the latest scientific research and therapeutic insights. Finally, each chapter provides *Tools* for putting these proven strategies for success into action, and *Resources* to which you can turn for further insights and tools.

Chapter Four

Step One: Vision —
The Science of Figuring Out
What You Really Want
from Life

"The world always steps aside for people who know where they're going." Miriam Viola Larsen

A FEW YEARS AGO, I vacationed in Peru, hiking the Inca Trail to the famed ruins of Machu Picchu, a site of intense interest to adventure travelers, archeology buffs and New Agers alike. One of the most interesting aspects of this amazing trip was the people who, like me, had been drawn to this destination. It was very much a "workaholic-young-professional-in-search-of-meaning" vacation. My fellow trekkers included a lawyer questioning whether he could ethically represent tobacco companies, a writer who had just left her husband-to-be at the altar, a Mormon college student about to go on his two-year mission overseas, a devout Christian questioning his faith and his sexuality, and several professionals suffering burn-out and contemplating career changes. We were all on personal vision quests, navigating life transitions and trying to figure out what we really wanted from life, because we all understood one bit of common knowledge about success: successful people know what they want...

. . .

COMMON KNOWLEDGE:
SUCCESSFUL PEOPLE KNOW WHAT THEY WANT

Successful people envision their futures and specify the outcomes they desire so that they can channel their effort toward those ends. Society conveys this message through clichés like "If you don't know where you're going, you'll get there," "If you aim for nothing, you'll hit it," and "If you fail to plan, you plan to fail." Popular success writers have echoed this idea for decades. According to Stephen Covey, for example, one of the seven habits of highly effective people is "beginning with the end in mind." Interestingly, the rationale for visualizing the future provided by success writers has evolved over time. Enthusiasts of the 19th century "New Thought" movement – an early self-help movement philosophically similar to Christian Science – offered religious or mystical explanations, believing that one's visions of the future literally created the future. In the early decades of the 20th century, followers of Freud popularized the idea that visions of the future influenced the unconscious, subtly but unknowingly pushing one closer to desired end states. Today, as psychology has become more practical and pragmatic, explanations have focused more on the role of Vision in focusing efforts and clarifying priorities.

Successful therapy is focused on the future, and begins with therapist and client collaborating to identify desired results. Therapy is commonly criticized for being overly focused on the past, particularly by "competitors" such as personal coaches and success writers who stand to gain if negative perceptions of therapy spread. But this criticism glosses over the fact that there are many different forms of therapy. Some, like psychoanalysis, do focus primarily on the past and tend to be less effective, at least in the short-term. But the more effective varieties focus on problems in the present and how to overcome them to create desired future outcomes. The University of Pennsylvania's Martin Seligman, one of the world's foremost authorities on psychotherapy, concludes that "therapy that reviews childhood endlessly... that views a better future as incidental to undoing the past, has a century-long history of being ineffective. All therapy that works for depression, anxiety, and sexual problems focuses on exactly what is going wrong now and on how to correct it."[20]

Like researchers studying therapeutic effectiveness, business leaders have also concluded that Vision is crucial to sustained success. Harvard marketing guru Ted Levitt contends that "the future belongs to people who see possibilities before they become obvious," and we even label such people (and companies) as visionary. Polls confirm that "the Vision thing" is considered a top criterion for business leadership, rivaling people skills, outside-the-box thinking and technology smarts.[21] Over time, companies that pursue compelling Visions with a consistency of purpose far outperform those that vacillate from one strategy to the next under the auspices of revolving door CEOs.[22] Little wonder then that envisioning corporate futures is a massive industry. Large companies maintain entire strategic planning departments to envision the future of the company, anticipate emerging trends, and capitalize on those Visions with strategic plans, mission statements, and so on. Hundreds of consulting firms aid this effort, the largest of which are training grounds for future corporate CEOs.

One of the best examples of the power of Vision in business highlights the importance of thinking about one's future when making career choices. In the early 1980s, Apple Computer had launched the personal computer revolution and had attracted a small group of loyal fans, but it needed seasoned managers to lead its transition from entrepreneurial startup to Fortune 500 mainstay. Co-founder Steve Jobs believed Pepsi president John Sculley was the best man for the job, but Sculley remained uncertain even after numerous enticements. Finally, Jobs asked a question that focused not on money or stock options, but rather on Sculley's Vision for his own future: "Do you want to spend the rest of your life selling sugared water, or do you want a chance to change the world?" Sculley described himself as "haunted" by this challenge to his Vision of the future, and eventually took the job at Apple.[23]

• • •

Future Selves:
Envisioning "Who" As Well As "What"

The example of Steve Jobs and John Sculley highlights an important lesson: successful people not only envision *what* their future will be like, they envision *who* they will be in the future. Scully decided he wanted to be a world-changer, not a soda-seller. University of Michigan psychologist Hazel Markus and her colleagues have pioneered the scientific study of this phenomenon by exploring "future selves" – mental images of whom we might become and what we will be like. Most people consider a wide range of possible futures for themselves. In one study, college students examined 150 potential descriptions of themselves, including personality traits such as creative and selfish, physical descriptions such as athletic and wrinkled, potential lifestyles such as health-conscious or alcohol-dependent, and possible professions such as artist, judge and taxi driver.[24] When asked which items described them now, participants chose an average of 51 items, but when asked which items described "possible selves," participants chose an average of 80 items, with some choosing as many as 147 items. Nearly half considered all 50 of the positive items to be possible futures for themselves.

Envisioning our future selves is not only common, it actually plays an important role in our performance and our psychological well being. Far from idle daydreams, images of our future lives contribute to our self-esteem, our happiness, and the sense that we can control our own destinies.[25] Moreover, empirical research backs up the very old notion that those who envision themselves as successful perform better, particularly if they envision themselves as being successful as a result of their own hard work.[26] Future selves provide concrete ways of understanding how accomplishing our goals will change our lives, boosting motivation. "Some possible selves are symbols of hope, whereas others are reminders of weak, sad, or tragic futures that are to be avoided. Yet all of these ideas about what is possible for us to be, to think, to feel, or to experience provide a direction and impetus for action, change, and development. Possible selves give specific cognitive form to our desires for mastery, power, or affiliation, and to our diffuse fears of failure and incompetence."[27]

The ability to envision positive, empowering futures for ourselves leads to more than just enhanced performance on routine tasks – it is also crucial to our ability to recover from tragic events.[28] For example, the current self-concept of those recovering well from serious life crises (such as divorce or death of a spouse) differs little from those recovering poorly. Instead, the key driver of recovery lies in Visions of future selves. Those who recover well are more likely to envision their future selves as motivated, independent, rich, creative, powerful, intelligent and attractive. In contrast, those recovering poorly are more likely to envision their future selves as unpopular, unimportant, and weak. They are also more likely to envision themselves dying young, having a heart attack, and having a psychological breakdown. Ask yourself: When something bad happens to you, do you envision yourself as resilient or cursed? When you experience a business setback, do you envision yourself as Donald Trump or as *Death of a Salesman*'s Willie Loman?

Just as positive future selves can aid in the recovery from traumatic events, the loss of a potential future self can trigger a psychological crisis. When an individual is paralyzed after an accident, for example, physical injury is compounded by the psychological trauma of once-valued future selves becoming seemingly unattainable. Questions such as "What will I become?" and "Who will I be?" predominate. Mid-life crises are often triggered when it becomes clear that workplace goals and visions for one's future are no longer tenable. Consider the psychological "crises" triggered by the loss of future selves among the 18 year old who realizes she will not become a rock star, the 30 year old who realizes he will not become a captain of industry, the 40 year old who realizes he will no longer be attractive to college co-eds, and 65 year old who realizes she will never be young again. Each is a loss, not of the current self, but rather a psychological crisis triggered by a possible future self being extinguished.

. . .

The Power of Passion, and the Barrier of Ambivalence

Successful people not only envision positive future selves, they are selective and focus their attention on the future selves that excite them the most. Indeed, when one examines the lives of highly successful people, passion is a common theme. History's most accomplished people, including artists, writers, composers and leaders, all tended to find their calling relatively young. Thomas Stanley, author of *The Millionaire Mind*, found that financially successful people typically identify what "lights their emotional fire" at a relatively young age, and translate that passion into a profitable business venture. Just as the three keys to real estate success are location, location, location, Stanley believes the three keys to wealth for most millionaires are vocation, vocation, vocation. Joseph Campbell, who studied the psychological meaning of mythology, offered three simple words of advice for those seeking to make their way in the world: "Find your bliss." Those who devote themselves to their passion not only accomplish more, but they enjoy the process. To those who have found their bliss, "work" does not have negative connotations, and doesn't "feel like work."

Dostoyevsky wrote, "The secret of man's being is not only to live but to have something to live for. Without a stable conception of the object of life, man would not consent to go on living." That may be a bit of poetic overstatement, at least as it pertains to daily life. But under extreme circumstances, a passion and a purpose may indeed provide more than direction in life – they may be essential for life itself. That's precisely what psychologist Victor Frankl observed during his horrific experiences in a Nazi concentration camp.[29] In this most dehumanizing of circumstances, most of the goals and expectations that prisoners once had for their lives were completely stripped away and rendered unattainable. Some individuals found new goals and meanings in life, ranging from the very tangible –

striving to obtain food, information, or jobs within the camp – to higher-level purposes such as easing the pain of others, or remembering events in detail for future historians. But others did not find new goals to strive for, and that lack of purpose was often associated with a sense of passive resignation, a feeling of aimlessness, physical and psychological deterioration, and ultimately death.

Fortunately, most of us will never experience such intense dehumanization. But it's fair to say that in today's world, compelling Visions of "what to live for" are increasingly elusive, and that probably plays a major role in today's epidemics of depression and anxiety. The numbers are dramatic. Over the past century, rates of major depression have increased 10 times overall, and up to 20 times among women.[30] Depression now afflicts people, on average, ten years younger then it did just a few decades ago.[31] The average child in the 1980s felt more anxiety than child psychiatric patients just three decades earlier.[32] Many factors fuel these epidemics, including a greater awareness of the problems and a lessening of the stigma attached to them. But perhaps the primary driver is the social changes that have made meaningful personal Visions much harder to find. In previous generations, meaning in life flowed more naturally from relationships between individuals and something larger: God, country, family, ideals, etc. But in the post-World War II era, religiosity has declined, divorce rates have skyrocketed, and consumerism too often supercedes idealism. Individualism, for all its benefits, also means that people must create meaning in their own lives, and must increasingly find their own unique Visions for their futures. Non-shared Visions are not only harder to find, but they result in a lack of connectedness with others, and less social support in pursuing those Visions.

Ambivalence and uncertainty, in many ways the polar opposites of passion and vision, are in fact associated with depression and host of other negative consequences.[33] People who have conflicting goals or are ambivalent about their goals[34] are more likely than others to...

• Experience negative emotions such as depression and anxiety.

- Be less happy and less satisfied with their lives.
- Have more physical illnesses & doctor's visits.
- Be indecisive, uncertain and rebellious.
- Be easily distracted and procrastinate.
- Spend more time thinking about their goals.
- Spend less time taking action toward their goals.

These last two items are particularly important, and when combined form a psychological pattern called rumination. Ruminative animals such as cows chew their cud – in other words, they chew partially regurgitated food for extended periods of time. This isn't a particularly attractive image, but then again, neither is rumination when it occurs in people. This pattern of thinking about one's goals but not taking action – a paralysis of analysis – is characteristic of underachievers, depressives, and a number of other groups to which you'd rather not belong.

Ambivalence and goal conflict are clearly barriers to success and personal change. In fact, people who attempt to make life changes but fail ("non-changers") are six times more likely to be uncertain about what they really want and to question whether they truly want to change.[35] Consider the ambivalence of this Non-Changer: "It seems all my adult life I've been trying to figure out what I'd like to be when I grow up." Or the lack of passion exhibited by this Non-Changer: "Part of my difficulty in achieving this goal is that I cannot figure out what it is that I will enjoy – I have a lot of interests, but no one main passion." After years of research, two experts on the psychology of relapse reached a similar conclusion about detrimental effects of ambivalence, describing those who fail to change this way: "They want to drink (or smoke, or purge, or gamble), but they don't want to. They want to change, and they don't want to."[36]

. . .

The Vision Thing Poster Child

Just as we admire those who avoid rumination and have a clear, passionate sense of their future, we are harsh on those without a sense of vision. Those who miss the big picture and fail to anticipate the future are derided for "missing the forest for the trees" or "rearranging deck chairs on the Titanic." Fairly or unfairly, George Bush (the elder) was widely criticized when he admitted not having "the Vision thing" – clearly Americans want visionary presidents. Perhaps the most vivid "poster child" for the Vision thing is not a real person, but rather a literary character: Hamlet. Even 500 years after it was written, the play remains popular not only because it is beautifully poetic, but because it is a strikingly accurate character study – Shakespeare's portrayal of the psychological effects of ambivalence is very consistent with modern scientific findings.

A quick review of the plot: Hamlet is the prince of Denmark, son of the king. Hamlet's uncle murders the king – his own brother – and marries the queen. Killing one's brother and marrying his wife is a crime of biblical proportions, and Hamlet swears revenge, vowing to kill his murderous and (by some definitions incestuous) uncle. But Hamlet was plagued by ambivalence – he wasn't certain what he really wanted, or if he could truly bring himself to kill his uncle. And with Hamlet's ambivalence comes the pattern we would expect based on psychological research: anxiety, angst, rebellion, restlessness, procrastination, rumination, and an inability to act (they didn't call him "the melancholy Dane" for nothing). Throughout the play he encounters opportunities to take revenge upon his uncle, but he passes each one up, showing the classic ruminative combination of talking endlessly about his goals, but not taking action to accomplish them. Ambivalence and a lack of clear Vision even drive Hamlet's most famous characteristic: the tendency to engage in long ponderous monologues about vaguely relevant topics. Today, the modern reader may marvel at the beauty of the words in Hamlet's soliloquies, but at the same time impatiently implores: "Hamlet, buddy, do something. Anything! Just take action!!!" Hamlet's inaction causes him to lose control of his future and fall victim to the schemes of others. Indeed, the final act of Hamlet has a body count like a Schwarzenegger movie. Ambivalence leads to rumination, and rumination leads to a downfall. Shakespeare's message: If you don't know where you're going, you leave your destiny to chance.

. . .

Delaying Gratification

The tale of Hamlet underscores another insight into success: *thinking* about the future isn't enough. Hamlet thought about the future endlessly, but without a clear Vision, he was unable to *act* consistently toward a desired future. A dozen times a day, we are all faced with the choice to do what feels good in the moment at the expense of long-term ambitions, or to act in a less satisfying way now so that future rewards will be greater. The ability to delay gratification, and to act with an eye toward the future, is a potent predictor of life success. It manifests itself even at a very young age. Numerous studies have presented toddlers with the choice of a small pile of M&M candies now, or a big pile later, and found that how pre-schoolers respond to this brief, artificial task at age four predicts an amazing amount about them years later.[37] Those who delay gratification at age four tend to become pre-teens and teenagers who are . . .

• More academically and socially competent.
• More verbally fluent and articulate.
• Better able to cope with stress and frustration.
• More thoughtful, reasonable, attentive and reflective.
• More resourceful and skillful.
• Better able to concentrate, focus, make plans, and think ahead.
• More effective at setting and pursuing goals.

Kids who resist temptation at age four even score better on the SATs when they apply to college over a decade later! Conversely, preferring immediate rewards to long-term satisfaction lies at the heart of most varieties of self-destruction and underachievement, including overeating, oversleeping, overspending, procrastination, crime, and addiction.

There are several ways to improve your ability to delay gratification. One is distraction. Kids who sing songs or make up games or play with toys delay gratification longer than those who stare longingly at the candies. Another is abstraction. Kids encouraged to think about the enticing aspects of M&Ms ("Mmmm... chewy chocolate and a crunchy candy coating") give into temptation much faster than kids encouraged to think about less arousing aspects of M&Ms ("they are shaped like buttons, and won't melt in my hands"). A third is substitution, like thinking about salty, crunchy pretzels rather than M&Ms. But perhaps the most powerful strategy for delaying gratification in daily life has no analog in abstract studies of kids resisting M&Ms, and that is to have a very clear, compelling, inspirational Vision. In other words, unlike Hamlet, you have to know what you really want...

. . .

How Do You Figure Out What You Really Want?

Throughout history, people have sought to occasionally "get away from it all" and figure out what they really want from life. The specifics of how and when people engage in this soul-searching have differed across time and place, as have the labels placed on the process, but still there are striking commonalities. Many Native American tribes have Vision quest rituals in which those on the brink of adulthood go into the wilderness alone to find their guardian spirit, and by extension, to find a Vision and purpose to guide their lives. Today many people engage in a secular version of this process when they spend time alone seeking to "find themselves." Businesses spend millions annually to do the same, but find it awkward to put "Vision quest" on expense reports, so they call them "off-site" meetings and "strategic retreats." In the modern techno-nerd-geek equivalent of a Vision quest, Microsoft's Bill Gates regularly takes "reading vacations" in which he gets away from his day-to-day responsibilities, and reads extensively as a way a spurring strategic thinking about his company in particular and technology in general.

Our next step, then, is clear: we need to go on our own personal Vision quests. Our aim will be to identify our passions – what we really want from life – and erase any lingering, debilitating ambivalence about our objectives. Of course you don't want to think about your future in any old way. You want to think like a genius...

. . .

UNCOMMON KNOWLEDGE: HOW TO THINK LIKE A GENIUS

Fortunately, psychologists have learned a great deal about the thinking patterns of successful people. First we'll explore six key characteristics of the thinking styles of highly successful people, and then we'll structure our Vision quest process so that it practically ensures that we think like geniuses.

. . .

Genius Guideline #1:
Successful People Are a Little Crazy

Anecdotes and conventional wisdom have long suggested that successful people are a little crazy. We've all heard of mad scientists, crazy artists, and maverick business leaders. Although the notion of the crazy genius may be a bit overstated, it is based on a kernel of truth. In both science and art, those who tend to be a little eccentric do tend to be more successful, productive and influential.[38] Only about a third of the general population suffers from mental illness in their lives, but rates are significantly higher among highly achieving artists and scientists (rates vary dramatically by discipline: poets 77%, actors 74%, psychologists 51%, journalists 47%). [39]

It should be emphasized that successful people are, in general, a *little* crazy. With some exceptions, their "craziness" generally doesn't manifest itself as major mental illnesses such as schizophrenia. Instead, it more commonly takes the form of unconventional thinking, a rejection of traditional beliefs, a lack of concern with what others might think, and the confidence to take on ambitious projects from which more "sane" people would shy away. Moreover, they have some control over their eccentricities, and even put them to good use. Dean Simonton, an expert on psychological studies of famous historical figures, concluded the society's high achievers are poised between average people and true psychotics, possessing "just the right amount of weirdness. They are strange enough to come up with odd ideas, and to pursue those ideas no matter what the rest of the world says. Yet creators are not so outlandish that they lose all contact with reality."[40] Historian of science Derek Price agreed, concluding that top scientific minds are characterized by "*mavericity*, the property of making unusual associations in ideas, of doing the unexpected.... who, in doing the word association test, responds to 'black' not with 'white' but with 'caviar.'"[41] Financial success benefits from a bit of craziness as well. Three-in-four millionaires, for example, believe that learning to "think differently from the crowd" has been a key factor in their economic success.[42]

. . .

Genius Guideline #2:
Successful People Are Overly Optimistic

Compared to those who are less successful, highly successful people are often *less* accurate in their perceptions of themselves and the world around them. For example, relative to depressed people, those who are more psychologically healthy tend to...[43]

• Overestimate how much others like them.

• Have unrealistically positive views of themselves.

- Remember compliments better than criticisms.
- Remember successes as greater than they were.
- Take too much credit for success, while excessively denying responsibility for failures.
- Perceive events as more controllable than they are.
- View themselves as unrealistically unique and exceptional.
- Believe they are more likely than average to have good things happen to them.
- Believe they are less likely than average to suffer negative experiences (i.e., experience the illusion of "unique vulnerability").

Back in the 1980s, one psychologist summarized these phenomena with the phrase *totalitarian ego*.[44] Totalitarian regimes manipulate information in a very biased way, disseminating positive information about themselves while suppressing negative information, constantly casting themselves in an unrealistically positive light. These days I call it the *spin doctor self*.

Just as successful people are a little crazy, it's important to realize these cognitive biases are modest as well – successful people obviously can't be totally unrealistic and still get by in life. But these effects are pervasive and far-reaching. Whether it is memories of the past or expectations about the future, one's self-concept or perceptions of others, the pattern is clear: in a phenomenon sometimes called *depressive realism*,[45] depressed people and those with low self-esteem are less happy but slightly more realistic in their outlook, whereas successful people tend to be overly optimistic. Similarly, people with mild dysfunctions like low self-esteem or moderate anxiety have equal numbers of positive and negative thoughts, whereas psychologically healthy people have nearly twice as many positive thoughts as negative ones.[46] We'll explore the power of slightly excessive optimism and other cognitive biases more fully in the Persistence chapter.

. . .

Genius Guideline #3:
Successful People Are Flexible Thinkers

Several diverse lines of research converge on the notion that successful people are flexible thinkers. For example, when historians are asked to rate American chief executives on various dimensions, their ratings of presidential flexibility are among the best predictors of overall presidential effectiveness. A list of history's most flexible presidents reads like a *Who's Who* of history's greatest presidents, including Thomas Jefferson, Abraham Lincoln, Franklin D. Roosevelt, and John F. Kennedy. Jefferson is a prime example – although he was concerned about excessive power in the hands of the executive branch, he was willing to overlook his own concerns to make the Louisiana Purchase, which he knew to be in the nation's best interest. In contrast, the opinion of history is much more divided about the effectiveness of history's least flexible presidents, a list that includes Woodrow Wilson, Andrew Johnson, Herbert Hoover, John Tyler, John Quincy Adams, and Andrew Jackson. In addition, the terms of less flexible presidents were marked by conflict and gridlock; relative to more flexible presidents, less flexible ones made more vetoes, had their vetoes overridden more often, and had their Cabinet and Supreme Court nominees rejected more often.[47]

Research also confirms that flexible thinking is a prerequisite for creative thinking. Based on his interviews with highly creative achievers, including Nobel and Pulitzer Prize winners, psychiatrist Albert Rothenberg identified two flexibility-related elements crucial to creative thinking.[48] The first was the ability to conceive of an idea and its opposite simultaneously (which he called *Janusian thinking*, after the Roman god Janus who had two faces looking in opposite directions; in the previous chapter, we saw that this same god inspired New Year's resolutions among ancient Romans). The second he called *homospatial* thinking: the ability to conceive of two different objects as occupying the same space simultaneously, and to visualize the new object which would result. Just as individual creative thought benefits from these flexibility-inducing techniques, so does group decision-making. Groups often make more effective decisions when one individual is assigned to the role of "devil's advocate," repeatedly questioning the assumptions of the group, and constructively pointing out possibilities contrary to those being considered.[49]

Inflexible thinking styles lead to several forms of psychological dysfunction. Low self-esteem, for example, is often driven by two types of beliefs – first, that one must get constant love and approval from everyone, and second, that one must accomplish all of his or her goals perfectly.[50] Inherent in both of these beliefs is a lack of flexibility in thinking, as well as an unwillingness to accept the imperfections and conditional nature of life. Similarly, depressed people tend use too many shoulds ("I should lose weight"), perfectionisms ("I must accomplish my goals perfectly"), and unflattering comparisons ("I am a loser, compared to X").[51] Influential therapist Albert Ellis believes this type of inflexible thinking (which he sometimes labels "musturbation") lies at the heart, not only of psychological disorders, but of most human unhappiness as well.[52] Ellis' Rational Emotive Behavior Therapy encourages therapists to help clients develop flexible, conditional styles of thinking to replace inflexible, self-destructive beliefs such as awfulizing beliefs ("No one likes me"), I-can't-stand-it beliefs ("I can't take one more minute of this!"), and self-damnation beliefs ("No wonder she doesn't like me – I'm a total loser").

. . .

Genius Guideline #4:
Successful People Look To Mentors and Role Models

Trial-and-error is an extremely inefficient way to learn life lessons, and successful people prefer to learn from others such as mentors and role models. Generally speaking, the number of highly successful creators and political leaders in a given generation can be predicted by the number of highly successful people in the preceding generation.[53] In other words, the more highly successful role models there are, the more successful people there tend to be in the next generation. Over half of Nobel Prize winners, for example, studied closely under another Nobel Prize winner.[54] Even Albert Einstein looked to others for ideas and inspiration, decorating his study with pictures of his role models such as pioneering physicist Isaac Newton. As Joshua Reynolds put it, "He who resolves never to ransack any mind but his own will be ... obliged to imitate himself, and to repeat what he has before often repeated."

We saw earlier that highly successful people are adept at combining unusual ideas in unique ways, and combining several role models can be an effective strategy for insuring that one becomes an innovator, not an imitator. Just as I have been described as a cross between Tony Robbins and Mr. Spock, creative combinations can lead to new insights and pique the interests of others. By extension, having a sophisticated, multi-dimensional self-concept enables people to better deal with negative or potentially stressful events.[55] If you only think of yourself as a "successful business person" and your business does poorly, the result will be considerable emotional turmoil. But if you view yourself as a successful businessperson, great mom, fantastic lover and world traveler, then a bad day at the office will not be as emotionally upsetting.[56] And it's not just your "current self-concept" that plays this stress-reduction role – "future selves" plays the same role when it comes to dealing with information about your future potential. For example, art students with complex, multi-dimensional future self-concepts are less upset than those with simple future self-concepts by feedback indicating they scored poorly on a test of creativity, implying that their future as an artist might be in doubt.[57]

. . .

Genius Guideline #5:
Successful People Take Risks

Uncommon accomplishment requires uncommon ambition; as Robert Kennedy said, "Only those who dare to fail greatly can ever achieve greatly." Highly successful people, therefore, show an open-ness to taking risks. Great leaders typically earn the label of great-ness by making bold decisions in difficult times. Artists and writers often pursue their passion while risking financial ruin. Entrepre-neurs often risk that fate as well. Pioneering scientists risk the out-rage of those committed to the status quo, as when Galileo was im-prisoned by the Catholic Church for espousing the heretical belief that the earth revolved around the sun. Even today, innovative sci-entists risk the outrage of those with entrenched views and the dis-dain of conservative academic institutions. The risk taking of most successful people is not a "throw-caution-to-the-wind" type of fool-hardiness, but rather recognition that life often involves a risk-re-ward tradeoff and a willingness to take some risk for the potential of high rewards. Most millionaires, for example, did not inherit their wealth, but rather saw an economic opportunity overlooked by oth-ers, and took the risk necessary to capitalize on it. Indeed, "there is a strong correlation between one's willingness to take financial risk and one's level of wealth. It is less about investing in the stock mar-ket and much more about investing in ourselves, our careers, our professional practices, our private businesses, and so forth."[58]

. . .

Genius Guideline #6:
Successful People Ask Questions

Twenty-five hundred years ago, the Greek philosopher Socrates taught his pupils, not by giving answers, but by asking questions. Rather than categorizing their answers as right or wrong, he asked even more questions, continually pushing them to think more deeply and question their own implicit assumptions. Two millennia later, this Socratic method of teaching is still used widely, particularly in law schools. Many psychotherapists are trained in Socratic ques-tioning, and typically strive to be "non-directive" – in other words, they focus on asking questions and eliciting responses rather than providing direction or giving instructions (prompting the old joke that psychologists respond to every statement with the question: "And how does that make you feel?").

Businesses too know the power of questions. Thomas Watson, chairman of IBM during its most explosive period of growth, said: "The ability to ask the right question is more than half the battle of finding the right answer." CEOs who lead their companies from average to exceptional habitually ask questions, not in a threatening way ("Don't you agree?") but in a manner that facilitates communication ("What issues should we focus on?" or "Can you help me understand?").[59] Salespeople are trained in asking the same types of questions to uncover the needs and desires of prospects.

Einstein said: "The important thing is not to stop questioning." But if you're still not convinced, then consider the implications of not asking questions. Recognize this quote? "Never question yourself out of a good story. You have got to know when to stop asking questions." It's the motto of Eddie Clontz, editor of *Weekly World News*, the supermarket tabloid known for quality stories like "I Was Bigfoot's Love Slave."

· · ·

TOOLS: THE VISION QUEST-ION PROCESS

Plotinus: "Vision needs no special gift or effort, but only the use of a faculty which all possess but few employ." Now it's time to put this faculty into action. With these basic principles of thinking like a genius, you are prepared to think about your future in a very specific way – you are ready for the Vision quest process. In this process, you will answer a series of thought-provoking Vision Quest-ions, and follow six simple rules that ensure genius-level thinking as you plan your future, identify your passions, and consider the future selves you desire.

Rule 1. Be alone. Be very alone. In contemplating the future, learn from the isolation common in Native American Vision quests and be alone for the process. Being around others is not only distracting, it inherently focuses you on the expectations that others have of you rather than what you truly want for yourself. This is a time to focus on yourself, your goals, your passions, your vision of the future. Einstein: "I am a horse for a single harness, not cut out for tandem or teamwork, for well I know that in order to attain any definite goal, it is imperative that one person should do the thinking and commanding."

Rule 2. Choose the right time. Obviously you want to engage in your Vision quest when you are in an energetic state, and for most people, that means doing it in the morning before becoming distracted by the ebb-and-flow of daily events. Research also suggests two times in particular to avoid: 3-5pm, and 3-5am. The basic human rest and activity cycle (or circadian rhythm) generally hits its lowest points at these times, and as a result, we have the least energy and think least effectively at these times. In the afternoon, 3-5pm is a great time to get out and exercise rather than think strategically about your future, while 3-5am is a great time to be asleep (note that accidents involving human error often occur between 3am and 5am, including the wreck of the Exxon Valdez and the nuclear accident at Chernobyl). Some self-improvement seminars run late into the night, using sleep deprivation and hunger to break down defenses and make attitudes more malleable; for our immediate purposes, such extreme measures are unnecessary and counter-productive.

Rule 3. Don't worry, be happy. When under stress, people find it difficult to think about the big picture. Instead, they revert to "low-level" thinking about mundane, everyday issues to dull the pain and distract themselves from the stress.[60] This is most apparent when the stress is intense. For example, women married to soldiers listed as missing in action often become preoccupied with low-level tasks such as paying bills and cleaning house as a way of avoiding stressful thoughts.[61] Under the even more extreme circumstance of torture, victims find the focus of their attention narrowed to the minutest details of their experience. Stress limits the ability to think in abstract and creative ways, and must be minimized for a successful Vision quest.

Good moods trigger a different kind of thinking. When people are in good moods, positive events suddenly seem more likely and more plausible.[62] Creativity is also boosted by good moods, even if the mood was triggered by something as small as watching a few minutes of a funny movie or getting a small bag of candy.[63] If you're struggling to get happy, try this simple Mood Booster exercise: spend 10-15 minutes thinking happy thoughts. Accentuate the positive, as the song says. Mentally relive your successes and triumphs. Recall times when you have felt particularly loved and connected with others. Research shows that, after thinking about happy events for just 12 minutes, people are more focused on past successes, feel better about themselves, and have higher expectations about what they can accomplish in the future; on the flip side, those who think about negative events for just 12 minutes rate themselves as less self-confident, friendly, popular and intelligent.[64] Keep in mind that the Mood Booster brings about only a very temporary boost in mood. The power of "positive thinking" is limited, and it's not a strategy for lifelong happiness,[65] but it will serve our purposes for now.

If the Mood Booster doesn't work at first, try one of these two ideas:

• Get more specific with your thoughts. Clinically depressed people encode and retrieve information – particularly memories of positive experiences – on a very general, abstract level. As a result, they often have difficulty bringing to mind specific positive memories that would help combat their negative mood.[66] Even among non-depressed people suffering a more fleeting negative mood, the recall of specific positive memories can help "repair" a negative mood.[67] In both cases, specificity is the key.

• Schedule a time for stress. If you find that negative thoughts keep creeping into your mind, try setting aside a specific time later in the day to get stressed. It may sound a little odd, but it tends to work.

Rule 4. Choose a stimulating environment. Places of natural beauty are ideal for Vision quests, as they can have stimulating, rejuvenating, and inspiring effects. Such environments can also help us break out of our habitual patterns of thought. For example, psychologists have studied the beneficial effects of writing about negative emotional experiences. We'll review these findings in greater detail later, but for now the relevant finding is this: Even though people were alone during these studies, they were generally reluctant to open up when the study was conducted in a "typical" setting such as a classroom or a cubicle. But if the cubicle was modified with unusual wall coverings and unique lighting, creating a very unconventional setting, people were more willing to let down their usual defenses, open up, and break out of traditional ways of thinking.[68]

Rule 5. Just say no. As I travel the country speaking about the scientific research on success, I sometimes get the question: "A Vision quest: Don't I need drugs for that?" The answer is clearly no. Certainly many societies do incorporate drugs such as peyote or hallucinogenic mushrooms into their Vision quests or related processes, and drugs became widely associated with secular Vision quests during the 1960s (as LSD guru Timothy Leary exhorted at the time, "turn on, tune in, and drop out"). But to assume that drugs help clarify one's Vision or purpose is an unnecessarily limiting belief, and there is little or no compelling evidence that drugs contribute to creativity and insight in a manner that outweighs their negative effects. Consider, for example, the conventional image of heavy-drinking writers. Writers do have above-average rates of alcoholism, but that does not mean that alcohol helps them write. In fact, evidence suggests the opposite. Among successful writers who are also heavy drinkers, more than three-in-four believe that alcohol hinders their writing, whereas less than one-in-ten believe alcohol helps.[69]

Two additional examples from history make the most compelling case for "drug-free Vision quests." The first involves William James, one of the first American psychologists and brother of novelist Henry James. An open-minded chap, William James experimented with nitrous oxide, the "laughing gas" still used by some dentists. While under the influence of the drug, James felt as though he were having tremendous insights, but when the drug wore off, his "insights" seemed random and meaningless: "The keynote of the experience is the tremendously exciting sense of an intense metaphysical illumination. Truth lies open to the view... of almost blinding evidence. The mind sees all the logical relations of being with an apparent subtlety and instantaneity to which its normal consciousness offers no parallel; only as sobriety returns, the feeling of insight fades, and one is left staring vacantly at a few disjointed words and phrases.... I have sheet after sheet of phrases dictated or written during the intoxication, which to the sober reader seem meaningless drivel, but which at the moment of transcribing were fused in the fire of infinite rationality.... [He gives examples of his intoxicated insights, and concludes] The most coherent and articulate sentence which came was this: There are no differences but differences of degree between different degrees of difference and no difference."[70] So, if you're looking for great insights like that, then using nitrous oxide on your Vision quest may be for you.

The second example is evident in the career of Dr. Andrew Weil. Today, he is known as a best selling author and authority on integrative medicine. His recent books include *8 Weeks to Optimal Health* and *Eating Well for Optimal Health*. But few people realize that, earlier in his career, Weil had a very different focus. Few realize, for example, that Weil authored *From Chocolate to Morphine: Everything You Need To Know About Mind-Altering Drugs*. And even fewer remember that his first book was *The Natural Mind: A New Way of Looking At Drugs and Higher Consciousness*. And hardly anyone knows that he wrote the forward to *Psilocybin Mushrooms: An Identification Guide* (yes, psilocybin mushrooms are the hallucinogenic kind). Clearly his thinking has evolved. An open-minded young man, he explored the world of drugs on his own personal quest for meaning and purpose. But over time, he came to recognize that altered states of consciousness could be brought about more safely and effectively without drugs, and today he advocates the use of meditation and breathing techniques as part of a healthy, spiritually-fulfilling lifestyle. Other pioneers of drug use (including Timothy Leary and Stanislov Grof) evolved in similar ways. We have seen that successful people prefer to learn from others rather than by trial-and-error, and we can all learn from the evolution of Weil and others toward drug-free Vision quests.

Rule 6. Think like a genius. We've explored six key characteristics of how highly successful people think. The rules for answering the Vision Quest-ions on the facing page will ensure genius-like thinking during the process. Some of these rules will sound familiar to anyone who has done brainstorming, a technique first pioneered in the 1930s, but which really took off as World War II spurred interest in group dynamics (and government funding spurred research on the topic). It quickly became standard practice for helping businesses visualize creative solutions to problems. Brainstorming, like our rules for the vision quest process, is designed to bring about a "Jekyll and Hyde" type of thinking, helping us set aside our critical judgments (the rational Dr. Jekyll) and think in more unconventional ways (the outrageous Mr. Hyde).

Too often we think "in a rut," with the same thoughts repeatedly cycling through our minds. We replay the same events in our minds, and imagine the same possible scenarios for the future. Moreover, we are often rewarded for taking the "safe path" rather than pursuing true creativity. When he wasn't sucking down nitrous oxide, William James wrote eloquently about the "stream of consciousness." He pointed out how our thoughts flow through our minds like water through a riverbed, but too often our consciousness flows repeatedly through the same channels, cycling through the same patterns of thoughts and imagined events. If our thoughts are a stream of consciousness, then the rules for our Vision quest will create a *thought flood*, helping consciousness overflow its normal boundaries and flow through new channels of thought and possibility. Although some of James' language seems outmoded and archaic today, his description of the "highest order of minds" is precisely the kind of thinking that we will try to bring about in our Vision quest: "Instead of thoughts of

Characteristics of genius-level thinking	Rules for answering Vision Quest-ions
Successful people are a little crazy	Commit to being a little crazy during the process. Write down every idea that comes to mind, regardless of how outlandish or ridiculous it may seem. Strive for unusual ideas in odd combinations.
Successful people are unrealistically optimistic	Commit to intense optimism during the process. Consider what you really want to accomplish and who you really want to become. Strive for quantity over quality. Delay judgment and criticism. When your inner critic says "you can't do that," make your motto, "Pay no attention to what the critics say; no statue has ever been erected to a critic" (composer Jean Sibelius).
Successful people are flexible thinkers	Commit to being open-minded during the process. As you consider answers to the questions, consider the opposite of those answers as well (in some ways, the questions will force this kind of flexible thinking).
Successful people look to role models	Consider those you admire during the process. Consider how your role models might answer various questions (again, some of the questions themselves will force you to do this).
Successful people take risks	Think big. Think really big. Remember that great success requires ambitious goals. Recall the words of Thomas Carlyle: "Every noble work is at first impossible." Or better yet, remember the words of Mark Twain: "Twenty years from now you will be more disappointed by the things that you didn't do than by the ones you did do."[1]
Successful people ask questions	The process itself is obviously focused on questions, but even beyond that, take this opportunity to question your assumptions about what you really want from life. Ask "why"? Consider why you aspire to the things for which you now strive.

concrete things patiently following one another in a beaten track of habitual suggestion, we have the most abrupt cross-cuts and transitions from one idea to another, the most rarefied abstractions and discriminations, the most unheard-of-combinations of elements, the subtlest associations of analogy; in a word, we seem suddenly introduced into a seething caldron of ideas, where everything is fizzling and bobbling about in a state of bewildering activity, where partnerships can be joined or loosened in an instant, treadmill routine is unknown, and the unexpected seems the only law."[72]

. . .

The Vision Quest-ions

OK, enough psychological foreplay. Let's get to the questions. They are organized into nine different scenarios. Write as much as you can in response to each.

1. The Ideal Life Scenario. Take a few moments and envision the ideal life you would like to have ten years from now.

• What will I be doing?
• Where will I be living?
• Will I still have a job? If so, what would it be? How much will I be making?
• Who do I want to be? What roles do I want to have in ten years? (such as entrepreneur, athlete, parent, etc.)
• If I had three wishes today, what would they be?
• What makes me laugh? How would those things be part of my daily life in ten years?
• What celebrities or historical figures do I most admire? In what ways would my ideal life be like theirs?
• Try writing a resume that reflects your accomplishments over the next ten years.

2. The Lottery Scenario. Take a few moments and envision your life if you won the lottery.

- If I had enough money to retire today, what would I do with the rest of my life?
- Near-term: What would I buy? Where would I travel? Who would I visit?
- Longer-term: After buying "stuff" gets boring, what would I do?
- What kind of job would I be so happy in that I would do it even if I didn't need money?

3. The Ideal Day Scenario. Maybe ideal lives and winning the lottery are a little hard for you to imagine. Try imagining that you have the day off tomorrow with no responsibilities. What would you do? (If you said "Sleep," then write about what you would do the next day).

- What would the day be like for me to wake up totally excited?
- What time would I wake up?
- What would I do?
- Who would I spend time with?
- What kinds of experiences do I find totally engrossing? In other words, when I am engaged in them, I forget everything around me?

4. The Forgotten Dreams Scenario. Take a few moments and remember the dreams and ambitions of your youth.

- When I was young, what did I want to be when I grew up?
- When I was young, who were my heroes and role models?
- When I was young, what were my favorite subjects in school?
- How did I end up in my current profession?
- If things had been different, what other careers might I have ended up in?

5. The Deathbed Scenario. Imagine that you are on your deathbed, and you are looking back over your life.

- If I could live my life over, what would I do differently?
- Knowing what I know now, would I have chosen different goals and ambitions?
- What were my happiest moments in life? The saddest?
- At what point was I most excited about my future?
- What did I really want to do in life, but didn't try to accomplish, because I lacked confidence or someone talked me out of trying?
- What was my best decision? My biggest missed opportunity?
- What remains on my "things to do before I die" list?

6. *The Beyond the Grave Scenario.* Now imagine that you have passed away.

- How would I like my family and friends to remember me after I have passed away?
- How will my family and friends remember me after I have passed away?
- Try writing two obituaries for yourself: a "likely" obituary as if you were to pass away today, and an "ideal" obituary as you would like it to be.

7. *The Road-Not-Taken Scenario.* Consider the following list of values. Now rank them, with 1 being the value that has been most important to you in the past, and 10 being the value that has been least important to you.

———— Family
_____ Success
_____ Contribution
_____ Wealth
_____ Love
_____ Security
_____ Variety

_____ Contentment
_____ Excitement
_____ Growth

Now consider how your life would have been different if you had different patterns of values.

• What if my least important values had been my most important?
• What career would I be in today?
• Would I be married?
• Would I have the same friends?
• Would I be more financially secure or less?
• Would I be happier?

8. *The Brutal Honesty Scenario.* This one is a little different. Try being brutally honest about your life. At its core, what is your life really about? What is your job really about? Recall Steve Jobs asking John Sculley if he wanted to change the world or sell sugared water. Is your life about selling sugared water? If it is, what do you really want your life and your job to be about? I once worked for a consulting firm, and convinced myself that I was "helping companies become more profitable, and thereby boosting the free enterprise system." But when I became brutally honest with myself, I had to acknowledge that my job really involved "helping companies sell more stuff." It wasn't long before I changed jobs. Maybe when you do this, you come up with a very positive answer. As I've worked with members of the U. S. armed forces, for example, they often feel their job is "protecting the Constitution." At Fannie Mae, which provides government-backed mortgages, executives believe they are in the "American dream business," strengthening "the whole social fabric of America" by making "home ownership a reality for thousands of Americans."[73] But many people come up with much less satisfying answers when they get brutally honest with themselves, and the process helps them clarify what they would find more satisfying.

9. Targeted Vision Quest-ions. The Vision Quest-ions above are useful for helping clarify a Vision for your life as a whole. That's obviously a big task. In seminars with limited time, I often ask people to focus just on one area of life, and answer the questions below.

- *What*: In this area of your life, what do you want to accomplish? In this aspect of your life, what would you try if you knew you could not fail?[74]
- *Who*: In this aspect of your life, who do you want to be? What is your ideal future self? What roles and identities do you want to have? Who do you admire?
- *Why*: Why do you want this? In this aspect of your life, at what point were you most excited about your future? (In the Persistence chapter, we'll explore why this final question is so psychologically telling.)

Resource Reccommendation

If you are intregued by the Vision Ques-tion process, you might enjoy reading *What Color Is My Parachute? A Practical Manual for Job-Hunters and Career-Changers* by Richard Nelson Bolles. For nearly three decades, this book has been a leading guide for job hunters. Updated annually, it is much more than a manual on writing resumes or negotiating salaries. Ultimately it focuses on two questions, both of which get to the heart of our Vision quest process: What do you want to do? Where do you want to do it? You may also want to check out the book's companion web site, www.jobhuntersbible.com.

. . .

A Vision Quest Example:
See Dick and Jane Clarify Their Passions In Life

To summarize the concepts in this chapter, and to make them more concrete, we'll end with a brief example of two people seeking to achieve more in life. Dick takes the more common path, but achieves less. Jane takes the advice in this book to heart, even when it seems unconventional, and finds the road less traveled far more rewarding.

Jane is 28 and she's doing OK in life. She's got a decent job and a great family. She's doing better than a lot of her friends, but she's not exactly living the life of her dreams, either. Like many people, she's gone from one job to the next, earning higher salaries with each move, but not really thinking about what career would be most personally satisfying to her. She's so busy focusing on her day-to-day responsibilities and near-term obligations that she just doesn't have much time to think about her long-term aspirations.

Jane wants to take greater control of her life, and she realizes the first step is figuring out what she really wants, so she arranges an afternoon alone for an "off-site meeting with herself." She does a lot of hard thinking on her Vision quest. The most revealing aspect, although it was emotionally challenging, comes when she gets brutally honest with herself (scenario #8). On a personal level, she recognizes that she habitually puts the interests of others ahead of her own needs. Professionally, she acknowledges that she has become a cog in a bureaucratic machine rather than pursuing the more meaningful volunteer work and artistic pursuits that truly excited her when she was a student (#4). She thinks about what she'd do if she won the lottery (#2), and the process re-kindles her interest in art and travel. In addition to considering *what* she wants, she envisions *who* she wants to be (#1): an artist, an athlete, a world traveler, and a contributor to society as well as to her family. She wants to lose weight, but sees that more as a means to an end; her larger focus is getting fitter, feeling healthier, and having the energy she'll need to accomplish the other aspects of her Vision.

Like Jane, Dick is doing OK in life. He's a computer programmer, and he's fairly good at what he does. Still, he's behind many of colleagues because he spent five years in advertising before deciding that he didn't like it, and started over in an entry-level position in his new field. Now that programming is becoming a bit boring to him, he's considering another career change. Dick has a lot of interests, but with no defining passion, he drifts, rudderless.

He isn't totally clueless, though. He does recognize that he's underachieving in life, but unlike Jane, he distracts himself from that painful realization rather than face it. Eating is one of his favorite distractors, and because delay of gratification has never been his strength, he has put on 35 pounds in the past two years, although he prefers not to think about that, either. Whereas Jane made the time to develop a compelling Vision for her future, Dick prefers to think about the past, often pondering how his life might have been different if he had a different set of values (#7) or had made different decisions (#5). Unfortunately, he uses these thoughts as a form of escapism, rather than as aids in making better decisions about the future.

Chapter Five

Step Two: Strategy –
The Science of Turning
Lofty Ambitions into
Consistent Action

"If one advances confidently in the direction of his dreams,
and endeavors to live that life which he has imagined,
he will meet with success unexpected in common hours.
If you have built castles in the air, your work need not be lost;
that is where they should be. Now put the foundations
under them." Henry Thoreau

IN 1948, IBM CHAIRMAN John Watson predicted that in the future, there would be, at most, five computers in the world. By the 1970s it was clear that Watson's remark would go down as one of the most spectacularly wrong predictions in history. Still, computers were hardly household items; they remained massive, million-dollar machines run by white-coated engineers in large organizations. That's precisely how things remained until a new Vision emerged: average people empowered by fun desktop computers. Inspired by that Vision, Steve Jobs co-founded Apple Computer in his parents' garage and sparked the personal computer revolution.

But Vision, as we shall see, is a "necessary but not sufficient" condition for success. Jobs was ousted from Apple before the company's greatest successes in the mid-80s, displaced by none other than John Scully, the man Jobs enticed to Apple with his sugared water comment. Jobs excelled in creating and communicating an idealistic Vision of the future, but fell short in managing people, developing a corporate strategy, and steering the company toward profitability. Jobs was a visionary, not a strategist. His longer-lasting return to Apple in the late 1990s was possible only because he had enhanced his skills as a strategist. Although this example focuses on the corporate world, the same message is true for individual success as well: lasting success comes from having a compelling Vision and developing a Strategy for making that vision a reality.[75] Having only one or the other leads to underachievement. As we all know, successful people make plans for success...

. . .

COMMON KNOWLEDGE:
SUCCESSFUL PEOPLE MAKE PLANS FOR SUCCESS

Many entrepreneurs suffer from the Jobs syndrome – being a visionary with weak strategic skills – and have suffered the same fate of being cast out of the company they founded. Many high-profile dot-com failures exhibited the corporate equivalent, with lofty Visions (e.g., "the Internet will reshape the business world, and we're going to be a part it...") but poor Strategies ("... so let's sell dog food online!"). On an individual level, the Jobs syndrome underlies several types of psychological dysfunction. Perfectionists and procrastinators, for example, tend to have ideals so lofty or daunting that no Strategy could possibly be successful, leading to anxiety and avoidance. This combination – high-minded ideas but the inability to put them into action – is seen everywhere from television characters like Kramer on *Seinfeld* to social archetypes such as "hopeless romantics" and "absent-minded professors."

	Vision	
	High	**Low**
Strategy — High	• Henry Ford • Thomas Edison • Mahatma Gandhi • Martin Luther King Jr. • Ted Turner • Steve Case • Oprah Winfrey • Revolutionaries-turned-political-leaders • Characters played by Michael J. Fox	• The misguided • The indecisive • Perpetual students • Hamlet
Strategy — Low	• Steve Jobs (circa 1985) • Procrastinators • Perfectionists • Hopeless romantics • Absent-minded professors • Dot-com flameouts • Perpetual revolutionaries • Kramer on *Seinfeld*	• Slackers • Wanderers • Drifters • Depressed • George on *Seinfeld* • Bart Simpson

Of course, "high vision/low strategy" is not the only recipe for underachieving. The "low vision/high strategy" combination is perhaps best illustrated by a friend of mine. Although extremely smart, he drifted through life without a sense of Vision or purpose, never identifying a true passion among his many passing interests. While his friends went to graduate school, he could not decide what he wanted from his education, so he took class after class for nearly a decade, ending up almost accidentally with bachelor's degrees in philosophy and linguistics. After school, while his friends became successful doctors, artists and business owners, he drifted from one low-paying, dead-end job to the next. Without a Vision to provide direction in his life, his strengths in Strategy – for example, his ability to sign up for and complete classes – did not lead to the success worthy of such a smart, good-hearted man.

True success only comes from a combination of Vision and Strategy. Henry Ford had a Vision of America reshaped by affordable automobiles, as well as a highly successful Strategy built around mass production and mass marketing. Throughout history, successful business ventures – Ted Turner's CNN, Steve Case's America OnLine, Oprah Winfrey's inspirational empire – have all been made possible by the combination of Vision and Strategy, of insight and execution. Social and religious leaders such as Mahatma Gandhi and Martin Luther King Jr. had the same combination – an inspiring Vision of society's potential, coupled with Strategies based on inspiration and civil disobedience for helping make that Vision a reality.

Strategy requires a different kind of thinking from Vision. It is less crazy and more rational. It is less idealistic while being more complex and conditional. American presidents, for example, illustrate the transition from Vision to Strategy in their speeches and writings.[76] During elections, candidates speak in simple, straightforward, visionary terms. After all, idealistic, optimistic rhetoric tends to win elections. But within a month of inauguration, a dramatic shift occurs. The "integrative complexity" of their speeches and writings increases. Chief Executives stop presenting issues in black-and-white terms, and instead focus on the complexity of the problems at hand and the compromises needed to resolve them (interestingly, if the incumbent runs for re-election, the integrative complexity of their speeches drops as election season begins).

Revolutionaries who become successful politicians transition from Vision to Strategy even more dramatically.[77] Fostering a revolution requires unambiguous rhetoric ("the old regime is evil, but we are on the side of righteousness"), whereas running a country, particularly in the aftermath of a revolution, requires a different kind of thinking. During the American Revolution, the Founding Fathers presented issues in black-and-white terms (e.g., Patrick Henry's "Give me liberty or give me death"). After the revolution, some successfully made the transition to more complex, strategic thinking – Thomas Jefferson and George Washington did so and went on to be highly successful presidents. But others didn't. Alexander Hamilton was unable to shift to less rigid strategic thinking. He repeatedly failed to win a presidential nomination, lost the leadership of his own political party, became mired in America's first political sex scandal, and was killed in a dual with an old rival. Similarly, communist revolutionaries-turned-lasting-politicians (e.g., Lenin, Castro) made the transition from visionaries before the revolution to practical strategists afterwards. Those unwilling to taint their visionary ideals with strategic practicalities become perpetual revolutionaries with no place in the post-revolution power structure (e.g., Trotsky was assassinated, Che Guevara was killed trying to foster revolution in Bolivia). Before you start writing angry letters – I'm not saying that the Strategy or Vision of the communist figures was good. I'm simply illustrating the transition from Vision to Strategy based on the writings and speeches of these historical figures.

· · ·

Vision and Strategy in Everyday Life

Of course, the combination of Vision and Strategy isn't just required for building a business empire or cementing a place in history. It's required for success in daily life as well. "Flexible" thinkers who engage in higher-level visionary thinking as well as lower-level strategic thinking are, on average, physically healthier than people who consistently think at either level alone. Flexible thinkers have lower rates of drug and alcohol abuse as well.[78]

Making plans for success is crucial for wealth as well as health. The benefits of financial planning, for example, are well known. In *The Millionaire Mind*, author Thomas Stanley asked a nationwide sample of millionaires how they reduce fears and worries. The results indicate not an escapist attitude, but rather a mindset of proactive planning. Topping the list are hard work (94%) and believing in themselves (94%), foreshadowing the importance of Persistence and Belief that I'll highlight in later chapters. But ranking just behind are items underscoring the importance of planning: preparation (93%), focusing on key issues (91%), being decisive (89%), planning (87%), and being well organized (83%).

If true success requires planning, then it follows that a "motivational pump-up" alone will have only a modest effect. In researching this book, I've been to a number of "motivational" seminars at which it's common to see people jumping up and down, yelling "power phrases" like "I'm unstoppable!!," making fist-pumping "power moves," and dancing wildly to blaring music (for reasons I've been unable to discern, music by 80s hair bands seems to be preferred). I've got nothing against getting pumped up – it's fun, and in the right context, it can contribute to enhanced performance. But too often, people seem to leave such seminars thinking, "I'm motivated! I'm pumped-up!! I'm unstoppable!!! ...Now what do I do?" Motivation without a strategy might be fun, but it also tends to be fleeting.[79]

. . .

Goal Setting and Strategies for Success

It's been said that when myth replaces reality, believe the myth because it contains deeper, more fundamental truths. I don't particularly agree with that sentiment – I'm very much pro-reality. But it is nevertheless useful to examine these deeper truths inherent in myth. Urban legends are modern-day morality plays – they are dramatic, memorable stories used by elements of society to teach lessons or shape behavior. The urban legend that people only use 10% of their brains, although false, inspires people to set higher standards, try harder, and breakthrough self-imposed barriers. Similarly, the story of the Yale Study of Goals, although fictitious, is perpetuated because it makes the very valid point that goal setting can contribute to personal achievement. Real research, although less dramatic and more complex than the Yale Study of Goals, clearly demonstrates the beneficial effects of goals. People with highly important goals, for example, tend to be happier and more satisfied with life than those without important goals (in fairness, it should be pointed out that they are also more anxious).[80] Goals, when properly set, lead to enhanced performance, and can be an integral part of a Strategy for Success.

Psychologists agree that goals play a fundamental role in human behavior. Psychologist Alfred Adler wrote, "We cannot think, feel, will, or act without the perception of a goal." Another prominent psychologist even went to so far as to say that a goal-less state of indifference could be described as "psychological death."[81] Literally hundreds of studies have been conducted on goals, and hundreds more on related concepts with different names, including "current concerns," "personal strivings," "personal projects," "sales quotas," and "self-guides." Goals are far more than research topics of academic interest. Elite athletes are trained in goal setting techniques. Members of the U. S. Olympic ski team, for example, are required to write personal performance goals and submit them to their coaches on a regular basis. Many businesspeople are compensated based on whether they achieve their goals. The list of practical applications for goal setting is quite lengthy. Regardless of what they are called or how they are used, goal-like concepts lead to increased performance for three major reasons:

- *Direction.* Goals direct action. They channel and focus effort in the direction chosen by the goal setter. As a result, they are empowering tools, enabling people to steer their lives in the direction of their choosing. If you have ever decided to buy a particular kind of car, and suddenly began seeing that kind of car everywhere, you've experienced how goals direct attention as well as action, even without conscious effort.

- *Motivation.* Goals stretch and push, resulting in greater effort and persistence. Goals clarify and make concrete your desired ends. Being aware of the gap between where you are now and where you want to be creates motivation to close that gap. Further motivation comes about because goals engage your sense of pride, self-esteem, and (depending on the circumstances) possibly even competitiveness.

- *Strategy refinement.* Goal setting is merely one element of a Strategy for success. But it is a crucial element because goals accelerate and intensify the broader process of Strategy refinement. After setting challenging goals, people think longer and more creatively about how to accomplish them, and how to measure progress toward them.[82] Merely telling a salesperson to "sell as much as you can" will result in directed action and heightened motivation. But a challenging, specific goal (like selling a million dollars worth of products per year) will also engage the process of Strategy refinement – hard, creative thinking about how to accomplish the goal.

There's an important caveat to all these wonderful benefits of goals: they are only effective when set properly. They key to developing a potent Strategy, then, is understanding the six proven principles for effective goals...

. . .

UNCOMMON KNOWLEDGE:
SIX PROVEN PRINCIPLES FOR EFFECTIVE GOALS

. . .

Goal-Setting Principle #1:
Challenging

It should come as no surprise that, all else being equal, people who set more *challenging* goals tend to accomplish more than those who set more modest goals.[83] As Emerson said, "We aim above the mark to hit the mark." As goals are set higher and higher, performance increases by a comparable amount (in what's known as a "linear function"). But only up to a point. Challenging goals must, by definition, also be attainable. People with attainable goals tend to be happier and experience more well-being than those with unattainable goals; they also put forth greater effort and are less likely to give up in the face of obstacles.[84] Conversely, when goals exceed expectations of what is feasible (as when people have lofty Visions unreachable by any Strategy), people achieve less, become anxious, and often sink into depression.[85]

The most common reaction to unattainable goals is simply disengagement – people don't commit to them. In fact, commitment to a goal is predicted by a simple formula:[86]

Commitment to a goal = Goal Importance X Goal Attainability

People are most committed to important, attainable goals, but if either goal importance or goal attainability becomes zero, then commitment disappears. This formula also indicates why employees are often reluctant to commit to corporate goals set by senior management. Such goals are typically challenging (e.g., double profitability within three years), but are often considered unattainable. In fact, rank-and-file employees often think that management itself considers the goals unattainable, and merely set them outrageously high in a manipulative attempt to spur productivity. Successful companies enhance employee commitment by fostering the sense of attainability (e.g., via training, hiring additional staff, investing in technology). They also communicate why such goals should be important to employees as well as management (e.g., linking individual compensation to corporate performance, highlighting opportunities for career growth enabled by new corporate strategies).

. . .

Goal-Setting Principle #2:
Specific

The biggest boost in performance from goal setting comes when goals are not only challenging, but challenging and *specific*. Over 100 published studies support the notion that challenging specific goals result in better performance than easy goals, no goals, or situations in which individuals simply try to "do their best."[87] In fact, one team of psychologists and business experts who reviewed this research concluded "the beneficial effect of [specific challenging goals] on task performance is one of the most robust and replicable findings in the psychological literature."[88] And it is the breadth of findings, across different kinds of tasks and different types of people, that is particularly impressive. The beneficial effects of specific, challenging goals have been shown across different types of . . .

- *Studies*, from tightly-controlled laboratory studies lasting less than an hour to "real-world" field studies of employee performance lasting several years.
- *Tasks*, from typing to energy conservation, from brainstorming new ideas to repairing soda machines, from fund raising to bargaining.
- *People*, from elementary school children to Marine recruits, from logging crews with little formal education to highly trained scientists and engineers.
- *Industries*, from manufacturing to delivery services, from telecom-

munications to baking pastries.

- *Business functions*, from sales to customer service, from managing staff to loading ships and trucks.
- *Countries*, from the U. S. to Australia, from England to Israel, from Germany to Japan.
- *Goals*, from goals individuals set for themselves to goals (such as sales quotas) set by others.[89]

One irony uncovered by this very consistent body of research is that trying to "do your best" doesn't actually result in "your best." It leaves "wiggle room," creating the opportunity for a counter-productive combination of loafing and self-deception – easing up while convincing yourself (and perhaps others) that you in fact gave full effort. Specific, challenging goals minimize wiggle room, resulting in greater effort and persistence, as well as more Strategy refinement (e.g., planning, preparing, organizing).[90]

The benefits of specific challenging goals, from performance-enhancement to ambiguity-reduction, make them popular in the workplace, boosting both goal commitment and employee satisfaction. Air traffic controllers, for example, are evaluated in part for their ability to perform under stress. But instead of evaluating controllers on "the extent to which the ratee keeps control over the situation even while facing stressful circumstances," more specific behavioral goals tend to work better, like "When pilot reports emergency, subject instructs pilot with great precision while directing air traffic as usual." Similarly, instead of evaluating global dimensions such as whether one has the "knowledge to do the job," employees respond better when goals are framed in terms of specific behaviors like "updating pilots with flight information" or "navigating planes through clouds, relying on radar."[91]

. . .

Goal-Setting Principle #3:
Approach

True success in life comes from achieving things, not avoiding them. Although we may respect those who avoid conflict, drugs, guilt, or overeating, we truly admire those who build lasting businesses, nurture loving families, or contribute to society. Our goals should follow suit – pulling us toward desired outcomes rather than pushing us away from negative ones. In other words, we should set *approach* goals. Fortunately, most people understand this intuitively, and only about 10-15% of the goals set by most people are avoidance goals such as giving up smoking or avoiding alcohol.[92] And that's a good thing, because relative to those who focus on moving toward approach goals, people with many avoidance goals tend to …[93]

- Be less happy and less satisfied with life.
- Experience more anxiety and more physical illnesses.
- Report lower marital satisfaction.
- Feel less autonomy and control over their lives.
- Be less committed to their goals, and give up on them more easily.
- Be less happy when making progress toward their goals, but more upset by setbacks.
- View accomplishing their goals as less enjoyable and satisfying.

Avoidance goals have what one might (quite unscientifically) call a "soul-sucking" effect. Their pursuit leads to a decreased sense of self-esteem, competence, and vitality. Avoidance goals bring to mind negative experiences, conjuring up memories of accidents or thoughts of failures, whereas approach goals are mentally associated with positive memories and triumphs.[94] Avoidance goals trigger a "should" mindset with a focus on threats and self-protection, whereas approach goals trigger a "want" mindset with a focus on possibilities and opportunities. Perhaps all these challenges of avoidance goals are why the Old Testament's ten commandments are so often violated – eight of the ten are admonitions *not* to do something!

A few years ago, I attended an adventure racing school and learned that race car driving is similar to goal setting in one crucial way – in both cases, you want to focus on the outcomes you desire, not the ones you want to avoid. The first thing amateur racers are taught is to "look where you want the car to go." Where your eyes look, your body will instinctively steer the car. Most of the time, that's an easy rule to follow. But when the car spins out and careens toward a wall at 150 miles per hour, it suddenly becomes very tempting to look at the wall. Just as people can't resist gawking at car accidents they pass on the highway, apparently we're equally fascinated with car accidents that involve our own impending deaths. But this is precisely when it's most important to focus on approach goals, and look where you want the car (and your life) to go.

. . .

Goal-Setting Principle #4:
Measurable

In business it's often said, "What gets measured gets done." And although that may be a bit of an overstatement, it's clear that goals have a much bigger impact on performance if they are *measurable*. For example, people given the specific challenging goal of reducing their electricity usage by 20% are only successful in conserving if they are able to measure their progress; those getting periodic reports of kilowatt usage reduce consumption, but those not getting feedback fail to reduce their consumption.[95] Measurable goals have many benefits, including enhanced Strategy refinement. Feedback that your energy usage hasn't declined, for example, prompts a new action plan, perhaps lowering the thermostat instead of turning off lights.

Measurable goals also encourage consistent, steady progress – day after day, week after week. Consultant Laddie Hutar said, "Success consists of a series of little daily victories," and measuring progress fosters that mindset. Even creative work, which you might think takes place in "binges" when the artist is "inspired," is actually best accomplished by consistent, daily, measurable progress. Professional writers, for example, are just that: professional. They are disciplined, writing day-in and day-out, in measurable amounts. Aldous Huxley wrote five hours per day, Hemingway six, and Flaubert seven; Joseph Conrad, whose novel *Heart of Darkness* inspired the movie *Apocalypse Now*, wrote eight hours each day.[96] Others measured not the number of hours worked, but the actual amount written. George Sand, a hard-drinking woman who posed as a man to publish her writing more easily, committed to writing 30 pages each day, regardless of her drunken state.

On a day-to-day basis, progress toward goals generally gets measured in degrees of success, not as pure success or pure failure. That's particularly important because dichotomous, black-or-white, success-or-failure thinking makes you vulnerable to the "snowball effect" – letting a minor setback "snowball" into a major relapse, and abandoning goals after a single slip. Psychologists call it the "what the hell" effect, or more formally, the "abstinence violation" effect[97] – bingeing after a single setback if you have forbidden yourself something (e.g., made a resolution to abstain completely from fatty foods or alcohol). In other words, when you fall off the wagon, sometimes you fall off big. For example ...

- Non-dieters who drink milkshakes in the initial phase of a research study go on to eat less in later portions of the study (because they aren't as hungry); dieters, in contrast, actually eat more because they figure they've broken their diet so "what the hell."[98]
- In supermarkets, obese people purchase more if they eat free food samples (because they feel they have broken the diet); non-obese people purchase less (again, because they're not as hungry).[99]
- Obese people make more impulse purchases in supermarkets, particularly products at the end of aisles or in checkout lanes, if they have recently eaten, as opposed to if they are hungry.[100] Non-obese people show the opposite pattern.

In all of these cases, the root cause is the same; people tend to suffer major setbacks when they think in "either-or" terms rather than thinking in terms of consistent measurable progress toward goals with inevitable ups and downs. As one group of psychologists put it, we must be wary of "zero tolerance" beliefs – in other words, beliefs that "no misstep, no violation, can be allowed, because it will lead almost inevitably to disaster. There is no gray area, no allowance made for minor indulgences, no sympathy for occasional backsliding.... The problem with zero-tolerance beliefs, however, is that if a lapse does happen, these beliefs may contribute to subsequent snowballing. And because people are not perfect and do not live absolutely by the rules 100% of the time, some of these lapses are likely to occur.... Zero-tolerance beliefs can be compared to a military strategy of putting all one's defense on the front line, with no reserves. The front line is defended maximally well; but if there is a breach, there is no fallback option, and catastrophe ensues."[101]

. . .

Goal-Setting Principle #5:
Proximal

Everyone knows that deadlines are very motivating. Among college students, for example, about three-in-four report finishing projects precisely on the day they are due.[102] As the deadline for a particular goal looms, people think more about that goal[103] and experience a burst of productivity. Even rats work harder as they approach their "goals."[104] So it makes sense to use this "imminence" effect to your benefit by setting *proximal* goals with relatively short time horizons. In other words, think weekly or monthly goals rather than yearly goals. In addition to the greater motivating power of proximal goals, it is also easier to measure your progress toward them – you'll quickly be able to assess if you are on track to accomplish your goal, and if not, you'll quickly be able to devise new strategies.

Children struggling in math asked to set near-term, proximal goals not only outperform those asked to set more distant goals, they also develop a heightened sense of personal control, confidence, determination, and even (gasp!) an interest in math that wasn't there before.[105] Proximal goals are ideal for kids (and anyone else with a short time horizon, or less able to make abstractions into the future). But they work for adults as well. Proximal goals lead to more weight loss than distant goals, and those who do lose weight setting distant goals do so only because they tend to "improvise" more proximal goals as well.[106] In a very real sense, satisfaction with life itself can be enhanced by proximal goals. Those who are most satisfied with life are those working toward enjoyable, moderately challenging goals of high short-term importance.[107] In contrast, those who consistently focus on very long-term goals are less satisfied with life. They also view their long-term goals as more difficult, more pressure-filled, and less enjoyable, while their near-term goals seem less relevant and satisfying. Similarly, members of the U. S. Olympic ski team are required to write long-term, intermediate and short-term goals, but the sports psychologists who work with them have concluded that "repeated daily focusing on long-term goals is often counter-productive. The focus is too far into the future and prevents the athlete from completing the intermediate steps essential to ultimate success."[108] Using the same logic, military leaders often "segment" or "compartmentalize" complex missions into smaller, "bite-sized" sub-missions.

Certainly there are some benefits to longer-term goals. They can provide a clear sense of the overall outcomes you are working toward. Businesses often emphasize annual goals because they can help in financial planning, estimating hiring needs, and so on. But top businesses also set quarterly or even monthly goals because they realize that, for the most part, annual goals are simply too far in the future to be motivating. Annual goals are too abstract. If you set a yearly goal, it is easy to find yourself sitting around for 9 or 10 months doing little about your goal, feeling uneasy and overwhelmed about such an ambitious objective, and then freaking out as the end of the year approaches.

Of course, it's possible to go overboard by making goals "too proximal." For example, students asked to make general monthly plans and goals perform better than those asked to make highly specific daily plans. They spend more time studying, study more effectively, procrastinate less, and get better grades.[109] Monthly planners experience more flexibility in crafting strategies for accomplishing their goals. They more easily adjust "on the fly" and are less easily "derailed" by changes in circumstance. A daily planner who gets a mild case of the flu quickly finds his daily goals unattainable, resulting in disappointment and a loss of momentum. General planners enjoy the process of planning more, gaining a sense of designing their lives, while highly specific planners get the sense of their lives being controlled by their appointment books and Palm Pilots. In short, it is best to set proximal goals that are monthly or weekly, and think in terms of daily progress, not daily planning.

· · ·

Goal-Setting Principle #6:
Inspirational

Finally, your goals should be *inspirational*. That term means different things to different people – in this context, it simply means that your goals should be important to you and consistent with your own ideals and ambitions for the future. People who pursue goals that others set for them must live with what psychologist Karen Horney called the "tyranny of the should." People whose goals are consistent with their needs and values, even when compared to others with the same skills, exhibit "more interest, excitement and confidence, which in turn is manifest both as enhanced performance, persistence and creativity, and as heightened vitality, self-esteem and general well-being."[110] Aligning goals with your long-term Vision also makes goals easier to remember, makes them more "top of mind," and enables better time management because you spend more time progressing toward more important outcomes.[111]

We all know people who have set non-inspirational goals (e.g., a friend who went to law school because his parents wanted him to, not because he was interested in law). But in corporate America, I'm sorry to say that non-inspirational goals are the rule rather than the exception. Consider the typical hour-long annual performance review. An Employee sits down with her Boss. The Boss spends the first two minutes praising Employee's strengths and accomplishments. Often, this can take the full two minutes. Then The Boss spends 56 minutes harping on The Employee's failures and weaknesses. We live in a politically correct society, so of course they're labeled "opportunities for improvement" or "areas for growth" or "deltas," but we all know The Boss really means "weaknesses." Then, in the final two minutes of the review, The Boss spells out The Employee's goals and objectives for the coming year. And in an effort to create "balanced" and "well-rounded" employees, those goals invariably ignore strengths and focus on improving weaknesses. In fact, advancement and promotion are generally tied to improving weaknesses to an adequate level. Interestingly, research on the most effective managers reveals that they do not fall into this pattern. They identify the individual strengths of their employees, set goals based on those strengths, and create environments in which those strengths can flourish while weaknesses can largely be ignored.[112] In other words, the best managers harness the power of inspirational goals.

. . .

Some Frequently Asked Questions about Goals

Got any tips for remembering these principles?

It's simple. Just think shrimp. Think pasta. That's right –think SCAMPI. Specific, Challenging, Approach, Measurable, Proximal, Inspirational. Remember, goals are effective for three main reasons, and each of the six SCAMPI principles makes at least one of those three reasons more prevalent.

	Reasons why goals are effective		
	Direction	Motivation	Strategy refinement
Specific	✔		✔
Challenging		✔	
Approach	✔	✔	
Measurable	✔		✔
Proximal		✔	✔
Inspirational		✔	

How big is the effect of setting goals? In other words, by how much do goals boost performance?

Obviously that depends on many factors. In some circumstances and with some people, goals have modest effects, whereas other studies document performance improvements of 50% or more. On average, goal setting alone typically leads to performance improvements of 10-15%.[113] In this book, we'll combine goal setting with other performance enhancement strategies, and that leads to profoundly better outcomes. In business settings, for example, when goal setting is combined with monetary incentives and bonus plans, performance improvements are more typically in the 40-50% range.[114]

I understand the power of proximal goals, but I always seem to underestimate how long it will take to accomplish my goals. How can I make better time estimates?

People and organizations are notoriously poor at predicting how long it will take to accomplish goals. Taking longer than expected to complete a task, even knowing that most similar projects have run late, is so common that psychologists even have a name for it: the *planning fallacy*.[115] We've all had the experience of sincerely expecting to tackle the dozen or so projects we set aside for the weekend, despite the fact that so many weekends have come and gone having tackled only one or two. College students, for example, report finishing about two-thirds of their projects later than expected. Even when they make worst-case scenario predictions about how long the project will take – assuming that everything that could go wrong did – roughly half still finish later than expected.[116]

The best predictor of future behavior is past behavior, and the best predictor of how long it will take to accomplish a given task is how long it took to accomplish similar tasks in the past. But too often we overlook past failures when estimating completion times, and go out of our way to construct scenarios about how it will be "different this time." When predicting how long a task will take, as much as 70% of a person's thinking is devoted to making future plans for that task, and very little time is spent thinking about potential problems, past experiences, or how long it has taken others.[117] This is one instance when our generally healthy tendencies to plan for the future and be optimistic can lead us astray. For more realistic deadlines, try…

- *Thinking back.* Focus on similar experiences you've had in the past, and relate those experiences to your estimate of how long it will take this time. Only about 29% of college students complete tasks within the time frame they predict. If they think in a general way about how long it took to accomplish similar tasks in the past, the success rate rises to 38%. But if they think about relevant past experiences and specifically base their prediction on those past experiences, then fully 60% complete their task within the time frame they predict.[118]
- *Getting help.* Try asking friends or co-workers to help you estimate how long it will take, because they will tend to offer a more objective view. They are more likely to use past occasions to estimate how long it will take, and are less swayed by your explanations of how it will be "different this time." Whereas you will tend to underestimate how long the project will take, others will tend to

overestimate,[119] so try "splitting the difference" for a more accurate forecast.

Should I set goals that focus on the end result, or on the process for getting there?

Try some of both. These two types of goals have complementary strengths, and weaknesses that cancel each other out.[120] "Product" goals that focus on the end result can be highly motivating, contributing to lofty achievements largely because they are easy to make very specific, challenging and measurable. But these strengths can be weaknesses as well. It is easy to make product goals so specific that they are less than exciting (e.g., making ten sales calls per day is very specific, but less than inspiring). It is also easy to make them so challenging that they are nearly unattainable, leading to a cycle of disappointment, disengagement and helplessness. For these reasons, it's useful to counterbalance product goals with "process" goals that focus on learning, mastering new skills, enjoying each day, and the like. Although generally less specific than product goals, these remain very attainable even if you doubt your abilities,[121] making them ideal for goals that focus on personal growth, new pursuits, hobbies, and so on. They are also well suited for developing the skills and confidence of children (e.g., goals that focus on learning new math skills rather than solving a specific number of math problems).

Another benefit of process goals is that they are highly "controllable." It may seem obvious that you should set goals for actions that you have some control over, but many people do quite the opposite. Most people can't wake up in the morning and say "I will lose weight today," yet it is the most commonly set goal. But you can wake up in the morning and have control over the process, telling yourself "I will exercise today" or "I will eat healthy food today." People with uncontrollable, externally-oriented goals, such as those focused on power or money, are more likely than others to have psychological problems.[122] Top college football coaches rarely set the goal of "winning the national championship" because such a goal depends on uncontrollable factors like the performance of other teams. Instead, they typically set controllable goals that focus on winning their conference and going to a post-season bowl game. Even more controllable goals are set by St. Louis Rams defensive coordinator Lovie Smith. Instead of focusing on outcome measures like yards given up or points surrendered, he focuses on performance-based process goals based on "loafs." He measures how many times his players "take a play off" by not giving their full effort. This simple emphasis on highly controllably process goals leads to a relentless, swarming defense that doesn't give up, regardless of what the opposition does.

An interesting variant of process goals are "identity" goals. Decide what identity you want to adopt – perhaps an entrepreneur, someone who makes the tough decisions, or a loving parent. Then set the goal of thinking about yourself in this way, and acting accordingly. What these goals lack in specificity they typically make up for in inspiration, and they quickly influence a wide range of behaviors across many situations, precipitating major change.[123] Similar benefits derive from "attitude" goals. Choose an attitude – such as living in the moment or seizing the day – and set the goal of living accordingly.

Why shouldn't I just set easy goals so that I'm never disappointed? And besides, aren't goal-oriented people prone to heart attacks, anyway?

There are several flaws in this line of reasoning. The biggest is that happiness and self-esteem don't result from accomplishing goals per se, but rather from the magnitude of your accomplishments, the feeling of approaching your potential, the sense of engaging your abilities in a challenging way, and (for better or worse) how you compare yourself to others. As a result, habitually setting low goals is a recipe for underachievement and self-disappointment. Nor will easy goals necessarily promote better health. The notion that being overly goal-oriented contributes to heart disease is something of an urban legend deriving from research on "Type A" personalities. Since first making headlines in the 1970s and 80s, research on this topic got bogged down because there are several different, only partially related components of Type A behavior, including competitiveness, hostility, being chronically pressed for time, and constantly striving for overly challenging goals. So before you abandon goal setting because of this research, consider these findings:

- Of all the components of Type A behavior, it is hostility, not goal setting tendencies, that accounts for the bulk of increased coronary risk.[124]
- Type A individuals routinely set goals in excess of their abilities, and that probably does contribute to stress and poor health. I advocate challenging but attainable goals, combined with highly attainable process goals.
- For all their faults, Type A people do in fact tend to accomplish more than Type B's. Among psychologists, for example, Type A's conduct more influential research that is cited more frequently by other scientists.[125]

You've focused on the process for setting effective goals, but what about content? What kinds of goals should I set? Should I aspire to career success, or to make a lot of money, or to have a great relationship, or what?

As a general rule, I try to help people figure out what they want from life, and help them get it, but I don't tell them what they should aspire to in life. In fact, I think this is one of the key differences between psychologists and cult leaders. Cult leaders tell people what to believe, whereas psychologists (and good success writers) help people identify their own goals and passions. Having said that, research has shown that certain kinds of goals tend to be associated with overall well-being, so I would ask you to consider two factors as you decide how to prioritize your efforts.

First, be wary of defining success in financial terms. Everyone wants to be financially secure, and there's nothing wrong with that.

But people who aspire to wealth and material possessions at the expense of other goals tend to be less happy and less satisfied with life, while suffering more depression and anxiety.[126] The cliché that money can't buy happiness, as we'll see in the Persistence chapter, is true. One problem is, as Richard Huber put it, "When made of money, the ladder of success is a topless ladder." Consider the experience of Jim Clark, the only man to have founded three billion-dollar companies (Netscape, Silicon Graphics, and Healtheon). When he got out of the Navy as a young man, his ambition was to make $50,000 a year. He did much better. But when he was worth $600 million, he was quoted a saying, "I just want to have a billion dollars, after taxes. Then I'll be satisfied." When he was worth three billion, he wanted to have more money than Oracle founder Larry Ellison. "Then I'll stop."[127] As Samuel Johnson wrote long ago, "Our desires always increase with our possessions. The knowledge that something remains yet unenjoyed impairs our enjoyment of the good before us."

Second, consider goals that focus on meaningful relationships with others. People whose goals focus on quality relationships with others, and have themes such as intimacy and affiliation, tend to be happier and less stressed than others.[128] Isolation, on the other hand, is a known risk factor for depression and underachievement, and those whose goals focus on power and exerting influence over others tend to be less happy and have more medical problems than others.[129]

. . .

TOOLS: THE SCIENCE OF TURNING LOFTY AMBITIONS INTO CONSISTENT ACTION

. . .

Strategy Formation Step #1: Create a Strategic Frame of Mind

As with our Vision Quest, we want to be in a positive state of mind when formulating a life Strategy. Setting goals while unhappy is less than ideal, but not for the reasons you might expect. When in negative moods, people set unrealistically high goals because they are focused on how well they would have to perform to make themselves feel better.[130] Needing to achieve a lot to feel happy, they set overly ambitious goals. This is one reason why depressed or anxious people often have goals and standards far in excess of their accomplishments and their expectations.[131] Even highly successful, non-depressed people tend to set overly risky, inappropriate goals if they find themselves in ego-threatening situations.[132]

So a positive mood is a must, and repeating the Mood Booster exercise from the Vision chapter is a good start. Simply spend 10 or 15 minutes thinking positive thoughts. But we don't necessarily want the same creative, crazy, "outside-the-box" mood brought on by the Vision Quest-ion rules. We need a thoughtful, down-to-earth mindset, more befitting a sitting president than a throw-caution-to-the-wind revolutionary. For this, we'll use a Fantasy/Reality Contrast exercise: Start by mentally focusing on the positive aspects of your Vision. Review your answers to the Vision Quest-ions, and create mental pictures of yourself achieving the outcomes you desire. After a few minutes, contrast that positive view of your future with the negative aspects of your current reality. How are they different? In what areas are you close to your Vision? What aspects seem truly unrealistic?

Repeat this process several times. The key to getting value from this exercise is contrasting the future and the present. Neither process alone is terribly helpful.[133] Focusing on negative aspects of the present isn't much fun, contributing to depression and rumination but not necessarily action. Fantasizing about the future is more fun, but is still simply that – fantasizing. Either of these alone leads to mediocre levels of commitment and motivation across the board, for realistic and unrealistic goals alike. But when you contrast the two, good things happen. First, elements of your Vision that seem unrealistic are mentally cast aside. But for those elements of your Vision that do seem attainable, a slew of good things happen: you set more goals, make more plans, get more committed, start faster, work harder, persist longer and perform better. That's quite a list. But remember that the order of these two activities is important: Fantasize first, then focus on the reality. This mentally casts the current reality as an obstacle to be overcome. If you focus on disappointing reality first and then fantasize about the future, the fantasy becomes a relief and you don't feel the motivation to act. This process will fuel the optimistic yet realistic mindset ideal for strategic thinking.

. . .

Strategy Formation Step #2:
Create Order Out of Chaos

The mythology of many cultures begins with order emerging from chaos. The next phase of your life will unfold from the same process. Your answers to the Vision Quest-ions were likely haphazard and unconnected (at least they should have been, if you followed the rules). With the Fantasy/Reality Contrast exercise, we started the process of sorting through the chaos and identifying the more immediately attainable elements. Now take your ideas and do two things:

- *Identify broader themes.* What elements of your Vision seem related? Maybe you've listed ideas like "lose weight," "get in shape," "go jogging regularly," and "run a marathon." Clearly there's a theme there. Where else in your answers can you identify "higher-order" ideas?

- *Identify synergies.* Could accomplishing some aspects of your Vision help you accomplish others? If you have a set of ideas about exercising more and another set about eating healthier, then those have synergist effects – they complement each other because eating healthy will give you more energy, and more exercise will likely make you prefer smaller, healthier meals. (You may have hoped that more exercise means you could more frequently abuse your body with fattening meals, but you will probably find you have fewer cravings for, and less tolerance of, non-healthy foods). Synergistic goals will help create success feedback loops – success on Goal A fuels success on Goal B, which in turn fuels further success on Goal A, and so on.

• • •

Strategy Formation Step #3:
Write SCAMPI Goals

Having sharpened the focus of your Vision, you're ready to write some goals.

- *Think SCAMPI.* Consider each of the six SCAMPI principles when writing goals. Try to balance highly specific product goals with broader, more inspirational process goals (particularly in areas new to you, or in which you doubt your abilities).
- *Write them down.* Literally. There is a power to putting things in writing. This simple act enhances commitment, and diminishes the wiggle room that opens the door to revisionist personal histories (e.g., not putting forth your best effort, but rationalizing it as "I never really set that goal, anyway"). Students who sign a commitment "to themselves" at the beginning of a course to complete all the assignments on time are in fact much more likely to do so, even if the contract is never mentioned again.[134] There is even evidence that writing about your life goals leads to better health and greater happiness.[135]
- *Strive for balance.* Balance is often elusive, even for people highly successful in one particular area of life. In fact, only 37% of Americans consider themselves very successful in balancing work and family.[136] Try setting a few goals in each of five life "domains": personal, physical, financial, interpersonal and professional. If you have independent goals in different areas of your life, of course it is more difficult to make progress toward all of them,[137] but the rewards are higher – a sense of balance and a fuller life. We saw

earlier that people with complex and multidimensional self-concepts are more even-keeled and show fewer intense mood swings – the same applies to goal setting and life strategies. Those with many different plans for accomplishing their goals have less extreme mood shifts, and fewer intense emotional ups and downs.[138] The message is simple: don't put all of your emotional eggs in one basket.

. . .

Strategy Formation Step #4:
Think Foundation and Focus

Plato wrote, "One man cannot practice many arts with success." It is very easy to overwhelm yourself with too many goals, and spread your efforts too thin. It is important to identify a few areas of focused effort that will be the foundation of your broader success.

• If necessary, pare your list of goals so that you have no more than 15 goals in total (preferably less than 10). If you have been struggling to make changes in your life, try starting with just two or three.

• Be sure that you have no more than three goals in each life domain.

• Identify two or three goals that will be your top priorities. These will consume the bulk of your thought and effort. College students, for example, spend about a third of their time thinking about their single most important concern, and about half of their time thinking about their top two concerns.[139] In business, the 80/20 rule (also known as the Pareto principle) states that 80% of the profits typically come from 20% of the customers. In life, you may well end up spending 80% of your thought and effort on 20% of your goals, so choose that 20% wisely.

• Create a "focusing plan" that will minimize distractions. As the German poet Goethe put it, "Things which matter most must never be at the mercy of things which matter least." First, identify at least one potentially time-consuming task in your life that you will begin delegating to someone else. Second, identify at least one potentially time-consuming task or obligation to which you will simply begin saying "no."

. . .

Strategy Formation Step #5:
Flesh Out Action Plans

For simple tasks in which performance is driven largely by effort, like doing more sit-ups or brainstorming more ideas, goals tend to have a large, immediate effect. For more complex tasks – managing staff, selling, research – goals still boost performance, but the effect is less dramatic and takes more time to unfold, in part because it takes longer to identify and refine ways of making progress toward those goals.[140] In other words, goals are only one element of an optimal Strategy for success, and the next step is to flesh out action plans to accompany your SCAMPI goals. Action plans boost performance, particularly for difficult goals, for busy people, and for people with a history of not accomplishing their goals.[141] For each of your goals, identify at least...

- Three actions that will take you closer to your goals. It is important to specify several actions in case some of them get "derailed by circumstance" or turn out to be less effective than you hoped.
- One action you will take today. Yes, today! We'll talk in a later chapter about the importance of momentum, but for now it's enough to say that the sense of progress is a key driver of success.
- One action that can be done daily. Daily progress is a key to success, but is easier for some goals than for others. If you are struggling for ideas here, try an action plan that focuses on reading. For goals in areas like personal finance, daily action is sometimes difficult to conceptualize, but reading about finances is an easy daily task.
- One major obstacle and three ways to overcome it. Henry Ford said, "Obstacles are those frightful things you see when you take

your eyes off your goal." But the fact is that obstacles are every-where (otherwise you probably would have accomplished your goals already!). Identifying them in advance makes them less disruptive when they emerge.

• One way to improve your skills in this area. Mark Twain wrote, "Each one of us has the substance within to achieve whatever our goals and dreams define. What is missing from each of us is the training, education, knowledge and insight to utilize what we already have." Can you take a class, go to a conference, or at the very least read a book that would be helpful? These are a particularly good idea if you are nurturing a new passion, and generally better than riskier, more immersive alternatives like quitting your "day job." In addition, training can speed up the performance-enhancing effect of goals, and boost your confidence that you can achieve your goal.[142]

• One "ritual" to denote that you've entered a new phase of your life. OK, this idea may seem a bit "out there," and you might not want to do it for each goal you set. But there is a very real power to marking transitions symbolically. Society has rituals for new bonds (e.g., marriage), new stages of life (e.g., transitions from childhood to adulthood), and new group memberships (e.g., joining fraternities and sororities). Creating personal rituals to mark the beginning of your journey toward your Vision can have a performance-enhancing or healing effect. In fact, the feeling of a fresh start – a decision or action that results in greater hope and brighter prospects for the future – is a strong predictor of recovery from depression.[143]

• • •

A Strategy-Formation Example:
See Dick and Jane Craft Strategies for Success

When we last left Dick and Jane, both were contemplating changes in several life domains, although Jane was off to a much better start.

For the sake of simplicity, we'll focus on one ambition they have in common: losing weight.

After allowing her imagination to run wild while contemplating her Vision, Jane switches to a more practical, Strategic frame of mind by contrasting her Vision with her current reality. She's spread herself too thin in the past, so focuses on just three goals relevant to her personal health. First, she decides to get at least 15 minutes per day of aerobic exercise. She recognizes this is only a starting point. She plans to increase her goal in five-minute increments every 2-3 weeks, and eventually incorporate light weight training and yoga to build strength and flexibility. But for now her objective is to start with an easily attainable goal that is very much under her control. She accomplishes these same objectives with her second goal: eating fruits or vegetables at least 4 times per day.

Jane's first two goals are very consistent with SCAMPI principles, as they are Specific, Challenging, Approach, Measurable, Proximal and Inspirational. They are perhaps a bit weak in terms of being Inspirational; although they are certainly consistent with her Vision and ideals, they are very practical, and lack a certain motivating, energizing quality. To compensate for this, Jane sets an "identity goal" of being an athlete. To her, this means acting like, thinking like, and being an athlete each day. This identity means a lot to her. She has a lot of positive associations with the concept of an athlete, and it brings back positive memories of her days playing competitive soccer. What this identity goal lacks in specificity and measurability it makes up for in added inspiration.

Jane's goals make action planning easy. She has set them in such way that she can begin making progress immediately, and keep that progress going daily. She joins a health club, enhances her workout skills by reading exercise books, and inspires herself by reading biographies of athletes like Lance Armstrong and Billie Jean King. She writes down her goals, and keeps this list on her coffee table next to brochures for adventurous vacations she plans to take (but for which she'll have to be in better physical condition). Finally, she creates a personal ritual to mark her transition into a new stage of life with a reclaimed identity. She burns some of her old clothes, and buys new ones that she can't yet fit into. Yes, her friends think she's a little weird for doing this, but that doesn't bother her because the ritual has personal meaning for her (and she recognizes that successful people are little crazy!).

Dick never achieves Jane's clarity of Vision, nor does he achieve her sophistication in formulating Strategy. He sets two resolutions, the first of which is to never eat pizza again. It's not as effective as Jane's SCAMPI goals, as it is an avoidance goal that brings to mind past failures to lose weight. It also emphasizes measuring success in all-or-none terms rather than promoting steady daily progress, and invites the snowball effect if his willpower wavers for even a single day. Second, he resolves to lose 40 pounds in the coming year. Unlike Jane's goals of exercising and eating right, this goal isn't particularly under his control – he can't wake up in the morning and say, "I will lose weight today." Nor is it a proximal goal. A year is so far in the future that this goal won't inspire many immediate changes in behavior. Dick also joins a health club, but otherwise doesn't flesh out a specific Strategy for accomplishing his objectives.

Chapter Six

Step Three: Belief –
The Science of Minimizing FUD
(Fear, Uncertainty and Doubt)

"An uninspiring person believes according to what he achieves. An inspiring person achieves according to what he believes." Sri Chimnoy

IT WAS NOT my typical weekend. I spent it with over 1,000 strangers who alternately laughed, screamed, danced, cried and, remarkably, walked barefoot over red-hot coals. I hadn't joined a religious cult, although I heard several less-than-humorous jokes about drinking Kool-Aid. Instead, I was in a major U.S. city with other business owners and educated professionals attending a four-day self-improvement seminar that could best be described as equal parts rock concert, business seminar, group therapy, and faith healing revival.

In researching this book, I've been to a lot of these seminars, and I've found them to vary considerably in price, quality and technique. As I'll detail later, scientifically measuring their effectiveness is not easy, in part because these commercial ventures measure their success by profits rather than by documented effectiveness, and therefore rarely submit to rigorous testing. But clearly some of them use techniques that can boost performance and enhance psychological functioning. At the heart of the more effective seminars are two key ideas. First, powerful emotional experiences are crucial to the process of personal growth. Second, conquering challenges can boost not only motivation but also belief in oneself, and as everyone knows, successful people believe they will be successful…

* * *

COMMON KNOWLEDGE:
SUCCESSFUL PEOPLE BELIEVE THEY WILL BE SUCCESSFUL

Belief is a powerful predictor of success. Research consistently shows that those confident in their ability to make life changes are far more successful in those efforts than those who question their ability to change. Clearly, the philosopher Spinoza was correct when he wrote, "So long as a man imagines he cannot do something, so long as he is determined not to do it, then it is impossible for him to do it." Henry Ford was more concise: "Whether you believe you can do a thing or not, you are right." Psychologists have studied these "expectancy effects," and it is clear that events we expect to occur are in fact more likely to occur.[144] For example, people led to believe they would be successful in quitting smoking (because psychological tests allegedly indicated "strong willpower and great potential to … conquer their desires") are in fact more successful at quitting.[145] Psychological tests had actually indicated no such thing about these people, but the expectation of success spurs Belief, and Belief has very real effects. Self-fulfilling prophecies based on beliefs that we can change are not urban legends; they are very real. Without the Belief that we can change, we would not even try – there would be no success books, weight loss programs, support groups (like AA), therapy, or even rehabilitation-based prisons. In cultures that view the future as completely unpredictable, such self-improvement institutions don't exist, and people don't even try to shape the course of their own lives.[146]

Of course, Belief comes in many flavors. Sometimes the crucial factor is our Belief in the things we tell ourselves. When stricken with depression, for example, everyone tries to "talk themselves out of it" using what psychologists call "self-talk" or "self-instructions" (e.g., "get over it" or "cheer up"). This simple technique works occasionally, but only for the people who truly believe the things they say to themselves.[147] Psychologists have explored many other varieties of Belief; I'll highlight the three most relevant to our study of personal success.

. . .

Self-Efficacy: The Belief You Can Do It

Self-efficacy is essentially "task-specific" self-confidence. It's not your level of self-confidence in general, but whether you believe you can act in a certain way or carry out a particular course of action. If you ask yourself "Can I do task X?" and the answer you give is "yes," then you are high in self-efficacy for that particular task. In study after study, self-efficacy is consistently found to be one of the most powerful predictors of change and success. Relative to those low in self-efficacy, people high in self-efficacy are more likely to...[148]

• Set specific challenging goals, and be more committed to those goals.
• Perform better and accomplish more.
• Be more proactive, more motivated, and work harder.
• Successfully follow through on their New Year's resolutions.
• Persist vigorously in the face of obstacles, and view setbacks as a source of motivation.
• Be successful in tackling problems of depression, anxiety, alcoholism, smoking and obesity.
• Prevent a single lapse from snowballing into a full-blown relapse.

. . .

Internal Locus of Control:
The Belief You Can Control Your Outcomes

Whereas self-efficacy is very task-specific, locus of control is broader and more philosophical. You have an "internal" locus of control if you tend to think your outcomes in life are dependent on your own actions; you have an "external" locus of control if you tend to think what you get in life is mostly due to luck, fate or the actions of others. An internal locus of control confers many of the same benefits as self-efficacy, including greater effort, persistence, and goal commitment.[149] It is also associated with more contentment in life and with fewer psychiatric disturbances. Therapy works, in part, because it tends to make people more internal.[150] A sense of control contributes to effective coping when negative events occur;[151] this is why many dentists now allow patients to control aspects of their visit, such as holding and controlling the "saliva ejector" (better known as "the thing that sucks water out of your mouth" or "Mr. Thirsty"). It works in more extreme circumstances as well. Two-thirds of breast cancer patients believe they have some control over their disease, and those women do in fact adjust better to their circumstances; conversely, those who tend to blame others cope more poorly, displaying more anger and resentment.[152]

Many of the benefits of having an internal locus of control result from greater pro-activity. Women with a sense of control over their breast cancer adjust better, in part, because they are more likely to learn about their disease, make dietary changes, or begin regimens of meditation and visualization.[153] Even in the absence of serious health problems, people with an internal locus of control engage in more precautionary and proactive behaviors like exercising, getting inoculated, having regular dental checkups, and wearing seat belts. Entrepreneurs with an internal locus are more active in building their businesses,[154] particularly during difficult times. When Hurricane Agnes pummeled the east coast in 1972, businesses were hit hard by extensive flooding. Internally-oriented business owners were less stressed and engaged in pro-active problem solving behaviors. Not surprisingly, owners who were less stressed did a better job of resurrecting their businesses. Externals were more stressed, and engaged more defensive coping strategies like withdrawal, denial and hostility. Over time, internals successful in turning around their businesses became more internal, whereas externals who struggled in getting their businesses back on track became more external.[155]

The good news: most people are already fairly internal. Nearly two-thirds of Americans believe "we each make our own fate."[156] In contrast, only one-third believe "success in life is pretty much determined by forces outside our control," and only about one-tenth think "there is little that people can do to change the course of their own lives."[157] If anything, people tend to over-estimate the control they have over events,[158] even to the point of believing they can control random events (e.g., superstitious behavior in casinos). Although this "illusion of control" can at times be destructive,[159] it is generally beneficial, like excessive optimism and the other "cognitive biases" discussed in the Vision chapter.

. . .

Hope: The Belief in a Bright Future

Ironically, classical mythology paints a very dismal portrait of the concept of hope. Zeus, king of the gods, wanted revenge not only on Prometheus, who had stolen fire from the gods, but also on all mankind for using the stolen fire. Zeus sent Pandora to earth with a box containing hope and all the world's ills: vice, labor, sickness, death, insanity, etc. When she opened the box, these evils spilled out, forever ruining the world of man, but she closed it before hope could escape. It remained trapped, forever. Bummer.

Certainly hope, by itself, does not guarantee success. Ben Franklin was right: "He that lives upon hope will die fasting." But perhaps Francis Bacon was more insightful when he said: "Hope is a good breakfast but a bad supper." Hope is a good breakfast because, like an internal locus of control, it inspires a pro-active, problem-solving orientation that spurs greater achievement. Compared to those with less positive views of the future, those with more hopeful outlooks...[160]

• Set a greater number of goals.

- Set more effective goals (in other words, base them on SCAMPI principles).
- Set goals in more areas of life, thereby putting their emotional eggs in more baskets.
- Achieve more and perform better in many domains, from academics to sports to social competence.
- Are happier, and suffer less anxiety, depression and burnout.
- Attribute failures to changeable causes (e.g., poor strategies) rather than unchangeable ones (e.g., not being smart enough).
- React better to difficult circumstances, including bad test scores, stressful jobs, paralyzing accidents, and chronic illnesses.
- Use more effective coping habits such as humor, regular exercise, and preventative care.
- Are better at preventing a single lapse from snowballing into a full-blown relapse.

· · ·

The Flip Side of Belief

Just as Belief comes in many flavors, so too does a lack of Belief. One is *learned helplessness*, a term derived from a series of now-famous experiments in which dogs were given mild electric shocks.[161] Some dogs were given the opportunity to escape the shocks by pressing a panel with their noses; others received shocks of the same intensity and duration, but were unable to escape the shocks. All the dogs were then placed in "shuttleboxes" and given additional shocks. Those who previously learned they could escape shocks now did so easily, jumping out of the electrified compartment of the shuttlebox. But those previously given inescapable shocks simply lay down and whimpered, unnecessarily suffering shocks that could easily be escaped by jumping out of the box. They had learned that their actions were futile – they had learned helplessness. Humans become helpless, too, but because they have a richer mental life than dogs, the process involves more complex patterns of thought. Specifically, human helplessness and depression tend to develop when people habitually explain negative events in personal, permanent and pervasive terms (e.g., your explanation for getting laid off is "I'm stupid" rather than "the company has a bad strategy"). This "3P explanatory style" for negative events is a very destructive form of disbelief, and tools for combating it are described in the Persistence chapter.

Lack of Belief is also evident in *self-handicapping*. Usually people try to avoid handicaps, but a lack of Belief can actually lead people to seek out handicaps that undermine their own performance. If you drink too much alcohol and fail at a given task, then you have a built-in excuse. If you drink too much and perform well, then your success seems even more impressive. For some, this self-handicapping manifests itself as alcoholism, but others use procrastination, lack of effort, panic attacks, asthma, depression, or grief.[162] In each case, the root cause is the same: a lack of Belief in their abilities triggers a wider insecurity. To protect the image of competency, they try to fool themselves and others by making performance evaluation difficult ("Was it his fault, or the alcohol?").

. . .

How Do You Create Belief?

We've seen the power of Belief, and the destructive effects that result from a lack of Belief. But the big question is: How do you come to believe, really believe, that you will be successful? True belief requires more than just thinking you will be successful. You need to *feel* you will be successful on an emotional level, believing with your gut as well as your head. You also need the confidence that comes from prior success and *action*; you need the confidence of someone who has done it before and knows they can do it again.

The human experience has been described in terms of thinking, feeling and acting for centuries. This three-dimensional framework has been used by philosophers from Plato to Kant, and is prominent in the teachings of religions throughout the world (for example, Hin-

duism refers to the three paths of knowledge, feeling and action). I'll
call these three dimensions *affect*, *behavior* and *cognition*. As we'll
see, positive cycles of these three kinds of responses create true
Belief. In other words, for true success, you need to understand the
ABCs of changing your life…

• • •

Uncommon Knowledge: The ABCs of Changing Your Life

Affect simply means emotion, and refers to feelings, the experience of pleasure and pain, and so on. *Behavior* obviously includes
actions, but also refers to verbal behavior, posture, dress, appearance, movements, etc. *Cognitions* are thoughts, and are (hopefully)
the more rational and logical elements of our experience. Cognitions
include beliefs, goals, and action plans, as well as broader and more
abstract elements of mental life such as metaphors ("life is like a box
of chocolates"), scripts (expectations of how certain events unfold),
and even one's self-concept and identity (beliefs about oneself).

These three related but distinct elements of the human experience are even controlled by different areas of the brain. The hippoc-
ampus, for example, transforms perceptions of new experiences into
the longer-term memories crucial for cognition. People with damage
to the hippocampal region can learn complex new behaviors such as
how to play tennis or poker, improving each time they play. But their
cognitions are flawed – they have no memory of having played before, thinking that each time is their first. People with damage to the
basal ganglia – the brain region involved in learning new skills and
behaviors – display the opposite dysfunction: they can play tennis
repeatedly, with perfect memories of playing before and accurate
cognitions about how to play, but they never improve. People with
damage to the amygdala and the brain's other emotion-related pathways are left a bit like Mr. Data from *Star Trek: The Next Generation*
– capable of thinking and processing information, but with a limited

capacity for feeling and expressing emotions. They can also be paralyzed by indecisiveness. Their cognitive skills allow them to weigh the pros and cons of various decisions, but they don't know how they feel about each possible course of action.[163] Pascal was right when he said, "The heart has its reasons of which reason knows nothing."

Although highly specific forms of brain damage can isolate affective, behavioral and cognitive responses, most of the time they interact and influence one another, turning isolated responses into broad, persistent ABC cycles. Our emotions shape our cognitions. In a phenomenon called "state-dependent memory," good moods bring to mind good memories, and bad moods bring to mind unpleasant memories.[164] Good memories in turn enhance good moods and encourage greater action; unpleasant memories amplify bad moods, spurring either corrective action or a helpless shutdown. Actions bring about rewards or punishments, which drive our emotions. Fully three-fourths of those who successfully make changes in their lives experience substantial positive changes in their emotions, compared to fewer than one-tenth of those who fail in making life changes.[165] We then spend time thinking about our actions, mentally celebrating our successes and (hopefully) trying to learn from failures. These inter-connections, driven by the powerful human need for consistency, are the glue that holds ABC cycles together.

Whatever your goals might be, and whatever elements of your life you want to change, success will involve changing broad patterns of affect, behavior and cognition. To succeed, and to truly believe you will succeed, you must turn negative ABC cycles into positive ones. To understand this better, let's consider a few examples…

- *Problem gambling.* Roughly 3-5% of Americans have a serious gambling problem.[166] You might think of problem gambling as a purely behavioral problem, but in fact it takes the form of a negative ABC spiral.[167] Gambling binges typically begin with negative *affect* – emotions such depression, sadness, disappointment, or anxiety over money. Gambling is a chance to escape, to focus completely on something else, and gamblers expect it will cheer them up. So they engage in the *behavior* of gambling. And more often than not, they begin losing. (The odds for all casino games are in the house's favor – one rarely sees casinos advertising: "Come on down! We're sellin' all the roulette wheels 'cause we're goin' out of business!") Over the long term, casinos will always win and gamblers will always lose. While most of us would quit after losing our self-imposed gambling allowance, problem gamblers don't because they have a whole set of *cognitions* that keep them going. For example, problem gamblers truly believe they can win despite the odds. They view losses as "near wins." They erroneously believe that superstitious rituals will improve their odds. And they fall victim to the gambler's fallacy – the belief that future outcomes can be predicted based on what happened in the past.[168] These cognitions keep the gambling behavior going. Over time, debts begin to mount, triggering a new wave of emotions like sadness, anxiety, and a feeling of desperation. This is in turn triggers another behavioral pattern called chasing – betting more and taking bigger risks. Losses mount further, and cognitive patterns change: self-esteem drops, and they begin thinking of themselves as "losers," further triggering negative emotions which in turn trigger more gambling. Over time, problem gamblers often engage in illegal behaviors (such as embezzling or passing bad checks), and the ABC cycle spirals out of control.

- *Panic attacks.* This condition, although relatively rare, is often debilitating as it creates a fear and avoidance of many everyday situations. Once widely considered a purely biological disorder best treated by drugs, panic attacks are today increasingly recognized as ABC cycles spiraling out of control. A typical panic attack begins with behaviors such as a "hyper-monitoring" or excessive awareness of physical symptoms like shortness of breath, rapid heartbeat, dizziness and sweating. These symptoms can indicate simple anxiety, but people who suffer panic attacks interpret these symptoms in a particular way – their specific cognition is the belief that these signal imminent danger or an impending death, often from a heart attack. This cognition fuels an emotional response – anxiety escalating into extreme fear. This emotional response fuels further physical symptoms, and the ABC cycle spirals into a full-blown panic attack. Treatments for panic attacks focus on changing cognitions to prevent the ABC cycle from spiraling, but these treatments involve emotions and behaviors as well. First, therapists induce the shortness of breath and other physical symptoms of anxiety, often by having the client breathe into a paper bag for a few minutes. Through repeated use of this hyperventilation exercise, clients learn that the physical symptoms are not the result of a heart attack, nor do they signal impending death. Clients learn a new set of cognitions – they reinterpret their symptoms as indicating anxiety, and begin addressing that anxiety as the root of the problem.[169] The result is a very different ABC cycle, and a heightened sense of self-efficacy about their ability to manage their emotions.

• *Depression.* Obviously depression is largely defined by affect – it is characterized by sadness and low mood, as well as feelings of worthlessness, guilt, and dread. But there are also numerous behavioral manifestations – lack of energy, passivity, avoidance of usual activities, social withdrawal, loss of appetite (food, sex), disrupted sleeping patterns, slowed movement, and sometimes even suicide attempts. Cognitive elements are important as well – the "3P explanatory style" outlined earlier, rumination, slowed thinking, poor concentration, low self-esteem, the inability to recall positive memories, hopelessness, the belief that life is without meaning, and so on. These affective, behavioral and cognitive components interact, amplifying the psychological distress. Treatments for depression typically focus changing cognitions, particularly the "automatic negative thoughts" that trigger negative emotions, but clearly have behavioral elements as well (for example, scheduling activities that provide pleasure or enhance self-efficacy).

• • •

Using ABC Cycles to Change Your Life

Virtually any area of life, whether a domain of success or an area of struggle, is a complex, dynamic cycle of affect, behavior and cognition. From negative ABC cycles like depression or addiction to positive cycles like outstanding professional or athletic performance, it is clear that ABC cycles have a greater psychological impact than the sum of their parts. This has a huge implication for personal change: You cannot expect that changing one cognition will lead to broad patterns of change in your life. Successful attempts at lasting change will result from changing cycles of affect, behavior, and cognition.

This is one reason why many common strategies for change are relatively ineffective. Making a New Year's resolution is simply adding one cognition to a much broader ABC cycle; repeating an affirmation simply "drills" that cognition into your consciousness. In both cases, these isolated new cognitions will quickly be swept away by more powerful ABC cycles. For example, anyone wanting to lose weight must contend with a complex ABC cycle centered on eating and exercise.

- *Cognitions might include:* "Others don't respect me because I'm heavy." "Losing weight would make me happy." "Dieting sucks." "Exercise sucks." "Sometimes you have to enjoy life." "I deserve a big meal."
- *Behaviors might include:* Quantity of food eaten. Quality of food eaten. Speed of eating. Exercise habits. Social habits like drinking with friends (where buffalo wings are consumed).
- *Affective responses might include:* The pleasure of eating. Dissatisfaction with appearance. Shame after bingeing. The temporary escape from negative emotions provided by eating. Discomfort and self-consciousness when exercising.

Simply adding the new cognition of "I resolve to lose weight in the coming year" will mean little if you believe that dieting sucks, derive pleasure from eating, have social habits that put you in tempting situations, and so on. Little surprise then that losing weight is the most common New Year's resolution and also the most rarely accomplished goal.

Success and Belief are much more likely if we focus on changing a whole constellation of affective responses, behaviors and cognitions. For example, those using only cognitive or behavioral strategies to quit smoking have short-term relapse rates of 55%, whereas those who use both cognitive and behavioral strategies have relapse rates of just 13%. And this heightened success doesn't simply result from using more strategies – it results from using the mixture of strategies most likely to get an ABC cycle rolling.[170] In fact, one of the most effective elements of formal treatment programs is that they encourage people to add behavioral coping strategies – like eating right, exercise, and substituting new habits – to the more commonly used cognitive strategies[171] (e.g., resolutions, willpower-related self-talk).

• • •

Turning Vision and Strategy Into ABC Cycles

Clarifying your Vision was a cognitive activity focused on your thoughts about the future. Your Strategy focused on behaviors for achieving that vision. Now a healthy dose of emotion is needed to turn your Vision and Strategy into an ABC cycle, and to start really believing you can accomplish them.

Inducing positive emotional experiences by pumping people up with music or inspirational speeches has long been a staple of success seminars. If these techniques result in heightened motivation, and that motivation is combined with a compelling Vision and SCAMPI goals, the result certainly can be ABC cycles, enhanced Belief, and better performance ("motivation without a plan," although fun, has few lasting effects). Positive emotions bring to mind positive memories and make the future seem brighter, which spurs more proactive behavior; in short, they build a sense of momentum by turning ideas about the future into full-fledged ABC cycles.

The granddaddy of seminar-based motivational techniques (and certainly the one that generates the most publicity) is walking barefoot across red-hot coals. Firewalking is definitely not an exercise in "mind over matter"; it can be explained by basic principles of physics, and is sometimes even used as a classroom illustration by physics professors.[172] I'm not saying it isn't dangerous. People have been seriously burned, even when the firewalking has been conducted by experienced firms that specialize in this kind of thing.[173] Firewalking is the ultimate "don't try this at home" experience, and definitely not something you want to try on your barbeque grill. Having said that, hundreds of thousands of people have done it without injury. When done well, seminars that incorporate firewalking start with exercises to clarify your Vision and Strategy (although they don't use those terms). The firewalk is then presented as a metaphor for the obstacles you'll encounter pursuing your Vision, and as a symbolic representation of facing your fears. And trust me – no matter how well-versed you are in the physics of firewalking, no matter how closely you paid attention to the safety instructions, there is a deep and primal fear that comes over you the moment you stand before a long row of burning coals. Adrenaline pumps furiously. An ancient part of your brain screams, and throughout millions of years of evolution your body would have listened, instantly and instinctively running away. But on this night, a seminar leader pumps you into an emotional frenzy, and encourages you to repeat a mantra (largely a distraction technique). You walk. I've done this twice, and both times I had the same initial reaction: ouch. With the first step, one thought shot through my mind: that's really, really hot. If you didn't know it was serious before, you know it with that first step. But virtually everyone who tries it (like me) overcomes the fear, focuses, and moves on. As you step off the coals, you wipe your feet on wet grass (removing any bits of coal that may have stuck to your feet), and celebrate with your fellow firewalkers. It can be a very powerful experience, even for skeptical scientists. If the resulting motivation and emotion are channeled in the direction of your goals, it can be a very positive and productive experience.

As I've said, I think there are sound scientific reasons to think that firewalking and other emotion-inducing experiences, when done in the right context, can contribute to a longer-term boost in personal productivity. Having said that, I can't point to controlled scientific studies that compare firewalkers to control groups of non-firewalkers. But there are dozens of studies about a similar if less dramatic technique: "adventure education." You might not be familiar with that term, but you probably are familiar with the leading brand in this category: Outward Bound. To some it is synonymous with wilderness courses for troubled youth, but this 60-year-old institution offers adventure education programs for all types of people throughout the world. In 1994 alone, over 40,000 people took Outward Bound courses.[174] Typically two to four weeks in length, these programs are longer than most success-oriented seminars, but otherwise they share many of the same elements: mentally and physically challenging tasks designed to "stretch" participants and nurture personal growth. And the results are impressive. Documented effects of Outward Bound programs include improved leadership skills among managers, higher grades among students, and lower recidivism among delinquents. Many of the benefits seem to result from heightened Belief; graduates have been shown to display significant improvements in independence, assertiveness, confidence, self-efficacy and locus of control. These are not "illusory placebo effects," and they don't seem to reflect mere "post-group euphoria" – in fact, some of these improvements get even larger in the months following the program (as ABC cycles begin spiraling in a positive direction). Obviously not every course they offer changes lives, and much depends on the frame of mind of the participants. A dysfunctional company with no Strategy that goes on an adventure retreat will probably end up being little more than a temporarily pumped-up dysfunctional company with no Strategy. But the scientific findings, coupled with anecdotal reports about firewalking, indicate a clear pattern: in the right context, tackling challenges and overcoming fears can induce positive emotions, build Belief, spur ABC cycles, and result in a generalized improvement in performance.

• • •

Using Negative Emotions to Build Belief

Positive emotions can build traditional forms of Belief like self-efficacy. Negative emotions can inspire a different but equally potent form of Belief: the belief that change is a necessity, not an option. Those successful in making life changes are far more likely than others to have experienced negative emotions or major suffering related to that area of life.[175] Over half of those who have experienced sudden, dramatic changes in their lives report being emotionally distressed or upset at the time.[176] Recovering alcoholics and drug addicts often point to the powerful emotional experience of "hitting bottom" as a turning point in their lives.[177] In fact, severe alcoholics are more likely than moderate alcoholics to recover, largely because their lives are more disrupted by alcohol – they are therefore more likely to have an intensely negative experience that they label "hitting bottom."[178]

Hitting bottom is one instance of what psychologist Roy Baumeister calls a *crystallization of discontent* – an emotional experience in which seemingly unrelated dissatisfactions with life suddenly seem to "come together."[179] A crystallization of discontent causes a person previously aware of isolated Problems W, X and Y to realize that these problems are merely symptoms of Pervasive, Damaging Mega-Problem Z, and the emotional pain of that realization motivates real change. It is a recognition that the whole is greater than the sum of the parts, and that the larger problem will continue into the future unless drastic changes are made. Many alcoholics realize their professional lives aren't all they could be, their relationships aren't ideal, and their health could be better; but until they face the seriousness of these problems, and recognize they are just symptoms of a destructive addiction, change is unlikely. Divorce often follows a similar pattern. Initially, isolated negative aspects of a marriage are viewed as troubling but solvable. When they coalesce into a global perception that the relationship is systemically flawed, preparations for divorce often follow. People who join non-traditional religious groups (a less judgmental term than "cults") often have isolated negative experiences such as losing some personal freedoms or being assigned menial tasks. Those who "defect" or "de-convert" from these religions often experience a crystallization of discontent in which these dissatisfactions become part of the larger perception that the religion is less than holy.[180]

Given that negative emotional experiences can create the belief that change is a necessity, it should come as no surprise that change experts like therapists routinely induce emotional experiences intentionally. Freud pioneered this technique over a century ago, basing his therapy in part on the notion that patients must do more than talk about their traumatic experiences – they need to feel the pain of the incidents on an emotional level to begin healing. Many of Freud's ideas have not aged well, but they remain prominent in popular culture and popular imagination because he got this one idea right long before anyone else. Many people try to avoid thinking about traumatic events (Anais Nin: "A great part of our life is an invention to avoid confrontation with our deepest self"). Freud called it denial and repression; psychologists today call it inhibition. You might expect that not thinking about something is easy, but in fact it takes work and psychological effort. In the short-term, inhibition causes stress and physiological changes like increased sweating. Over the long-term, inhibition leads to physical illness and psychological problems.[181] Those who try to simply shut out feelings of grief over a departed loved one often take the longest to get over their grief.[182] Similarly, incest survivors who try to suppress thoughts of their brutalization can become particularly obsessed with traumatic memories.[183] Feeling the pain of negative experiences begins to reverse the process.

Although therapy has changed greatly since Freud's time (today it typically emphasizes the present and the future more than past), the notion of inducing negative emotional experiences to spur personal change still plays a central role. Sometimes it's a *corrective emotional experience*, which means helping clients feel the emotional significance of problems they had been avoiding, without feeling overwhelmed or helpless.[184] Sometimes it's simply helping phobics confront their fears, or depressives face their destructive patterns of thinking and feeling (an ancient Chinese proverb: "Go to the heart of danger, for there you will find safety"). On other occasions, it's bringing about change by having clients visualize the painful futures that await them if they don't change their lives.

Popular success seminars, which have a long history of borrowing ideas from therapy, also try to leverage the transforming power of negative emotional experiences. One famous example was Erhard Seminars Training, better known as *est*, which attracted well-educated achievers and more than one celebrity during its 1970s heyday. *Est*'s notoriety came from its "boot camp" mentality – it combined lectures on traditional success topics like taking responsibility and the power of Belief with verbal abuse and humiliation. Participants were called "shitheads" and "assholes" and any number of other profane names. According to many accounts, access to bathrooms was limited, and incidents of individuals wetting their pants or vomiting were not unheard of. Presumably these humiliating experiences helped bring about very negative emotional experiences, inducing an artificial form of "hitting bottom." As one *est* executive bragged, "we're gonna tear you down and put you back together."[185] Keep in mind that I'm not recommending this seminar, which exists today in a somewhat "kinder and gentler" form known as the Landmark Forum; I'm simply trying to illustrate how seminars try to induce negative emotional experiences to bring about change.[186]

Before leaving this topic, I'll give one more example of negative emotions triggering positive change. This example is the polar opposite of *est*; it's the television show *Fantasy Island*. Each episode was similar. Someone (let's call him Bob) comes to the island to fulfill a fantasy, perhaps going back in time to marry his high school sweetheart. About 45 minutes into the hour-long episode, Bob has a negative emotional experience that makes it plain his fantasy would not really make him happy. Bob and all of Mr. Rourke's other clients rarely have a rational realization that the fantasy is counter-productive; rather, it is an emotional experience that brings about true change in the character and drama to the show.

All of these experiences – therapy's corrective emotional experiences, *est*'s artificial hitting bottom, and *Fantasy Island* – share a common recipe for change: pain and a plan. Emotional pain enhances the motivation to change, creating the Belief that change must happen for psychological well-being, but that motivation is of little use unless the individual has a plan for change as well. Pain without a plan is just that – pain. Dissatisfaction boosts motivation and performance only if people have set effective goals and get feedback on their progress toward those goals.[187] You can relive negative events indefinitely, but without a plan for change, it is unnecessary pain that won't trigger a positive ABC cycle.

. . .

TOOLS: THE SCIENCE OF MINIMIZING FUD (FEAR, UNCERTAINTY AND DOUBT)

This section contains a dozen tools for maximizing Belief, managing ABC cycles, and minimizing FUD (Fear, Uncertainty and Doubt). "Eliminating FUD" would be a much sexier headline, but such a promise would be little more than success snake oil. Evolution has wired our brains to feel emotions like fear, uncertainty and doubt. They are deep-seated in our psyches, and remain important survival mechanisms even in the modern world. Still, our daily lives are too often ruled by these emotions, and we can certainly learn to manage them more effectively, much like people who never fully recover from mental illnesses but learn to manage their conditions and function effectively regardless (*a la* John Nash in *A Beautiful Mind* – never completely cured of schizophrenia, he was able to manage the disease and went on to win a Nobel Prize[188]).

Building Belief is a less "linear" process than identifying Vision and crafting Strategy, so the dozen tools that follow are not laid out step-by-step. Instead, identify a few you think would be most helpful, plan to use them repeatedly, and add additional tools to your Belief-building repertoire over time.

· · ·

Belief Building Tool #1:
Crush the ANTs – Prevent Isolated Responses
from Spinning Into ABC Cycles

You can never eliminate FUD. There may always be a little voice in the back of your mind – an "inner critic" – that creates doubt. But you can learn not to listen to that little voice as much. An insight from Buddhism is particularly appropriate here: the inner monologue that has been cycling through your head since you learned to talk is not "you." In a sense, "you" are the listener rather than the voice itself. As the listener, you can shape the nature of that internal monologue, and choose to listen to a more positive voice. Most importantly, you can learn to prevent that little voice – those isolated cognitions – from spinning into full-blown negative ABC cycles that undermine your Belief in yourself.

Any kind of response – affective, behavioral or cognitive – can start an ABC cycle. But the most common pattern is a negative thought triggering a negative emotion that in turn triggers the broader cycle. The trouble often arises from ANTs – *automatic negative thoughts*[189] – that jump into consciousness quickly and reflexively. Different people have different ANTs. In response to a professional setback, some will automatically think, "I'm a loser." After a romantic disappointment, others instantly assume, "I'm unworthy." Schoolyard bullies often have automatic thoughts like "He is out to get me," causing them to infer threatening intentions from innocent actions, triggering a broader ABC cycle of aggression.[190] ANTs often have their ultimate origins in intense emotional experiences from childhood or adolescence, and although there is some value in reviewing the past to gain insight, it is important to realize that they have a life of their own, and that the path to resolving them lies primarily in the here and now. The key to more productive responses, and to building true Belief in yourself, is crushing the ANTs; you can't eliminate ANTs forever, but you can certainly minimize the extent to which they trigger negative ABC cycles.

Stopping a negative ABC cycle can begin with a conscious decision. If you find yourself spinning into a negative ABC cycle, yell "STOP!" Some therapists recommend carrying a 3x5 card with "STOP" written on it, and looking at it when negativity sets in. At this point, some introspection is needed: What triggered your ABC cycle? What was going on around you, and what were the very first thoughts you had? We're often not fully aware of our ANTs. They're not exactly "unconscious" in the traditional Freudian sense. "Preconscious" might be a better phrase, as they've been repeated so many times, and are such deep-seated assumptions about ourselves or the world around us, that we often don't realize they have crept into our thinking. But understanding your ANTs is crucial for the next tool...

· · ·

Belief Building Tool #2:
Argue With Yourself

By learning to argue with yourself, you can prevent your automatic negative thoughts from triggering negative emotions and broader ABC cycles. In a sense, you can short-circuit the ABC cycle before it really gets started. The first step is getting a little more specific in your thinking because it's hard to argue with such general statements as "I'm a loser." What triggered your ANT? Often ANTs result from counter-productive rules or "if-then" statements that we aren't fully aware of ("If I don't finish my project on time, then I am a loser"). Once you've fleshed out a more specific statement of your ANT, you're ready to argue with yourself in a productive way by asking seven types of questions in the table on the opposite page.

Resource recommendations: These first two tools – crushing the ANTs and learning to argue with yourself – play central roles in cognitive therapy, pioneered by Dr. Aaron Beck, and rational-emotive behavior therapy, pioneered by Dr. Albert Ellis. Both men have written several books, although primarily for clinicians rather than general audiences. One exception is *A Guide to Rational Living* by Ellis and Robert Harper, which has sold well over a million copies. A very practical book based on many of these same ideas is *The Feeling Good Handbook* by Dr. David Burns.

. . .

Belief Building Tool #3: Break the Links

Learning to argue with your ANTs "breaks the link" between cognition and affect – it doesn't stop you from having negative thoughts, but it prevents them from triggering negative emotions. Here's another way of breaking the links that therapists occasionally recommend: sing. Make up a song about your ANT and all the other thoughts that tend to flow from it. The lyrics of your song should contain the same words and terms that trigger the negative emotions of your ABC cycle. Then sing them over and over again, preferably in different styles (e.g., rap, country-and-western, heavy metal). Sing it with a low-pitched voice, and then with a high, whiny, mocking tone. This idea might sound like success snake oil, but this technique can break the links between cognitions and affect by making certain words or statements less emotionally charged. The ANT ("I'm a loser) may still pop into your mind, but you've repeated it so many times and in so many different emotional contexts that it doesn't trigger the negative emotions that it once did. The "scramble technique" used by Tony Robbins is based on a similar rationale: people repeatedly visualize a painful

Types of ANT-killing questions	Some examples for the ANT: "If I don't finish my project on time, then I am a loser."
Evidence: What is the objective evidence for this ANT?	• Does not finishing my project on time really indicate that I am a loser? • Haven't I completed lots of other projects on time? (if your answer is "no," then some problem-solving is called for)
Exaggeration: Is this ANT an exaggeration? Am I over-reacting? Am I over-generalizing?	• Isn't "loser" a little strong? • In concluding that I am a loser because I didn't finish my project on time, am I making a mountain out of a molehill?
Alternatives: What are some other possible explanations?	• Is it possible that I didn't finish my project on time because I didn't have the resources I needed?
Flexibility: Can I evaluate this situation in more flexible terms? Am I thinking in overly rigid, black-or-white, all-or-none terms?	• Just because I may have room to improve my project management skills, does that really mean I'm a loser?
Utility: Is this belief empowering or counter-productive?	• Does it really benefit me to think of myself as a loser just because I was late with one project? • Should my self-worth depend on this kind of thing?
Comparison: How have others fared in similar situations?	• Did everyone else finish their projects on time?[191]
Role reversal: How would I evaluate other people who performed as I did?	• Would I consider everyone who didn't finish their project on time a loser?

situation as a cartoon, each time varying aspects of the visualization, until the situation can be imagined without the painful emotional association. Breaking the links between thoughts and emotions in these ways are not panaceas for underachievement or depression, but used in conjunction with other techniques, they can help.

. . .

Belief Building Tool #4:
Feel Your Pain
(In Other Words, Plan an Emotional Outburst)

We saw earlier that expressing negative emotions can lead to better health and psychological functioning. It may not directly spur greater Belief in yourself, but it "frees up" mental and emotional resources for the positive ABC cycles you are trying to create, and contributes to the sense that change is a necessity. Repressing negative thoughts takes work, and expressing them begins the process of "moving on." We'll put that idea into action in a very simple way: writing.

Many studies have documented the benefits of writing.[192] One of the most compelling was done with senior engineers who were suddenly laid off from a computer company. Half were asked to write about their deepest thoughts and feelings concerning being laid off, while half wrote about less intense topics such as time management. Several months later, 53% of those who had written about their emotions had new jobs, whereas only 18% of those who wrote about more superficial topics had new jobs, even though those in both groups had been on the same number of job interviews. Those who had written about their emotions were better able to move on – they were less angry, and had been able to derive some broader meaning from their experiences.[193]

The benefits of writing don't result from simply venting emotions. People often ruminate about negative experiences, mentally re-enacting events endlessly, but it is putting them into language that fosters a sense of insight and meaning. Humans have been storytellers for millennia, and it is precisely the process of weaving disjointed images and emotions into a meaningful story that facilitates psychological healing. You'll derive the greatest benefits from your writing if you use "meaning" words that convey why things happened (e.g., because, effect, reason, why, cause, source, attribute, bring about) as well as "insight" words (e.g., understand, realize, know, explain, comprehend).[194] Psychotherapists often ask their clients to write about their ANTs for homework, a process that heightens awareness of cognitive processes and helps to put ANTs in perspective.

I recommend writing for at least 15 minutes per day, preferably in the morning (before getting distracted by daily events) or at night (as way of putting the day in perspective, and preparing for the next). Although you certainly don't need to write daily to get the psychological benefits, it is clear that dispersing your writing over time tends to be more beneficial than "bunched" writing.[195] As you write about negative experiences, you might find the process upsetting. The benefits evolve over time, and people often feel somewhat distressed during or immediately after writing. And you don't just need to write about negative events, although that certainly provides "cleansing" benefits; as we saw in the Strategy chapter, writing about your Vision or Strategy leads to health benefits and greater happiness as well.[196] As long as you don't specifically avoid writing about the emotional aspects of your life, you will likely benefit.[197]

If writing just isn't for you, try verbally confiding in someone you trust. There is a natural tendency to keep traumatic emotional experiences to yourself, but confiding in others about those experiences provides many of the same physical and psychological benefits as writing. Even brief conversations about severe trauma are beneficial. For example, survivors of Nazi concentration camps frequently relive the horror of those experiences in their minds, but only about one-third have discussed them. When interviewed about their experiences, those who opened up the most were significantly healthier in the year following the interview. Even 40 years after their imprisonment, personal disclosure in a brief interview had measurable effects.[198]

Obviously you should exercise caution in applying this tool. If you feel your writing experiences are too upsetting, seek the advice of a qualified therapist.

Resource recommendation: For more on the benefits of writing, check out *Opening Up: The Healing Power of Expressing Emotions* by Dr. James Pennebaker. Pennebaker has conducted pioneering research on this topic, and provides many practical tips on writing and other techniques for opening up and moving on.

· · ·

Belief Building Tool #5:
Add a Dose of Positive Emotion

We saw earlier that tackling challenges and experiencing intense positive emotions can build Belief and get ABC cycles rolling. You can try doing these alone, but it feels a little forced and awkward to crank up some music, jump up and down, and "get motivated" by yourself. So I think a course or seminar is the best approach. Outward Bound, as we've seen, has a well-deserved reputation for quality courses. I also recommend the *Unleash the Power Within* seminar conducted by Tony Robbins. It features a firewalk and a number of other exercises that leverage the power of emotion, and is a fascinating experience for anyone interested in applied psychology. Note that I have no affiliation with either Outward Bound or Tony Robbins, and receive no money if people attend their courses. I simply offer these recommendations based on my research and experience.

· · ·

Belief Building Tool #6:
Build Belief with Behavioral Baby Steps

At my seminars, I'm often approached by people who tell me they just don't have confidence in themselves. Despite the various tools that I present for building Belief and positive ABC cycles, they assure me they have a "deeper problem." OK, maybe. They sometimes do indeed have deep-seated problems. But more often than not, even if the root of the problem lies in the past, the solution lies in practical ABC-management techniques in the present. They could spend years discussing their childhood problems, perhaps feeling better by blaming their problems on their parents, perhaps gaining a sense of importance from the process ("look at me – I have issues!"), but without any appreciable change in their lives. One of the most effective techniques for such people, even though they often aren't happy with the suggestion at first, is to build Belief with behavioral baby steps.

The ancient wisdom of the I Ching states that the process of change should begin with the easy and the simple. Two thousand years later, experts on psychological change concluded that there are two crucial rules for shaping your own behavior: *"(1) you can never begin too low*, and *(2) the steps upward can never be too small*. When in doubt, begin at a lower level or reduce the size of the steps."[199] Successful people assess a situation and get started, even if it's just in a small way. Depressed people, in contrast, tend to evaluate a situation and conclude they need still more information before acting, leading to rumination and a paralysis of analysis.[200] As Liz Smith put it, "Begin somewhere; you cannot build a reputation on what you intend to do."

The best way to start building Belief with behavioral baby steps is to start with "guaranteed successes" – things you know you can do. For example, be sure that you've set at least a few process goals in addition to product goals. As highlighted in the Strategy chapter, if you set goals in terms of the process of learning or reading or developing new skills, then you can be confident in your ability to start making progress. You may question your financial skills, but you can certainly be confident in your ability to pick up a financial book and start reading. Another aspect of beginning with behavioral baby steps is investing a lot of effort in the process of change early. This is why your action plan called for at least one action you could take today. Create some easy, early successes; celebrate them and build on that momentum. This works well for anyone, but behavioral baby steps are particularly good for building Belief among children.

· · ·

Belief Building Tool #7:
Act Like a Success

Another way to begin with behavioral baby steps that falls into the category of "guaranteed successes" is to just start acting like a success in minor, easily achievable ways. People often ask me how they can come to be viewed as a leader by their co-workers. The easiest way to get the ball rolling is to just start acting like a leader: take the lead on projects, speak like a leader, act like a leader, dress like one, etc. It's obviously not the ultimate solution, but it's a start. And it begins to change how you think about yourself. One key to successful change is adopting a new identity, particularly a public identity. The process of kicking a drug habit, for example, often begins when addicts begin thinking about themselves differently, abandoning old identities (drug addict, rebel, non-conformist) and adopting new ones (parent, responsible adult).[201] Choose the identity you want, and begin acting accordingly; soon the expectations of others and your own internal need for consistency will get ABC cycles spinning in the right direction.

Just as you can take on outward appearances to shape public perception, you can also take on outward appearances to create internal emotions and build Belief. Psychologists call this idea the *emotional expressivity effect*: express an emotion physically, and you will feel that emotion internally. This idea is actually an ancient one. From Homer's *Iliad* to Shakespeare's *Henry V*, literature documents how soldiers have long been urged to express anger physically as a way of pumping themselves up for battle. In science, Charles Darwin first explored the idea systematically: "He who gives way to violent gestures will increase his rage; he who does not control the signs of fear will experience fear in a greater degree."[202] Actors routinely take on the facial expressions, poses and postures of their characters, even when off-camera, not only to create outward appearances, but also to better feel the emotions of their characters. Today, everyone from sports coaches to popular success writers urge people to exhibit the "physiology" of successful people. Certainly depressed people are prone to specific postures (head down, shoulders slumped); the postures don't cause their depression, but they can definitely help perpetuate a negative mood.

Here's a very mild example of the emotional expressivity effect: hold a pen in your mouth using your teeth (not your lips) for a minute or two. How do you feel? (Don't say "silly"!) If you are like many people, you will feel slightly happier because you are adopting the facial pose of smiling, and that facial expression can actually drive a slight increase in mood. Now try holding it with your lips – this causes you to adopt a frowning facial pose and results in a slight drop in mood. People holding pens in their teeth (i.e., smiling) rated Far Side cartoons as significantly funnier than those holding pens in their lips (frowning).[203] Of course, arbitrary facial expressions like these, that you took on only because someone (or some book) told you to, have very mild effects.[204] But if you use your whole body, and more spontaneously express emotions relevant to your goals, the effect is much more powerful. You will begin to feel the emotions you express physically, and the phenomenon of state-dependent memory will bring to mind thoughts and memories from when you experienced the same emotion in the past; soon, you'll feel the momentum of a positive ABC cycle. That momentum will get a boost from the people around you because your outward expressions will change how people respond to you – if you act like a success, people are more likely to start treating you that way. Of course, you'll need some goal-oriented behavioral successes to keep the cycle going, but acting like you are already a success is a good way to get the ball rolling.

· · ·

Belief Building Tool #8:
Visualization

Visualization is another "guaranteed success" – even if you doubt your ability to carry out a certain course of action, you can certainly visualize yourself doing it successfully. Much like "acting like a success," mental rehearsal is obviously no substitute for actual behaviors, but as a supplement it can enhance performance, primarily by enhancing Belief. Simply thinking about an event makes it seem more possible, as you begin to construct mental scenarios of how it might occur and how you might make it happen.[205]

Visualization creates more than a Belief-inspiring self-fulfilling prophecy – by focusing your attention on your future, it boosts the likelihood that you'll set inspirational goals based on your unique personality and values.[206] Visualization also provides many of the benefits of practice, and world-class athletes are routinely trained to visualize performing well in competitive situations[207] (in *Golf My Way*, Jack Nicklaus wrote, "I never hit a shot, not even in practice, without having a very sharp, in focus picture of it in my head. It's like a color movie"). Visualized behaviors can generally be practiced more quickly, easily, and frequently than actual behaviors, and research confirms that visualization can boost athletic performance, particularly when alternated with deep relaxation.[208] It can even help with more "mental" aspects of the sport – athletes with anger management problems can visualize staying calm when opponents try to tempt them into outbursts.[209]

Visualization can also reduce stress, and is frequently used in business and therapy to help individuals practice behavior that would be too frightening or intimidating to perform in reality. In this context, visualization can have an inoculating effect; salespeople who fear rejection perform better by visualizing themselves facing – and bouncing back from – rejection, and therapists ask phobic patients to visualize themselves facing their fears as a way of easing them into actually confronting those fears. Roughly two-thirds of millionaires visualize their future success as a way of reducing anxiety.[210] Visualization is also beneficial for practicing behaviors that are too dangerous to perform in person, as when recovering alcoholics visualize themselves facing – and resisting – tempting situations such as parties or restaurants.

Visualization must be done properly to be effective. Improperly done, it can be a waste of time, or even worse, actually hamper performance. There are four keys to successful visualization.[211]

- *Correct.* Visualization improves performance if you visualize the appropriate behavior, but visualizing incorrect behavior will hurt performance. Visualization enhances the performance of elite athletes, but hampers the performance of less-skilled athletes because novices mentally practice the wrong skills (e.g., novice basketball players mentally rehearse poor form in free throw shooting). So until you have become relatively skilled, you are better off forgoing visualization and focusing on real practice, learning from skilled performers, taking lessons, getting training, etc.

- *Precise.* Visualization must be precise, vivid and detailed to be effective. Popular success books often advocate envisioning broad ends like "being richer" or "having less fear," and this may in fact temporarily boost your motivation, but greater benefits – reduced anxiety, heightened planning and enhanced performance – result from envisioning the specific means to those ends.[212] Don't envision "having a great sales year," but instead envision going to specific sales meetings, your actions in those meetings, the reactions of others, and how you will specifically overcome obstacles and persist in the face of rejection. Use all your senses – as you imagine the actions of others, consider how they might dress and the sounds of their voices. When visualization was used with the 1976 U. S. Olympic ski team, for example, precision and detail were crucial to the process: skiers visualized themselves careening through the entire course, experiencing each bump and turn in their minds. That team performed unexpectedly well, and precise visualization has since become a standard tool in training Olympic athletes.

- *Distributed.* Visualization sessions are most effective when distributed over time, rather than "bunched" into fewer, longer sessions. This "spacing effect" holds true for any kind of practice or preparation. For example, in preparing for a test, short bursts of studying distributed over time (e.g., one hour per night for four nights) lead to better results than cramming (e.g., four hours in one night).[213]

- *Focused on ABC cycles.* Experience your visualization as if you are really living it, not just observing or remembering it. Experience each element of the appropriate ABC cycle: think the thoughts, feel the emotions, vividly imagine the behaviors. For example, a college football wide receiver dropped a pass and soon fell into a negative cycle of affect (worry, anxiety about dropping more), behavior (tentative, overly cautious) and cognition (questioned his skills, developed a new identity as a "dropper").[214] By mentally rehearsing catching passes and scoring touchdowns, he was able to restore his confidence, but touching on each element of the ABC cycle was necessary.

· · ·

Belief Building Tool #9:
Schedule Your ABC Cycles

Here's another Belief builder: schedule your ABC cycles. If you lack confidence in your ability to get your positive ABC cycle rolling, try scheduling a time when you will engage in positive goal-oriented behaviors, regardless of how confident you might feel. If you find doubts creeping in, just tell yourself that you'll have plenty of time to plague yourself with self-doubt later, but for now, just focus on the behavior. If you're having trouble with goals focusing on "living in the moment" or just having fun, then schedule a time for them and follow through. Scheduling fun activities can be an effective (if short-term) mood booster even for clinically depressed people, but they are typically too depressed to do it.[215] If you find yourself scheduling positive ABC cycles but not following through, try scheduling them for early in the morning before distraction or self-doubt set in.

You can prevent negative ABC cycles from overtaking your whole day by limiting them to a very specific location or time of day.[216] In research and case studies, frequent sulking has been lessened by limiting it to a "sulking chair," smoking reduced dramatically by limiting it to an inconvenient and uncomfortable "smoking chair," and anxiety lessened by limiting it to 30 minutes a day and only in a "worry chair." If your ABC cycle creeps into non-scheduled time, just tell yourself that you'll have plenty of time for it later. You may be surprised how effective this simple tool can be.

· · ·

Belief Building Tool #10:
A Vacation from ABC Cycles –
Meditation & Relaxation

Western minds often have trouble understanding why many Buddhists consider nirvana – which generally translates to "emptiness," "extinguishing" or "the blowing out of a candle" – the ultimate aim of life. Here's one way to think about nirvana that might make the idea a little more accessible: it's a "vacation" from ABC cycles. If you're like most people, sleep has been your only respite from ABC cycles in years (and even during sleep, the brain remains quite active). "Stilling" your mind, and temporarily halting all affective, behavioral and cognitive responses, can be profoundly relaxing and rejuvenating (Theodore Rothke: "A mind too active is no mind at all"). Meditation is both the path to nirvana and a very practical technique for quieting your ABC cycles.

Most major cultures throughout the world have developed systems for meditation. Although they differ slightly in philosophy and technique, they share a focus on stilling ABC cycles and focusing attention in a non-verbal way on breathing or a mantra. They all tend to be about equally effective, providing documented benefits for such dis-orders as anxiety, stress, chronic pain, heart disease, sleep disorders, and even alcoholism.[217] There is some evidence that meditative tech-niques like Transcendental Meditation (TM) are more effective than clinically-oriented procedures like progressive relaxation,[218] but the reasons why aren't totally clear. It may simply be that TM tends to bring about an easier, more effortless form of meditation for many people. The details of the techniques are less important than the amount of time you spend practicing them, so I'd suggest trying a few different varieties and picking what works for you.

Here's a very simple technique. Sit alone in a quiet place. Relax and just notice your breathing. In many cultures, the words for "breath" and "life" are nearly identical, but too often we're not in touch with this vital element of our existence. You'll probably notice your breaths getting slower and deeper; that's a good sign that your body's "relax-ation response" is kicking in. As you focus on your breathing, thoughts will probably come to mind. Remember that "you" are not those thoughts, and "you" are not your inner monologue; "you" are the listener, and you can choose not to listen right now. You will be very tempted, in true Western fashion, to "go" with these isolated thoughts, spinning them into stories or letting them trigger memories, and soon you'll be swept away by an ABC cycle. But resist that temptation. Tell yourself that you can engage in that ABC cycle later, and just return to concentrating on your breath. Then try repeating the mantra "one" or some other short phrase that "works" for you. Just say it quietly to yourself, and feel it resonate through your body. Many people find that mantras help them shut out unwanted thoughts, but if you find it distracting, simply go back to observing your breathing. Another ben-efit of mantras is that, with practice, they become associated with relaxation, just as Pavlov's dogs came to associate a bell with food; the mantra will be able to trigger relaxation quickly, just as the bell quickly triggered hunger in the dogs.

Resource recommendation: J. C. Smith has written several good books on meditation. His *Relaxation Dynamics* (1985) is particularly interesting as it provides a summary of nine techniques from throughout the world. Many meditation and relaxation techniques are also described on the Internet; for a good start, try some of the resources at MentalHelp.Net (e.g., http://mentalhelp.net/psyhelp/ chap12/chap12c.htm).

. . .

Belief Building Tool #11:
Distraction

This is the tool to use if you find yourself saying, "Help! I've fallen into a negative ABC cycle and I can't get up!" Find an activity that will absorb your attention, focusing you outward on some unrelated task rather than internally on your ABC cycle. This obviously isn't a permanent solution, but can help in the short-term. The activity can be anything from exercise to music to watching a movie, as long as it absorbs your attention.

Just as people in negative or depressed moods tend not realize how much they will benefit from scheduling positive ABC cycles, they also tend to underestimate how much they will benefit from distracting activities, and as a result tend not to engage in them. Instead, thinking that wallowing in their negative ABC cycle will yield insights into themselves, they tend to ruminate about their problems, pondering why they have taken hold, how pervasive they are, how long they will last, etc. Over time, ABC cycles tend to spiral, or at the very least perpetuate themselves, so rumination exacerbates poor moods rather than reducing them.[219] Similarly, expressing anger usually intensifies the emotion rather than having a cathartic, reducing effect.[220] When struck by bad moods, women tend to ruminate, whereas men tend to engage in distracting activities; this contributes to the greater prevalence of depression among women.[221] Depression isn't the only negative ABC cycle that can benefit from constructive distraction. People trying to start exercise regimens often get bogged down in negative cycles of affect (disappointment,

feelings of incompetence), behavior (tiredness, soreness) and cognition (thinking of themselves as weak and out-of-shape). But distraction can help. Beginning runners who think distracting thoughts while
exercising are more likely to stick with it over the long-term.[222]

Avoid eating as a distraction technique. It works in the short-
term, but only as long as you are actually eating. When you're fin-
ished, the negative ABC cycle will return, and it may well be compounded by "overeater's remorse." Exercise is better. If you are feeling
depressed, a sugary snack can improve your mood and energy in the
short-term, but even a moderate amount of exercise (as little as a 10
minute rapid walk) has much better effects over the next few hours,
and more extensive exercise regimens can even help combat more
severe depression.[223] Another distractor to avoid: alcohol. Drinking
alcohol creates a kind of "myopia" – it focuses you on immediate
stimuli rather than on delaying gratification to achieve longer-term
goals, and can actually increase your focus on negative ABC cycles.[224]
One team of psychologists summarized the research this way: "Although there is quite a bit of folk wisdom suggesting that eating favorite foods to be nice to oneself, drinking alcohol, or smoking a
cigarette will help one calm down or to cheer up, there is little empirical support for these beliefs. In fact... there is even considerable
evidence suggesting that these efforts... will actually serve to worsen
one's bad mood."[225]

. . .

Belief Building Tool #12:
Think "Substitutes"

If you've developed a Vision and set SCAMPI goals, then you've
already got a clear sense of the ABC cycles you desire. But often
people are better at identifying what they don't want. So if you've
gotten to this point and only know what you don't want – and only
have ABC cycles you want to avoid – then this is the time to clarify
what you do want. If you know only that you want to lose weight, you

need to recognize that you probably have patterns of inactivity and unhealthy eating that must be faced and replaced with new patterns of exercise and health eating. It's very difficult to "destroy" old ABC cycles, but it's much easier to "replace" them with substitutes.

Successful change does not come from simply trying to stop current ABC cycles. Repressing and denying negative emotional experiences not only have detrimental effects (as we've seen), but they actually lead to "rebound" effects. Suppressing thoughts about sex can lead to more physiological arousal than actually thinking about sex,[226] and dieters who try to suppress food-related thoughts become particularly obsessed with food, sometimes even going to the extreme of binge eating.[227] Simply trying to abolish an ABC cycle creates a psychological vacuum into which the old ABC cycle can rush back.[228] It is very difficult to get compulsive fingernail-biters to stop altogether, but it is much easier to get them to replace their destructive habit with a more constructive one like grooming their nails.[229] Similarly, people who talk too much in meetings find it difficult to become silent, but much easier to replace their compulsive talking with highly attentive listening.[230] In fact, one the best predictors of recovery from alcoholism is the development of substitutes to occupy one's time and attention (e.g., hobbies, exercise, social activities, immersing oneself in work or religion).[231] Remember the old saying, "If you don't know where you're going, you'll get there." If you only know what you don't want, then this is the time to really flesh out what you do want. And if you do decide that what you really want is just to get rid of some habit or thought process, then work on developing substitutes.

Practically every major non-pharmaceutical treatment for depression involves substituting negative thoughts and beliefs with more positive ones. This can take the form of the complex process of learning to argue with yourself, but it can begin with very simple substitution. There's a documented case of an individual whose intense fear of driving past cemeteries at night grew to the point where he avoided driving at night altogether. He felt "an overwhelming compulsion to stop the car, turn the inside light on, and look at the back seat." On the advice of a therapist, he made a new habit driving past a local cemetery, but this time substituting his fearful cognitions with thoughts of having sex with his wife, timing it so that he was maximally aroused when he passed the cemetery. He practiced this substitution 30 minutes a day, and his anxiety subsided within just a few days.[232]

The cognitive aspect of ABC cycles is almost always more than just a few isolated thoughts, encompassing a collection of related thoughts, ideas, theories, stories, etc. Substitution can be applied to all of these. The fact is that the language we use has implications for our ABC cycles, and substituting empowering terms for disempowering ones brings many benefits; for example, people who consider obstacles to be "challenges" or "opportunities" maintain their physical health better under stress than those who consider them "threats."[233] A writer who is "blocked" will tend to blame herself (the term implies a failure of something that should happen naturally), whereas a writer suffering the same problem but who considers herself "empty" will take proactive steps toward filling her "creative well."[234] We saw earlier that people often relive traumatic events without putting them into words, but crafting meaningful stories about them brings psychological and health benefits. In other cases, we have stories but they no longer serve us well, and benefits come from replacing them with more positive stories. Memory is a fluid, malleable interpretation of events, not a precise record of events, so "rewriting your personal history" is a definite possibility; as Gerald Johnson put it, "Nothing changes more consistently than the past... the past that influences our lives [is] not what actually happened but what [we] believe happened." In fact, the stories we tell about our lives often morph with changes in circumstance. Happily married people, for example, tend to tell idealized stories about their romantic meeting, whirlwind courtship, and pleasant marriage. But if they divorce, history is rewritten – their meeting is now viewed as a chance accident, and their relationship depicted as a fight-marred matter of convenience.[235]

Some might argue that substituting thoughts or ABC cycles is too "superficial" because it doesn't address why the old ABC cycle is there. Obviously there is some benefit to understanding the old ABC cycle – it can provide personal insight and help diagnose why certain goals haven't already been accomplished. Your old ABC cycle, whatever it may be, is there for a reason. They are often shaped by strong emotional experiences or cultural beliefs, and they are often reinforced over the years because, at least at some level, they "work" – providing some kind of psychological benefit, even if they are ultimately counter-productive. But there is a fine line between constructively revisiting your ABC cycle to gain insight and destructive rumination. You wouldn't watch a really terrible TV show a thousand times, but that's precisely what some people do with negative ABC cycles. ABC cycles are analogous to computer software – before installing the new version of a program, you need to uninstall the old one. Of course there is some value to understanding how that old program got there, and how it's different from the new program, but you want to spend the bulk of your time looking forward and using that new program. At some point, you have to make the decision to get over it and move on. It won't happen instantly, and you'll likely backslide at some point, but the decision to move forward needs to be made.

Resource recommendation: For more on managing unwanted thoughts, and substituting them with more positive ones, check out *White Bears and Other Unwanted Thoughts: Suppression, Obsession and the Psychology of Mental Control* by Dr. Daniel Wegner. It's an interesting read, and nicely combines sound research with practical applications.

. . .

A Belief-Building Example:
See Dick and Jane's Quest for Confidence

When we last left our intrepid duo, Jane had laid the foundation for Belief in herself with SCAMPI goals and a well thought-out action plan, while Dick's resolutions about losing weight and never eating pizza seemed to be setting himself up for a Belief-destroying "what-the-hell" setback.

Jane starts the Belief-building process with some guaranteed successes to boost her sense of self-efficacy and get positive ABC cycles rolling. By setting attainable but moderately challenging goals like exercising only 15 minutes per day, Jane can begin with behavioral baby steps (Belief Builder #6) and still feel the excitement that comes with making real progress. She also starts acting like a success (#7) by volunteering to coach a local girls soccer team; she may not be as spry as she once was, but just being out there on the field makes her feel more athletic, and gives her a sense of pride by contributing to her community. Another guaranteed success that boosts her overall sense of well-being is using meditation to take a vacation from all her ABC cycles (#10).

She starts keeping a journal to track her burgeoning exercise habit, but soon finds it healing to also write about past negative experiences, and motivating to write about her Vision and Strategy (#4). Writing also helps her recognize the automatic negative thoughts (ANTs) like "I'm not worthy" that often trigger her negative moods (#1). With greater insight into her cognitive processes, she finds it valuable to argue with herself (#2) and in particular question whether her ANT of "I'm not worthy" is an exaggeration and an over-reaction. On a purely cognitive level, she recognizes the irrationality of her ANT, but it still seems to pop into her head instantly at the slightest failing. Her ANT doesn't disappear, but over time and with practice, she finds that arguing with herself short-circuits the negative ABC cycles that used to be triggered so quickly by her ANT.

Dick takes a very different, more dramatic approach to building Belief. He goes to a motivational seminar, complete with firewalking experience, that pumps him into an emotional frenzy. At the seminar, he repeats his resolutions over and over again as affirmations, drilling these two cognitions into his consciousness. He also learns about visualization (#8) at the seminar, but doesn't do it in the most effective manner. He visualizes his desired ends (himself as thin) rather than the means for achieving those ends (healthy eating and exercise), and bunches his visualization in a few long sessions rather than many shorter sessions. Still, the seminar works, temporarily. It does indeed boost his resolve to avoid pizza and lose weight, but without a compelling Vision and well-crafted Strategy, that heightened motivation begins to fade after a week or two.

Unfortunately, Dick's attempts at change have been almost entirely cognitive. His two resolutions are isolated cognitions at risk of being swept away by a broader, longer-standing ABC cycle composed of affect (positive emotions evoked by memories of pizzas past), behavior (continuing to hang out with friends at the pool hall next to his favorite pizza joint) and cognition (his belief that he "deserves to treat himself"). The behavioral elements of his action plan are very limited, and his attempt to spur positive ABC cycles with the emotional boost from the seminar was short-lived. Although distraction (#11) can be effective under certain circumstances, Dick uses distraction to remain in denial about his lack of Vision and underachievement in life, preventing him from hitting bottom and feeling the emotional pain of his situation.

Even the cognitive strategies that he uses are relatively weak. His cognition that he deserves to treat himself isn't inherently bad, but he never re-structures what he means by "treat" – he continues to think only in terms of "treat equals big pizza," and never finds an appropriate substitute (#12). Perhaps the more fundamental cognitive impediment to Dick's success is his sense of fatalism – he's got low self-efficacy about his ability to lose weight, and his belief that people have relatively little control over their lives belies his inherent external locus control.

Chapter Seven

Step Four: Persistence – The Science of Drive and Determination

"We are what we repeatedly do. Excellence, therefore, is not an act but a habit." Aristotle

THIS IS THE LONGEST CHAPTER in the book, mostly because it's the step at which people most frequently run into problems. We've all known people who have underachieved in life despite a clear Vision, a reasonable Strategy for making it happen, and at least at first, true Belief they could do it. For such people, Persistence is usually the problem – they start enacting their Strategy, encounter obstacles, suffer setbacks, and give up.

Achieving true success is challenging not just because of its inherent difficulty, but also because of its unpredictability. For example, we've seen that quitting smoking usually takes several failed attempts before "it sticks." But still, success is unpredictable: the number of previous attempts to quit smoking does not predict success on the next attempt.[236] In other words, someone who has failed to quit five times is just as likely to be successful on the next attempt as someone attempting to quit for just the second time. As mutual fund companies are fond of reminding us, "past performance does not guarantee future results." Success is difficult to predict or forecast, and therefore requires persistence in the face of uncertainty.

Attempts to change often have unexpected consequences – sometimes we will face the surprise of quick success, but too often we must contend with the surprise of repeated failures.

It's easy to underestimate the importance of Persistence. It isn't "sexy." It isn't glamorous. You might go into the wilderness for a dramatic, life-altering Vision quest, but nobody goes into the wilderness on a Persistence quest. Even its clichés aren't glamorous – you "plow ahead" or "toil away" or just "keep on keepin' on." Persistence often goes unnoticed and unrewarded, "flying below the radar screen" of others, even after it produces remarkable results. After a great achievement, everyone wants to know "the secret of success," but when they are told "persistence," they turn away disappointed and keep searching for a sexier answer.

This unheralded role of Persistence is precisely what Jim Collins discovered when he researched extraordinary companies for his book *Good to Great*. Persistence is just as crucial to corporate success as it is to personal success, and is just as often overlooked. Executives who transform companies from good to great typically can point to "no single defining action, no grand program, no one killer innovation, no solitary lucky break, no wrenching revolution.... [there was] no name for their transformations. There was no launch event, no tag line, no programmatic feel whatsoever. Some executives even said that they weren't even aware that a major transformation was under way until they were well into it."[237] When prodded for some deeper secret to success, some dramatic insight, these executives become frustrated. One exclaimed: "Look, it just wasn't that complicated! Once we understood the concept, we just moved straight ahead."[238] Many echo Sam Walton, who described his Wal-Mart empire as an overnight success 20 years in the making. They downplay formal change processes like motivational exercises and corporate "encounter groups," emphasizing instead "fanatical consistency" or "consistent execution" or a "crawl, walk, run" approach. They talk less about "explosive growth" and more about "sustainable, organic growth." They use mergers and acquisitions to maintain momentum rather than create it from scratch. They don't fall head-over-heels for the Internet, but rather carefully plot out a strategy and execute consistently, even if it means not being first to market. But the media are often unsatisfied with such "mundane" explanations. Persistence makes a boring headline, so the business press features stories of critical "inflection points" or "celebrity CEOs" or other dramatic if largely irrelevant factors.

Certainly change can happen very suddenly. The decision to change can be dramatic. But true success comes from Persistence. As we all know, even if we don't like to admit it ourselves, successful people don't give up, and they work hard...

· · ·

COMMON KNOWLEDGE:
SUCCESSFUL PEOPLE DON'T GIVE UP,
AND THEY WORK HARD

Perhaps because Persistence is so easily overlooked, success writers and motivational speakers go out of their way to highlight famous examples of persistence. Many point to Thomas Edison, whose 1,093 patents remains a record, citing his famous remark that success is 1% inspiration and 99% perspiration (although I prefer his quip, "Everything comes to him who hustles while he waits"). Another favorite is Abraham Lincoln, who persisted despite being born into poverty, failing in business, going deeply into debt, and losing several elections. Still others point to Albert Einstein, who achieved the "overnight success" of his theory of relativity only after a decade of laying the foundation through intense study and thought. Other tales of persistence, featuring less familiar names but offering even more inspiration, are staples of the motivational speaking circuit. W Mitchell, a popular speaker whose story is told by others as well, suffered burns over nearly two-thirds of his body in a fiery motorcycle accident. His persistence during years of physical therapy and 32 operations was impressive, and he recovered to the point of even being able to fly a plane. Then fate struck again – Mitchell's plane crashed, leaving him permanently confined to a wheelchair. At this point, many people would simply give up, their spirits crushed. Mitchell, however, persisted and prospered, eventually becoming a mayor and running for statewide office; he even poked fun at his own disfigurement by running with the slogan, "Not just a pretty face."

Writers are often cited as examples of Persistence, in part because success writers are (obviously) writers themselves, but also because writing is one of the most rejection-filled professions. Persistence is a prerequisite for writing success. I'll spare you my own stories of agents and publishers who told me it was "impossible" to publish the book you now hold in your hands. (An actual conversation: Me: "I realize it's challenging..." Allegedly respectable agent: "No! Not challenging!! IMPOSSIBLE!!!!" I've since sent her an autographed copy). Other tales of writing Persistence are far more impressive than mine. *M*A*S*H, Gone with the Wind,* and Dr. Seuss's first book were each rejected over 20 times; each became a classic and sold millions. *The Good Earth* was rejected 14 times; Pearl Buck went on to win a Pulitzer Prize for it. Louis L'Amour was rejected 350 times before first being published; he went on to write over 100 novels. Jack London was rejected over 600 times before publishing his first story; he went on to write hundreds of short stories and over 50 books, some of which have been translated into 70 languages. Another writer received rejection letters every week for four years, and later spent nine years working on a project that nearly drove him to suicide; but as he contemplated throwing himself off a ship into the Pacific Ocean, that writer, Alex Haley, heard the voices of his ancestors telling him, "Don't give up!" *Roots* went on to change America. These examples all come from *Chicken Soup for the Writer's Soul,* itself a Persistence success story. The first *Chicken Soup* book was rejected by 123 publishers before selling millions and spawning dozens of sequels.

Persistence is a key theme, not only in inspirational tales, but also in pithy quotes repeated so often they become clichéd. Some emphasize bouncing back from obstacles. (Confucius: "Our greatest glory is not in never falling, but in rising every time we fall." Mary Pickford: "This thing that we call 'failure' is not the falling down, but the staying down.") Others emphasize hard work. (Thomas Jefferson: "I find that the harder I work, the more luck I seem to have." Anonymous: "The road to success is dotted with many tempting parking spaces.") But perhaps the ones that resonate most strongly are those that capture the essence of Persistence itself. Aristotle is often quoted as saying, "We are what we repeatedly do. Excellence, therefore, is not an act but a habit." But that sentiment had clearly gone mainstream when basketball's Shaquille O'Neil said the quote embodied his philosophy during his MVP season, and asked reporters to henceforth call him "The Big Aristotle."

Persistence is clearly a social value, an American ideal deeply engrained in our culture. It is inherent in popular theories about success. Over 90% of Americans agree that "willpower and hard work" are primary reasons why a person's life turns out well or poorly.[239] Roughly two-in-three believe hard work plays a bigger role in "getting ahead" than luck or help from others;[240] in contrast, only about one-in-three believe "success in life is pretty much determined by forces outside our control" or "hard work offers little guarantee of success."[241] We admire perseverance; 86% choose their heroes in large part because they are exemplars of Persistence.[242] We teach Persistence as well – the popular children's story *The Little Engine That Could* conveys two values: Persistence and Belief ("I think I can... I think I can"). Persistence permeates adult media experiences as well; consider, for example, the common theme of Persistence prevailing over unrequited love.[243] We've all seen this movie: Boy meets Girl, Boy falls madly in love with Girl, but Girl has no interest in Boy. In fact, Girl is typically engaged to Gorgeous-Rich-Obnoxious Guy. But Boy persists, sending flowers, engineering "chance" encounters, and sometimes charmingly disrupting Girl's wedding (often, for some reason, while wearing a gorilla suit). In real life, when Boy is so persistent, Girl takes out restraining order against

Boy. But in the movies, Persistence is rewarded, and Girl comes to realize that she loves Boy.

Although the benefits of Persistence are occasionally overstated, research confirms that the common knowledge notion of Persistence being crucial to success is no urban legend. Consider a sampling of relevant findings...

• People who successfully maintain their New Year's resolutions for at least two years report an average of 14 slips or setbacks during that time.[244] But they rebound, and a majority even say that their setbacks strengthened their resolve to make life changes.

• Among college students, each additional hour spent studying per week leads to only a 0.025 increase in grade point average. In other words, you'd need to spend an additional 40 hours per week studying to just raise your GPA by a full letter grade.[245]

• You probably knew that Persistence is crucial to losing weight, but you may not realize it's also the key to putting on weight. The average person gains only one pound over the holidays, and only a pound and a half over the course of a whole year. But the problem is Persistence: that weight goes on each year, typically staying on permanently, leading to a 10 pound weight gain in only seven years.[246]

• History's true achievers persist and work hard, producing both quality and quantity. In fields as diverse as chemistry, geology, geriatrics and linguistics, 10% of the people make about half of the scientific contributions.[247] Of the roughly 250 "classical" composers, for example, 16 account for half of all the works in the repertoire.

• Acquiring the skills and knowledge to change the direction of the field – not just contribute to it – typically takes a decade or so of 70-hour weeks.[248] Of course talent and other factors come into play, but Persistence is a necessary ingredient.

Research obviously confirms the common knowledge that successful people are persistent and work hard. But it also confirms a more elusive truth: Persistence is the key to happiness…

· · ·

UNCOMMON KNOWLEDGE:
PERSISTENCE IS THE KEY TO HAPPINESS

Scholars and sages have tried to unlock the secrets of happiness for centuries, but I think it's fair to say they've been more successful identifying what doesn't contribute to happiness than what does.[249] Consider the following "likely suspects," all of which have all been shown to have little or no impact on happiness:

- *Intelligence*. Ignorance is not bliss, nor are brilliant people particularly happy.
- *Physical attractiveness*. The beautiful are not happier than the rest of us, except among young women, and even then the effect is very slight.
- *Marriage*. Married people are moderately but not dramatically happier than their single counterparts. About four-in-ten married Americans describe themselves as "very happy," compared to only 24% of those who never married.[250]
- *Children*. As any parent will attest, having kids is no guarantee of happiness. In fact, childless couples are slightly happier than parents, but again the effect is very modest.

Even money has a smaller effect on happiness than one might expect. When asked what would make them happier, "more money" tops the list,[251] but in fact the relationship between money and happiness is relatively small and limited. Certainly it's difficult to be happy if you are very poor and have trouble meeting basic needs for food or shelter, but beyond a certain subsistence level, financial wealth is uncorrelated with happiness. Many people have trouble accepting this conclusion because it runs so contrary to our free enterprise ideology and today's glorification of entrepreneurs. A recent Lexus ad tried to convince us that "Whoever said money can't buy happiness isn't spending it right." A *New Yorker* cartoon questioned this conclusion in a more humorous way, depicting a man saying: "Researchers say I'm not happier for being richer, but do you know how much researchers make?" But the data are clear. For example, over the past 25 years, personal income in America has increased dramatically, while happiness levels have remained very stable; in study after study, about a third of Americans describe themselves as very happy, and an additional 55% or so say they are pretty happy.[252] If anything, happiness levels have declined slightly; 25 years ago, about 34% of Americans described themselves as very happy, compared to only 30% today.[253] Psychologist David Myers calls this *the American paradox*: "Compared with their grandparents, today's young adults have grown up with much more affluence, slightly less happiness, and much greater risk of depression and assorted social pathologies.... We are twice as rich but no happier. Meanwhile, the divorce rate doubled. Teen suicide tripled. Reported violent crime nearly quadrupled."[254] Clearly, money can't buy happiness.

The drivers of happiness have been so elusive that some psychologists have even concluded that a person's level of happiness is largely genetically determined, and that any fluctuations in happiness are at best temporary, and at worst illusory.[255] Studies of identical twins raised apart confirm that genes do play a role; there is a genetic component to personality traits like extraversion and optimism, and these traits in turn shape one's tendency to experience happiness or sadness. Certainly it is hard to permanently change your level of happiness; lottery winners experience an initial surge of excitement, but adapt to their new circumstances within a year and "settle back" to their previous levels of happiness.[256]

Perhaps it's the eternal optimist in me, but I'm not willing to concede that our level of happiness is immovable. It's psychologically beneficial to believe that you can become happier, even if it isn't true; fortunately, I believe that it is true. I agree with University of Missouri psychologist Ken Sheldon who concluded, "If you're a more gloomy, pessimistic person, you're probably never going to be really deliriously happy, but you can get into the high end of your possible range and stay there."[257] But if happiness isn't driven by money, marriage, procreation, beauty or intelligence, then what's left? In a word, Persistence.

. . .

Persistence, Progress and Happiness

Happiness is ultimately about progress. It is about moving forward, just as in the old saying about the journey being more important than the destination. Happiness is the emotional juice that emerges from a sense of momentum, from overcoming inertia to get the ball rolling toward inspirational goals. Psychologist Roy Baumeister summed it up this way: "The best prescription may be a slow crescendo of successes, allowing one to celebrate and savor each increment in achievement or each improvement in circumstances... Everyone may want to get to the top, but if you want to enjoy it, you should take the stairway rather than the elevator."[258] The American constitution guarantees "life, liberty and the pursuit of happiness" – not happiness itself. But as it turns out, the pursuit of happiness *is* happiness.

Happiness is about progress toward goals rather than accomplishing them per se. We've already seen that lottery winners aren't happier than the rest of us. You probably haven't won the lottery, but you probably have labored long and hard toward goals only to find that accomplishing them was less satisfying than expected. Psychological crises often driven by accomplishing a goal and being left with nothing more than a profound feeling of "Is that it?" As my man Mr. Spock once said, "After a time, you may find that having is not so pleasing a thing, after all, than wanting. It is not logical, but it is often true." You may recall the Vision Quest-ions that asked about when you were most excited about your future. I've found that most people answer with stories, not of accomplishing goals, but of the excitement inherent in initial progress. They tell tales of an inspiring

Vision, an achievable Strategy, Belief in themselves, and the joy that comes with "getting the ball rolling". In other words, they talk of the excitement that comes with progress, Persistence and momentum.

Happiness is one of only a handful of basic emotions. Psychologists debate the exact number, with most estimates falling somewhere between five and ten. These emotions are innate and universal; people from all cultures throughout the world use the same facial expressions to convey these emotions.[259] Many of these emotional states are largely determined by the status of your goals. Happiness, as shown in the table on the next page, is the affective component of ABC cycles that take hold after Persistence leads to solid progress toward goals.[260]

This chart obviously simplifies complex dynamics. For example, not all progress is created equal; the direction and velocity of progress are important to understanding how ABC cycles will unfold. Progress only brings about happiness if you are moving toward inspirational goals that reflect your Vision,[261] and if you progress at a pace you consider acceptable.[262] These subtleties aside, it is clear that progress and Persistence are crucial to happiness, even if we are far from our goals.[263] Properly managed, ABC cycles can grow into ABC spirals. By setting goals, accomplishing them, and setting even more rewarding and challenging goals, happiness can increase in lasting and pervasive ways. College students who create ABC spirals not only experience greater happiness, they get better grades than would be expected based on their standardized test scores (even if their goals weren't about getting good grades), and exhibit more personal growth.[264] But again, Persistence is the key. Spirals require continual effort; it is easy to lose momentum and fall back into ABC equilibrium.

This notion of Persistence and progress driving happiness explains why money, intelligence and attractiveness aren't good predictors of happiness in general, but do predict happiness for some people. If money and attractiveness enable progress toward your goals, then having them in abundance can boost your sense of well-being.[265] The Beatles were right that money can't buy love, but if your goal is accu-

Status of goal	Affect	Behavior	Cognition
Progress toward goal	Happiness	Heightened motivation; further progress	Confidence; self-efficacy; recalling past successes
Lack of progress; loss of goal; failure	Sadness	Loss of motivation; giving up; learned helplessness; depression	Lack of confidence; pessimism; recalling past failures
Frustration; progress inhibited by others or by circumstances	Anger	Aggressive striving toward goal, or striking out at obstruction/obstructor	Problem solving; denigration of obstructor
Goal conflict; ambivalence; Vision but no Strategy; avoidance goals; external threats or dangers	Fear, anxiety	Freezing; flight or fight; procrastination	Rumination; paralysis of analysis

mulating a house full of stuff, then more money does tend to make you happier. Similarly, self-esteem is a stronger predictor of happiness in very individualistic countries, where it facilitates independence and the pursuit of individualistic goals, but a much weaker predictor in countries where community and collectivism are more valued.[266] Money, intelligence and the like don't create happiness directly, but if they are "resources" that facilitate progress toward your particular goals, then they will indirectly tend to make you happier.

The Persistence-happiness link may also explain why people in some countries are happier than one might expect. Across nations, happiness correlates with income and economic productivity – people living in poverty-stricken nations are unable to meet basic needs and tend to be unhappy. But some nations "over-perform" – people in Brazil, Chile and Argentina are happier than one would expect based on their income, whereas people in Russia and eastern European nations are less satisfied with their lives than one would predict from their income.[267] The reasons are complex, and not easily pinned down to a single explanation. But people in South American countries may, because of cultural factors, tend to choose highly attainable goals toward which they can make progress relatively easily; in contrast, people in former Soviet-bloc countries may tend to choose goals based on expectations shaped in previous decades, but which are now difficult to make progress toward because of political and economic impediments.

· · ·

The "Happily-Ever-After" Myth

If progress and Persistence are the keys to happiness, then you need to avoid thinking that permanent fulfillment is just around the corner if only you accomplish certain goals. In other words, you must avoid the "happily-ever-after" myth. Fill in the blank: "I would be totally, completely happy forever if only I _____." What did you say? Meet your soulmate? Get a certain job or promotion? Win the lottery? If winning the lottery doesn't lead to lasting happiness, then anything else you might list probably won't either.

The happily-ever-after myth is seductive and pervasive. People tend to be very work-oriented early in their careers, unrealistically expecting that a certain level of achievement would result in a stress-free, problem-free, happily-ever-after life. When those lifestyle transformations don't occur, the result is often disillusionment and a "mid-life crisis."[268] As the saying goes, "Be careful what you wish for – you just might get it."

Mythology and literature also warn us about the happily-ever-after myth.[269] The quest for the Holy Grail led to heroic adventures and brought out the noble, chivalric traits in King Arthur's knights. But those who actually saw the Grail quickly died; Sir Galahad even asked to die so that life afterward would not seem anticlimactic. The message: happiness comes from progress, not necessarily from accomplishing the goal. In Goethe's story of Faust, the devil offers a lifetime supply of earthly pleasures, until the moment that Faust finds something so enjoyable he wants it to last. Faust takes the bargain, confident in his belief that happiness is fleeting, resulting from progress. But he eventually becomes tempted, and the devil takes his soul. The message: the happily-ever-after fallacy is irresistible, and man is, metaphorically speaking, "lost to the devil" as soon as he begins to aspire to permanent, blissful happiness.

My favorite warning against the happily-ever-after myth comes from a classic Star Trek episode, *This Side of Paradise*. Captain Kirk and his crew are sent to the distant planet Omicron Seti III to check the status of an agricultural colony, where they uncover several mysteries. First, the planet is being bombarded with radiation that should have killed the colonists, but instead they are in perfect health. Also, instead of a thriving agricultural colony, they discover the settlers had only planted fields to meet their immediate needs; instead of being world-builders, they had become mere subsistence farmers. These mysteries are resolved when Kirk discovers a plant with spores that both protects people from radiation and induces a blissful state of happiness. The spores infect his entire crew. Ambition is lost. They abandon their duties, spending their days blissed out as if on drugs, dreamily finding shapes in clouds. But Kirk knew that, at some level, the happiness inspired by the spores was illusory. He argued the point with Sandoval, the governor of the colony:

> *Sandoval*: "... they give you complete heath and peace of mind."
> *Kirk*: "That's paradise." [skeptically]
> *Sandoval*: "We have no need or want, Captain."
> *Spock*: "It's a true Eden, Jim. There is belonging...and love."
> *Kirk*: "No wants? No needs? We weren't meant for that. None of us. Man stagnates if he has no ambition – no desire to be more than he is."
> *Sandoval*: "We have what we need."
> *Kirk*: "Except a challenge."

Eventually Kirk finds a way to counter-act the effects of the spores (the key to breaking their hold and bringing about personal change: strong negative emotions. Sound familiar?). When Sandoval "sobers up," he recognizes that the spores brought only an illusory happiness: "We have done nothing here. No accomplishments. No progress. Three years wasted." Dr. McCoy comments that man has been thrown out of paradise for a second time. But Kirk disagrees, and launches into what Spock calls "non-regulation poetry": "No, no, Bones. This time we walked out on our own. Maybe we weren't meant for paradise. Maybe we were meant to fight our way through. Struggle. Claw our way up. Scratch for every inch of the way. Maybe we can't stroll to the music of the lute. We must march to the sound of drums." It may be a classic bit of Shatner-esque over-acting, but this episode, based on the ancient legend of Odysseus and the island of the lotus-eaters, shows a keen insight into the notion that progress brings about true happiness.

. . .

TOOLS: TEN PROVEN PRINCIPLES
FOR PERSISTENCE AND PROGRESS

Our first three steps – Vision, Strategy and Belief – laid the ground-work for Persistence, progress and happiness. People work longer, harder and faster when they have clear objectives, SCAMPI goals, and both broad and task-specific self-confidence.[270] These three initial steps also increase your chances of rebounding from a setback, rather than letting a single lapse snowball into a more serious problem.

We've laid the groundwork for Persistence, but we have not guaranteed it. Persistence requires more. Motivation can help, but it too is often not enough. Chronic disease sufferers are highly motivated to follow the medical regimens prescribed by their doctors, and at first most do, but over time about half stop complying.[271] Boosting motivation doesn't help as much as you might expect, because educating people about the seriousness of their conditions, or about the specifics of how and when to take their medication, doesn't boost compliance rates.[272]

Persistence requires, not just a motivational pump-up, but rather the right tools and techniques, like the ten proven tools that follow. The more you use, the better. As we saw earlier, across different areas of life, from weight loss to smoking cessation, from academic success to dating, those who are more successful are those who use multiple techniques for change; moreover, they use those techniques more frequently, more consistently, over longer periods of time, and thoughtfully apply different techniques to different kinds of problems.[273]

. . .

Persistence Promoter #1:
Think Like a Genius

Each characteristic of genius-level thinking highlighted in the Vision chapter is a potential Persistence-enhancer. Particularly optimism. Over the years, this basic concept has gone by many names.

"Positive thinking" first took hold as a popular philosophy in the late 1800's, spurred by several popular religious and philosophical movements including Mary Baker Eddy's Christian Science, the New Thought movement, the Don't Worry Movement and the Gospel of Relaxation.[274] The basic tenets of these movement can still be found in popular success books today, but they reached their zenith in the 1950s when, amidst a religious revival as the World War II generation raised families, Norman Vincent Peale's *The Power of Positive Thinking* had a record-setting run on best seller lists. The message was simple: faith, prayer and positive thinking were the keys to a successful life. Devotees were to practice daily "mind emptying" – clearing the mind of all fears and anxieties while replacing them with positive thoughts. The book was just one element of Peale's far-flung empire of inspiration, which included a weekly syndicated newspaper column, a monthly magazine, published sermons, and long-playing records (forerunners of today's success audiotape programs). Peale was, in a sense, the Oprah of his day.

Today, psychologists generally prefer the term *optimism*, and its benefits are well documented. Optimism "has been linked to positive mood and good morale; to perseverance and effective problem solving; to academic, athletic, military, occupational and political success; to popularity; to good health; and even to long life and freedom from trauma. Pessimism, in contrast, foreshadows depression, passivity, failure, social estrangement, morbidity and mortality."[275]

The Vision chapter documented how successful people tend to be "overly" optimistic, but they also know when to "turn it on" and when to "tone it down." On your Vision quest, optimism is highly beneficial – turn it on, because the more, the better. When formulating strategy, tone it down – a more realistic mindset results in better decisions and more realistic deadlines. Of course, there is a fine line between beneficial optimism and destructive, unrealistic expectations. When former Vietnam prisoner of war and vice-presidential candidate Admiral Jim Stockdale was asked who didn't make it out of the POW camp, Stockdale raised eyebrows when he said, "the optimists." By that, he didn't meant those confident they would make it out eventually (optimistic in Vision), but rather those who repeatedly developed – only to be disappointed by – unrealistic expectations about *when* they would get out (overly optimistic in Strategy and timelines). Those who said, "We'll be out by Christmas," only to see Christmas come and go, and then said, "We'll be out by Easter", only to be further disappointed, soon had their spirits crushed.[276]

After you've formed your Strategy and defined your timelines, and it comes time to pursue goals and implement plans, turn the optimism back up,[277] because in no domain is optimism more crucial than Persistence. Summing up years of research, psychologist Martin Seligman concluded: "When pessimistic people run into obstacles in the workplace, in relationships, or in sports, they give up. When optimistic people encounter obstacles, they try harder. They go the extra mile."[278]

In "high-rejection" fields, such as writing or sales, the most persistent are often the most successful. As a result, many companies now incorporate optimism tests into their recruiting and hiring practices, sometimes with dramatic success. Before optimism testing, about half of Metropolitan Life's salespeople quit in their first year, and 80% quit before five years. Research confirmed that optimism and Persistence were powerful predictors of job success at Met Life; in one study, optimistic salespeople outsold their pessimistic counterparts by 21% in their first year on the job, and by 57% in the second year (a classic case of momentum – a positive ABC cycle fueling itself and spiraling over time). By hiring optimistic, highly persistent salespeople, Met Life was able to grow its sales force with people well-suited to the rejection-filled task of selling life insurance. Obviously the company benefited – market share increased nearly 50%, and as turnover decreased, hiring costs dropped dramatically. Optimistic job candidates benefited, obtaining jobs well-matched to their skills and personalities, whereas pessimistic candidates were spared the stress, burn-out and failure they would likely face in such a rejection-filled profession.[279]

Can you become more optimistic? Yes, to a degree. Just as you can become somewhat happier, moving to the upper end of a biologically-shaped emotional range, you can learn to become somewhat more optimistic, but don't expect to totally revamp how you view the future, at least not at first. And, unfortunately, the process is more complex than many popular success books would suggest. Simple techniques like Peale's "mind emptying" can lead to greater happiness and a heightened sense of psychological adjustment, but only as long you continue to hold those thoughts in your mind. When you stop thinking positive thoughts, the sense of happiness quickly fades (unfortunately, the effects of negative thinking can be much more pervasive and long-lasting – in a sense, "non-negative" thinking is more powerful than positive thinking).[280] So how do you become more optimistic? Try these three ideas...

- Focus on the belief-building tools "Crushing the ANTs" and "Arguing with yourself." These lie at the heart of creating positive ABC cycles that will have more lasting and pervasive effects than "positive thinking."
- Read Martin Seligman's *Learned Optimism*. It includes an optimism test as well as practical tools for becoming more optimistic.
- Use the next tool, manage your attributions, over and over and over...

. . .

Persistence Promoter #2:
Manage Your Attributions

Attributions are explanations of why things occur, and are some of our most influential cognitions. Successful people have a distinctive *attributional style*, displaying a natural tendency to take credit for success while attributing negative events to external, easily changeable causes. Winning athletes and their coaches typically take credit for success, attributing wins to hard work, great play, or a sound game plan; losing teams tend to deflect responsibility by blaming external factors such as the weather, poor playing conditions, bad officiating, or just plain bad luck.[281] Winning politicians readily take credit for electoral victories, pointing to the righteousness of their political stands or tireless campaigning efforts, while losers blame uninformed voters or ill-timed economic downturns.[282] As President John F. Kennedy put it, "Success has a thousand fathers, but failure is an orphan." Learning to make attributions in this way habitually and instinctively is one key to developing optimism and persisting in the face of obstacles. Everyone gets a little sad after negative events, but your thoughts and explanatory style determine whether you bounce back or get mired in depression.[283]

When good things happen, try to make "3P" attributions for them – in other words, try to understand why those events occurred in *personal, permanent* and *pervasive* terms. If you manage a successful project at work, take credit for that success – attributing it to your intelligence, for example, offers an explanation that is personal (you are intelligent), permanent (you'll always be intelligent) and pervasive (your intelligence will help on other projects as well). Of these three dimensions, permanency is the most seductive – attributing success to intelligence dulls your ambition and lures you into a comfort zone. As a result, "2P" explanations – such as hard work – are often even better. As an attribution, effort is personal (you worked hard) and pervasive (you can work hard on other projects), and although it's not permanent (you might or might not work hard in the future), it is certainly a factor under your control. Therapists routinely encourage their clients to take credit for their progress in these terms; successful parents do the same for their children. These explanations get ABC cycles rolling, fostering persistence and bold action.[284] In programs for weight loss, smoking cessation, and insomnia, those who take credit for their progress are most successful in maintaining their progress even after the formal program ends.[285]

Over time, if you continue to take credit for your successes, you may experience a "crystallization of contentment."[286] We saw in the Belief chapter that a crystallization of discontent is a motivating experience that occurs when people recognize that seemingly unrelated dissatisfactions in their lives are due to a larger, more fundamental problem. A crystallization of contentment is a lot more fun. It occurs when you recognize that seemingly isolated successes in your life are the result of a larger, more fundamental success – the fact that you've truly taken control of your life, and you're heading down the path of truly fulfilling your potential. The crystallization of contentment triggers a cascading effect, an avalanche of change; your identity begins to evolve, people begin treating you differently, and greater successes follow.

When negative things happen, avoid "3P" attributions. In fact, using the 3P attributional style for negative events is a prime cause of learned helplessness and depression. It undermines Persistence as well. People who explain setbacks in permanent, pervasive and personal terms tend to give up easily, letting single lapses snowball into full-blown relapses.[287] Similarly, those who have the greatest difficulty in recovering from psychiatric breakdowns are those who make 3P attributions for the negative events that preceded their breakdowns.[288] Instead, focus on explanations that are external (non-personal), temporary (non-permanent) and/or focused (non-pervasive). If a project you are managing goes poorly, obviously you want to consider the situation objectively and learn from it (more about the importance of learning from negative events in the next chapter). But over time and across projects, you will tend to be psychologically healthier if you focus on explanations that are external (I wasn't given the resources I needed), temporary (I didn't work as hard as I could have, but I'll work harder next time), and/or focused (I may not be the best project manager, but I'm still a talented person with a lot to offer in other ways).

Obviously you shouldn't deny responsibility for events that are clearly your fault, and you must believe your attributions to derive psychological benefits from them. But the fact is you'll be happier and more persistent if you don't beat yourself up for every failure, and take some credit for your successes. Managing your attributions takes time and practice, so don't expect immediate effects, but over time, this is a very powerful tool for Persistence.

There's an important caveat to the principles outlined here: tone down or moderate your explanations when you make them publicly. People who publicly take too much credit for success are viewed as braggarts, whereas those who publicly deny too much responsibility for failures are viewed as slick or untrustworthy. If you are a manager, and you're asked to explain publicly the successes or failures of your group, reverse the normal attributional pattern: give credit for success to others, and personally accept the blame for failure (but be sure that your explanation for failure emphasizes how performance can be improved next time).

. . .

Persistence Promoter #3: *Surround Yourself With Excellence*

Humans are social animals, and the people around you are among the most potent influences on your successes and failures. Your popularity in the third grade is a better predictor of your mental health functioning at age 18 than just about anything else, including your IQ, academic record, and scores on psychological tests.[289] Among adults, social support is one of the most powerful influences on physical and psychological health. For virtually every cause of death, from heart disease and cancer to accidents and suicide, those with significant social support (for example, are married or have close friends) have lower death rates and are less at risk than those who are socially isolated.[290] Similarly, losing social support – as happens when interpersonal ties are broken through divorce, death of a spouse or losing a job – leads to lower immunity and increased mortality. Social support doesn't just "predict" good health; it has a causal effect, even after controlling for pre-existing physical conditions, income, age, education, smoking, drinking, exercise, blood pressure, cholesterol, access to health services, and satisfaction with life. In terms of magnitude, the beneficial effect of social support on health is comparable to the negative effects of cigarette smoking, obesity and lack of exercise. "Social support" even works among animals; being around members of the same species helps rats and goats avoid ulcers when subjected to stress.

Obviously, better health facilitates Persistence, but social support has more direct effects on Persistence as well. Supportive friends and family encourage progress toward goals, providing advice and emotional comfort after setbacks; they also encourage a wide range of pro-active "self-care" behaviors that facilitate progress and Persistence, including exercising more, eating better, and obtaining preventative medical care. Social support also has a "buffering," minimizing effect on stress, and stress is a prime cause of goal abandonment. These pathways of psychological influence combine to make social support one of the most potent drivers of Persistence. Those with social support persist more vigorously and successfully in response to life's hardest challenges; they more effectively kick addictions, maintain weight loss, stick to exercise programs, grieve lost loved ones, and make a variety of beneficial life changes.[291]

Social support also contributes to success because the expectations others have of you have a way of coming true. We saw in the Belief chapter that expectations for yourself can morph into reality, not by some mystical process, but via self-fulfilling prophecies. The expectations of others can create their own realities in a similar way. Literally hundreds of studies have documented this effect.[292] If teachers are led to believe their students are about to bloom intellectually, then those students do in fact go on to have better grades. Why? Because teachers with higher expectations of their students spend more time with them, set more challenging goals for them, are more encouraging, and so on. It even works with animals. If scientists are led to believe that laboratory rats have been bred to be highly intelligent, then those rats do in fact go on to run mazes more quickly because the researchers handle them more often, provide more stimulating environments, etc. Fortunately, Vision, Strategy and Belief have "stacked the deck" in your favor, making it more likely that others will have positive expectations of you. For example, compared to avoidance goals, approach goals are more supported by others, and are considered more desirable, more attainable, and more associated with success.[293]

The good news: seeking supportive relationships is not only a highly effective tool for enhancing persistence, it is one of the most commonly used techniques for change and growth.[294] And it's relatively easy to put into action, using any or all of the following six techniques...

- *Start building a "web of support."* Simply asking for help is a start. Social support need not involve constant displays of encouragement; instead, the more important factor is minimizing negative comments, or at least maintaining a reasonable proportion of supportive versus negative comments and actions.[295]
- *Bring people into your Vision.* Asking for help is good, but better results come from actively involving others in your Vision and Strategy. Those who are most satisfied with life tend to set goals and initiate projects with others, whereas those who set goals and work toward them in isolation tend to be less satisfied with their lives.[296] A working relationship with a skilled partner is more beneficial than simply being around someone who offers uniform encouragement, in the same way that motivation without a specific Strategy does little to boost performance. Merely having a supportive spouse doesn't aid weight loss, but if the spouse is given training in the kinds of techniques highlighted in this book – measuring progress toward SCAMPI goals, rewarding productive behaviors, and so on – then weight loss is significantly greater.[297] Similarly, problem drinking can be reduced if spouses of alcoholics are trained, not just in giving general support, but in stopping "enabling" behaviors such as reinforcing drinking or protecting their spouses from the negative consequences of their drinking.[298]
- *Create a Dream Team.* Creating a Dream Team or Mastermind Group

means going a step beyond surrounding yourself with "support-ive" people. It means surrounding yourself with excellence. It means identifying and regularly interacting with "peer role mod-els" – people of integrity with similar ambitions who will encour-age and reward your success. Too often people are resentful about the success of others; such people are not good Dream Team can-didates. Your Dream Team might meet weekly or monthly, sharing resources and encouraging one another. Set SCAMPI goals in one meeting, and report on your progress during the next. It works. Among artists, scientists and inventors, those with the most pro-fessional contacts in their fields are more productive and judged as greater talents by history.[299] Roger Bannister, the first man to run a four-minute mile, trained using a variation of the Dream Team idea. He used what he called "rabbits" – different friends who paced him for different miles. Running with just one friend for all four miles offered little challenge, but by having different friends pace him for different miles, he structured his social envi-ronment to push him and maximize his performance. Ask your-self how you can do the same. Who can be the rabbits in your life?

- *Know when to be alone.* When sad or depressed, many people in-stinctively withdraw from others, and the resulting isolation can intensify those negative emotions.[300] It's a natural reaction that you should be aware of, and avoid when possible. But if you are highly stressed on a habitual basis, try "unwinding" alone before seeking social support. People with stressful jobs, for example, have better family relationships if they spend time alone "decom-pressing" after work rather going straight home.[301]

- *Ask yourself if you need to fire some "friends."* Just as supportive people bring out the best in you, negative or conflict-prone people can have the opposite effect. Those who live with depressed people, for example, tend to become depressed themselves.[302] Upon leav-ing drug rehabilitation centers, people are routinely told not to socialize with their old drug-using friends; similarly, those who successfully battle alcohol abuse are in fact likely to have changed their friends, whereas not changing friends is a risk factor for relapsing.[303] Of course, I'm not suggesting that you "fire friends" cavalierly. If you have "friends" who chronically affect your life in negative ways, you should obviously try helping them first. But people don't change unless they want to, and addicts often insist they don't need or want to change. There are times when it's in your best interest to fire some "friends," keeping in mind that they aren't really friends at all.

. . .

Persistence Promoter #4:
Reshape Your Physical Environment

Reshaping your social environment is a powerful and commonly-used technique for enhancing persistence; reshaping your physical environment can be just as powerful, but is frequently overlooked.[304] Laboratory rats reared in enriched environments (e.g., lots of ramps and ladders for climbing) have heavier, more complex brains than those reared alone in barren cages ("solitary confinement").[305] Humans, of course, are not rats, but it is clear that stimulating environments benefit people as well.

• *Do a "cue purge."* Negative ABC cycles are often triggered by environmental cues. People trying to quit smoking, for example, are often lured back into their habit by tempting cues like cigarettes, ashtrays, lighters, bars, meals, or even sex – anything they previously associated with smoking.[306] Mahatma Gandhi reportedly demonstrated his ability to resist tempting cues by sleeping next to attractive young followers yet maintaining his chastity.[307] Few people have the willpower of the Mahatma, so I'd recommend eliminating tempting cues from your environment, a Persistence-enhancing process psychologists sometimes call *situational management* or *stimulus control*. Those who successfully battle alcohol addiction tend to get rid of all the alcohol in their homes, avoid former drinking places, and change their daily routine to avoid temptations.[308] During the Vietnam War, about half of all American soldiers tried heroin or opium, and about 20% were regular users; upon returning home, the vast majority kicked the habit relatively quickly, thanks to environmental changes and the elimination of drug-related cues.[309] About half of all "broken diets" are due to tempting cues.[310] Indeed, one of the reasons that success rates for losing weight are lower than those for quitting drugs or alcohol is that, because everyone has to eat, it is impossible to remove all food-related cues and temptations from the environment. If you're mired in very destructive ABC cycles, consider moving to a different part of the country for a massive change in physical and social environments; those successful in making life changes are significantly more likely to have moved than those who attempt life changes but fail.[311]

- *Create a motivating environment.* After purging your environment of cues that might trigger negative ABC cycles, it becomes time to "accentuate the positive." Restructure your physical environment so that it nurtures the positive ABC cycles you are trying to create. Post your goals where you can see them, and consider adding photos to create a "Vision collage" with more emotional impact. If accomplishing your goals requires breaking long-standing habits, then alter elements of your physical environment to bring change in your life more generally. Rearrange the furniture. Change your daily routine. Make success easy. Think alignment: How can you align your physical environment with your ambitions? Attendance at AA-type meetings can be predicted by how far people have to travel to get to the meetings.[312] You may not be an alcoholic, but it is worthwhile to ask yourself how you can make the resources you need for success more easily accessible.

. . .

Persistence Promoter #5:
Leverage the Power of Commitment

People who are highly committed to their goals work harder and persist more vigorously after setbacks. How can you get more committed? The Strategy chapter documented that putting goals into writing enhances commitment. Now take it further with these two techniques...

- *Go public.* Publicly expressing your goals is an infrequently-used but powerful technique proven to lead to stronger commitment and better performance.[313] We all want to appear successful to others, and public expression channels that desire into goal-directed behavior. It also minimizes the "wiggle room" that enables you to be satisfied with substandard performance, or give up altogether by denying you ever really set that goal. Public expression has important "internal" consequences as well. When you tell others about your goals, you also end up making more determined statements to yourself,[314] and these more assertive cognitions facilitate Persistence and perpetuate ABC cycles.

- *Get pre-committed.* Author Franz Kafka wrote, "From a certain point onward there is no longer any turning back. That is the point that must be reached." Pre-commitment means committing yourself in advance to your desired course of action in such a way that when temptations arise, you will have no choice but to go forward. Victor Hugo, author *Les Miserables* and *The Hunchback of Notre Dame*, used pre-commitment to resist being tempted into ABC cycles of distraction and procrastination. He instructed his valet to hide his clothes, forcing Hugo to work naked in his study until the valet returned at the pre-arranged end of the writing session.[315] The mythological character Odysseus used a different approach, tying himself to the mast of his ship so he could listen to the beautiful yet normally suicide-inducing songs of the Sirens without harm; when the urge for suicide took hold, he was safe because he had pre-committed himself to safety. Today you might place your alarm clock on the other side of the room before going to bed, or cut up your credit cards before going shopping. In each case, the principle is the same: make decisions that commit you to a course of action when you feel strong, before temptation arises. A friend of mine procrastinated an important career step: taking exams that would let him become a Certified Financial Planner. I suggested a form of pre-commitment: sign up for a study course, or even the exams themselves, even before feeling ready. Commit first, and get confident later. Ask how you can push yourself past the point of no return, and apply the power of pre-commitment to your goals.

. . .

Persistence Promoter #6: Reward Success

Perhaps the most fundamental law in all of psychology is the *law of effect*, which states that actions resulting in rewards are strengthened and likely to recur. We saw earlier the beneficial effects of taking credit for success, and that in and of itself is a kind of reward. Setting up more formal rewards for personal success, known as *contingency management*, is one of the least frequently used techniques for change,[316] but one of the most powerful, particularly when combined with goal-setting.[317] Those who accomplish their goals or successfully make life changes are significantly more likely than others to use some kind of self-reinforcement strategy.[318] It has proven beneficial in aiding weight loss, smoking cessation, writing productivity, kicking addictions, battling depression, boosting self-efficacy, and adhering to prescribed medical regimens.[319]

The process is simple but powerful. Identify your most important goal, and a few rewards that you value, perhaps dinner at a nice restaurant or an afternoon hike. If the goal is relatively modest, then reward yourself for achieving the goal (a "bonus" system). If the goal is more ambitious, identify a key milestone (e.g., making it halfway) or some measure of progress (e.g., ten hours of goal-directed work per week), and reward yourself for that progress (a "piece-rate" system).[320] Writer Jack London committed himself to writing at least 1,000 words a day, and rewarded himself for achieving that goal by drinking in saloons, but if he wrote less than 1,000 words, he didn't allow himself to drink. Of course, we saw in the Vision chapter that alcohol actually impairs creative work, but you get the idea. In institutional settings such as mental hospitals or homes for the mentally retarded, psychologists often formalize principles of reinforcement by instituting a "token economy." Patients receive plastic coins or tokens for engaging in appropriate behaviors such as getting up on time, cleaning their rooms, or cooperating with others; they can then "spend" those tokens on rewards like watching TV, taking trips into town, or upgrading to a nicer bedroom.[321] Whatever your system is, just remember that you'll be more likely to stick with it if you keep it simple.[322]

The most common stumbling block to using self-reward systems is *contract infidelity* – making a self-reward plan, but not sticking to it. To avoid this problem, combine self-rewards with pre-commitment by using the *deposit-and-refund* technique.[323] Suppose you want to lose 10 pounds. Give a good friend $500, and have him or her return the money at the rate of $50 per pound lost. Commit to spending the money on something enjoyable. Soon you'll find yourself very focused on your goal, and very persistent in the face of setbacks. There are a lot of natural rewards that come with losing weight, such as looking and feeling better. Unfortunately, those rewards are weeks and months into the future. Pizza, in contrast, can be delivered in 30 minutes or less. For better of worse, we live in an instant gratification society. And therein lies the power of the deposit-and-refund method – it makes instant gratification work for you. Lose just one pound, and you get an immediate reward. ⁻

Some have called the deposit-and-refund method a process of making "side bets,"[324] but if you make these bets on your most important goals, then there is nothing "side" about them – they are main bets crucial to your future. This process can work even with small amounts of money,[325] and you'll find it brings other processes into play, such as public commitment and social support. Consider this example from a college student who applied the deposit-and-refund method to his goal of participating more in class: "I gave a good friend five dollars to hold for me. He would give it back to me one dollar at a time after he had checked my records once a week to see if I had spoken up in class according to my goals. Two other friends ... displayed a lot of interest in my self-modification plan, and this put some social pressure on me. They would also compliment me when I reported my results for the week. The use of my friends in my plan was quite effective. They seemed to set off a positive emotional response in me that was very motivating."[326] Once the ABC cycle is rolling, it takes on a momentum of its own. One study found that weight lost using this process was maintained for a year, even though the self-reward period lasted only a few months.[327]

For even greater effectiveness, combine self-rewards with the Dream Team concept. Each team member deposits money, and each gets money back based on group, not individual, performance. Again using the example of weight loss, suppose you and four friends each want to lose 10 pounds, and you each deposit $100. Your group, therefore, wants to lose 50 pounds, and has deposited $500; the payback rate will be $10 per pound. When the group loses 10 pounds, it gets $100, to be split equally among the members of the team. Obviously, you should only do this if everyone on the team is committed, and you don't want people who are just "along for the ride." But the group setting provides social support, and perhaps even a bit of competitiveness, both of which can be highly motivating. And it works. People using the deposit-and-refund method in groups lose more weight, and keep it off longer, than those using the system individually.[328]

· · ·

Persistence Promoter #7:
Avoid Self-Punishment

In some ways, we live in a society more comfortable with punishments than with rewards. Husbands with obese wives, for example, make 12 times as many critical comments about their wives eating behavior than complementary ones.[329] That's unfortunate, because punishment is far less effective than reward.[330] In fact, people who struggle in making life changes consistently self-reward too little, and self-punish too much.[331] Blaming yourself for failures is a kind of punishment, and we've seen that blame-oriented attributions contribute to depression; depressed people are likely to punish themselves in other ways as well.[332] Binge eaters also fail to do enough "self-nurturing" – they are hard on themselves, and end up being "good" to themselves only by binging.[333]

There are many reasons for avoiding self-punishment as a strategy for boosting Persistence, even beyond its ineffectiveness. It doesn't encourage progress toward SCAMPI goals because punishment can only discourage old behaviors, not encourage new ones. And self-punishment obviously isn't much fun – that's one reason why people don't follow through on about a third of self-change plans that call for self-punishment.[334]

Overall, rewards are more effective than punishment, but if you insist on using self-punishment, here are a few principles to keep in mind.

- Give up money or something you enjoy as opposed to doing something painful or unpleasant.[335] You might try writing checks to political parties that you dislike, and have a friend send them if you do not accomplish your goal.[336]

- Make your impending punishment large enough to be a deterrent. Some personal coaches ask their clients to write them checks for thousands of dollars, and if the clients don't accomplish their goals, the coaches cash the checks and keep the money. The key to this punishment-oriented version of the deposit-and-refund approach is that the checks are large enough to motivate and shape behavior.

• Recognize that success is a process, and setbacks are common. Whatever your self-punishment system, build in ways to forgive yourself for setbacks, and recognize that sometimes things are truly outside of your control. Perhaps build in some loopholes, institute a "three strikes rule," or start with small punishments that gradually get larger. For example, one therapist used a rather unconventional treatment with a bulimic patient.[337] The patient agreed to pay the therapist one penny the next time she induced vomiting, and to double the penalty with each subsequent occurrence: two cents the second time, four cents the third time, eight cents the fourth time, and so on. It doesn't seem like much, but after calculating that she would owe thousands of dollars by the 20th vomit, she discovered a whole new level of commitment in dealing with her problem. Such "ordeal therapy" works under limited circumstances, but again, you'll find that self-reward is generally a more effective tool than self-punishment.

· · ·

Persistence Promoter #8:
Manage Your Attention

We saw earlier the importance of managing your attributions. Managing your attention is equally important. Much of the time you want to focus your attention inward, on your Vision, Strategy, and Belief, particularly when planning and preparing for the future. But an inward focus only helps if you have completed the previous steps in the process. Self-focused attention combined with SCAMPI goals enhances performance;[338] without SCAMPI goals, it intensifies anxiety and angst. Self-focused attention coupled with self-efficacy further boosts confidence; without confidence, it intensifies uncertainty and undermines motivation.[339] Test anxiety, for example, is the result of focusing inward when you lack confidence in your test-taking abilities.[340]

If you're confident in your Vision, Strategy and Belief, then try these half-dozen tools for focusing your attention inward.

- *Visualization.* In addition to building Belief, repeated visualization also has a very focusing effect, heightening your attention on your Vision and Strategy.
- *Keep your ambitions "top of mind."* People often set goals, only to forget about them amid busy schedules and daily distractions. Over 60% of U. S. workers report having unpredictable daily work routines, and nearly 40% are interrupted six or more times per hour.[341] Look for ways to keep your goals and action plans "top of mind" despite a cramped calendar. Writing them down helps, and posting them where you will see them often helps even more. Use them as the basis of your organizational system; devoting drawers and files to specific goals will keep them top of mind and aid in prioritizing tasks.
- *Start early.* Spend time thinking about your goals, and working toward them, first thing in the morning, before distractions mount. It is easy to begin the day by jumping into your obligations to others, but you'll find yourself more relaxed, productive and persistent if you begin the day jump-starting your positive ABC cycles.
- *Schedule "ABC islands."* In the previous chapter, we saw the Belief-building benefits of setting aside periods of time each day to focus on your goals. Building these prescheduled "islands" of ABC activity into your day can boost Persistence as well; it commits you to shutting out distractions and ensures daily progress. Managing by "to do" list tends to be less effective; you can create detailed to do lists, but if you don't preschedule islands of progress, you'll find that you have little to cross off your list at the end of the day. To do lists invite you to spend your day "putting out fires" and responding to the agendas of others rather than focusing on ambitions important to you.
- *Add mirrors.* OK, this idea might seem a little "out there." But research confirms that looking in a mirror heightens your self-awareness – that is, your focus on internal standards, principles

and goals. When asked to complete a test in a very short time period, 70% of college students worked beyond the time limit (a mild form of cheating). Taking the test in front of a mirror, which focuses attention internally on their values and sense of honesty, caused the cheating rate to drop to just 7%.[342]

• *Just say no.* Alcohol has the opposite effect of mirrors – it reduces self-awareness,[343] focusing your attention on the immediate environment rather than on goals and values. Alcohol lessens your internal sense of what behaviors are appropriate; it also makes you less aware of, and less concerned about, past behaviors and the good or bad things that resulted from them.[344] It should come as no surprise that these attentional effects of alcohol contribute to poor Persistence and weak progress toward goals.[345]

Of course, focusing inward isn't always good. Excessive self-focus can contribute to depression, sadness and other negative emotions.[346] After a failure or setback, we all get a little sad and focus internally. But non-depressed people redirect their attention outward with temporary distractions, and then move to a problem solving approach, short-circuiting negative ABC cycles;[347] depressed people, in contrast, maintain their inward focus, inadvertently extending their negative ABC cycles. So when negative ABC cycles take hold, as we saw in the Belief chapter, focusing outward or distracting yourself is generally a better strategy. Experienced joggers enjoy the process of running, and gain benefit from focusing inward, paying careful attention to body signals such as breathing, fatigue, and their own self-talk. Novice runners, however, must contend with boredom, soreness and low self-efficacy; they perform better and stick with running longer if they use distracting strategies such as focusing attention on music or non-running related thoughts.[348] Similarly, novice runners do better if they run outdoors, where they can be distracted by scenery, rather than running on an indoor track.[349] Distraction is also a good strategy if you are struggling with temptation. At the very least, focus your attention on the least appealing aspect of what tempts you. If you are trying to resist alcohol or drugs, then focus on memories of hangovers or disturbing mental images of addicts.[350] People faithful to their spouses do this naturally, focusing their attention on the unattractive features of otherwise attractive, potentially tempting people.[351]

If focusing inward is good for planning, and distraction is good while mired in negative ABC cycles, then how should you manage your attention when in a positive ABC cycle? Surprisingly enough, you want to stop thinking altogether. When competitive athletes describe their greatest moment, 95% say they weren't thinking about their performance, and a similar number say their attention narrowed so completely that they lost their sense of self-consciousness and became totally immersed in the activity.[352] Consider these experiences...

- *A cyclist:* "I am a vehicle for this. I initiate the performance and then the experience takes over."
- *A lacrosse player:* "It is a world within a world ... focused right here. I am not aware of the external. My concentration was so great I didn't think of anything else."
- *A skier:* "I was really blending into the snow, the mountain... I wasn't different from the hill."
- *A football player:* "It was effortless for me. I hit him and he just flew. Physically, I didn't put as much as usual into it."

This combination of clear focus, intense involvement and loss of self-attention isn't limited to sports – it accompanies peak performance in many areas of life.[353] Psychologist Mihaly Csikszentmihalyi calls it *flow*. Flow is the experience of being totally immersed in something, when thought and action merge, time slows, and the boundaries between self and environment seem to blur. Flow occurs when the challenges you face are matched by the skills you possess; it lies in the balance between stress and boredom, between being overwhelmed and being disengaged. Happiness pervades the moment, as happiness and flow are both about progress toward valued goals rather than accomplishing them (Csikszentmihalyi: "Climbers do not climb to get to the top but get to the top so that they can climb; chess players do not play to win but try to win so that they can play."[354]). Flow is created by a combination of factors familiar from previous steps: clear goals, a do-able strategy for accomplishing them, unambiguous feedback about progress, self-confidence, and persistent progress. And, of course, you have to stop thinking. *Resource recommendation:* For more on creating flow in your daily life, read Csikszentmihalyi's *Flow: The Psychology of Optimal Experience*, or his shorter and more practical, *Finding Flow: The Psychology of Engagement with Everyday Life.*

The opposite of flow is excessive self-attention while trying to perform. As we've seen, this is the essence of test anxiety – anxious people who doubt their test-taking abilities begin focusing inward, amplifying their anxiety. Test anxiety sufferers trained to "stop thinking" – that is, direct their attention away from themselves, and focus directly on the task – perform better.[355] Similarly, elite athletes who use a lot of self-talk (verbal statements to themselves) during preparation perform better than those who don't,[356] but they "quiet" that self-talk when performing; this quieting balances the highly verbal left hemisphere of the brain with the non-verbal right hemisphere that controls balance and coordination, enhancing performance. The sports equivalent of test anxiety is choking under pressure. Intense pressure can heighten self-awareness, hampering the ability to "stop thinking," and this self-consciousness can interfere with the performance of highly practiced, well-learned behaviors.[357]

. . .

Persistence Promoter #9:
Exercise

It should come as no surprise that exercise is one of the best predictors of long-term weight loss. But it also facilitates Persistence and progress in many aspects of life. It helps in smoking cessation; among smokers who become competitive runners (e.g., running in

10K races), about 80% give up smoking.[358] Exercise helps in battling alcohol and drug addictions, particularly if it is substituted for an end-of-day cocktail or drug session.[359] It moderates depression (at least in the short-term), minimizes the impact of stress on health, facilitates coping with chronic illnesses, reduces anxiety and improves self-efficacy.[360] It even enhances job performance[361] and financial achievement; about 60% of millionaires exercise regularly to reduce their fears and worries, while 50% use the mental toughness they developed in sports.[362]

For our purposes, the key finding is that exercise and participation in sports enhance Persistence, resilience and determination among both kids and adults.[363] If you're not already exercising, start (but seek a doctor's input before beginning an exercise regimen). As little as a 10-minute walk can boost energy levels and reduce stress for hours.[364] If you are already exercising, do more. The irony is that exercise only boosts Persistence in life if you are persistent about exercise – if you stop exercising, its benefits fade away.

· · ·

Persistence Promoter #10:
Have a Strategy for Setbacks

There's an old military saying: "A warrior prays for peace but prepares for war." Use that philosophy for thinking about progress toward goals – expect success, but at the same time, have a strategy for dealing with setbacks. It's like a fire drill[365] – you prepare for fires even though they are rare and you do everything possible to prevent them. Unfortunately, setbacks are more common than fires. Success is a dynamic process that ebbs and flows. One of the most popular psychological models of how people change is actually circular in nature, documenting how people typically move through cycles of making decisions, making progress, suffering setbacks, and then going back to re-evaluate and refine their initial decisions.[366] Smokers who quit permanently, for example, typically go through this process several times before quitting permanently.[367] Having a strategy for setbacks minimizes their negative effects, and speeds up the cycle. Among smokers who relapse but go on to overcome it, virtually all had planned in advance for a slip or two; among those who let a single lapse snowball into a full-blown return to smoking, only about half had a plan.[368] Our plan will focus on three objectives: minimizing the frequency of setbacks, preventing minor lapses from snowballing into full-blown setbacks, and learning from setbacks when they occur.

Setbacks can be made less frequent by using some of the Persistence tools described above, such as reshaping your physical or social environment and removing tempting cues that might trigger a reversion back to your old ABC cycle. But environmental cues tend to trigger temporary setbacks and isolated slips rather than full-blown relapses.[369] Instead, the primary drivers of major setbacks are stress and negative emotions. You try to make a change in your life, something happens that makes you sad or stressed, and you fall back into old habits. We've all done it. A lot. About half of all failures to quit smoking are driven by negative emotional states such as boredom, frustration, anger, anxiety and depression;[370] in contrast, only about 5% are attributable directly to physical withdrawal symptoms.[371] Negative emotional states don't necessarily kill motivation, drive goal abandonment, or create some wildly irrational urge to punish yourself through self-destructive behavior. Instead, they create a kind of myopia, focusing you on the immediate environment instead of on longer-term goals, and undermine your sense of self-efficacy, spurring the misguided belief that you can't deal with the upsetting event without reverting to your old ABC cycle.[372]

As the old saying goes, an ounce of prevention is worth a pound of cure, and certainly preventing stress and negative emotions is ideal. But it's obviously unrealistic to expect that you can eliminate them forever, so the key becomes dealing with them once they occur. Among those who lose weight and keep it off, virtually none eat when getting upset; however, of those who lose weight and regain it, about 80% eat in response to stress.[373] Try creating a "stress response plan" by filling in the blank: "When I feel stressed or upset, I will deal with it productively by _____ ." Identify two or three options that work for you. You might exercise, meditate, call a friend for support, distract yourself with immersive experiences like going to a movie, and so on.

Here are two more tools for pre-empting setbacks before they get started:

- *Surf.* Learn to "surf" unproductive urges or tempting feelings.[374] Just like a surfer rides an ocean wave, you can ride your temptation: feel the urge come upon you and peak, while you ride it out and let it pass. Try to experience it as an impartial observer. In the Belief chapter, we saw how the monologue in your head is not "you;" you are the listener who can observe thoughts come and go, without spinning them into stories and ABC cycles. The same goes for counter-productive urges and temptations; you can observe them, focusing on how they feel in the moment rather than on the negative ABC cycles that might follow, and then let them pass. If you are trying to lose weight and feel tempted by fattening food, notice your immediate thoughts and emotions, rather than focusing on how sinfully good certain foods would taste; then let the temptation pass, and return to focusing on your future goals.
- *Pause.* Learn to pause between the urge and the activity. Over time, gradually lengthen the pause. Cues and negative emotions can trigger ABC cycles quickly, almost automatically; pausing for even a minute or two allows the urge to pass, and gives you time to focus on your goals. If you are trying to quit smoking, for example, gradually increase the pauses between the urge to smoke and the act of lighting up.[375] If you are really struggling, commit yourself to a writing assignment during your pause, focusing on whether the actions you are considering will take you closer to your Vision, or farther away.

Setbacks are inevitable, no matter how diligently you pause, surf, and enact your stress reduction plan. The next element of an effective strategy for setbacks is minimizing the impact of setbacks when they do occur. For this, we'll use *psychological stop losses*. Stock traders often use the stop loss concept to minimize their downside risk. For example, if you buy a stock for $40 per share, you might decide to sell if it ever drops below $36. By instituting this stop loss, you can insure that you will lose no more than 10% of your money on this investment. Stop losses form the basis of a classic investment strategy: minimize your losses, and let your winners run. To prevent a single reversion to your old ABC cycle from snowballing into a major setback, try one of these psychological stop loss techniques:

• *Pause again.* We've seen that pausing after temptation, but before giving in to it, can prevent setbacks and negative ABC cycles. Pausing is also helpful after a minor slip, and can prevent a negative ABC cycle from gaining momentum. A two-minute pause in the middle of meals, for example, is an effective weight loss tool.[376] In this case, pausing not only provides time to step back and focus on long-term, but it also allows eaters time to "feel" they are full.

• *Review your Strategy.* Looking at your goals and action plans will put your setback in context. You have not broken a resolution. You have not committed yourself to "never again do X," so there is no need to say "what the hell" and give up completely. Instead, you've set SCAMPI goals and had one day of weak progress, which can be overcome with stronger progress tomorrow. Similarly, your action plan contained something you could do each day; maybe you didn't do it today, but you can do it tomorrow.

• *Manage your attributions.* Attributing setbacks to external and easily changed causes not only wards off depression in the long-term, it also prevents snowballing in the short-term. People who view setbacks as temporary obstacles that can be overcome are likely to bounce back. But those who attribute setbacks to permanent, personal or pervasive causes (such as personal weakness or lack of willpower) are most likely to "fall off the wagon" completely after a single lapse.[377] This isn't to say that you should deny all responsibility for your setback, but rather that you'll have more long-term success if you focus on what you can change and don't beat yourself up over minor failures.

The final step in dealing with setbacks is learning from them. Believe it or not, setbacks can actually have some benefits. In rigorous weight-loss programs, for example, people who struggle a bit at first tend to have more long-term success than those who initially find it easy.[378] Setbacks can have a strengthening, inoculating effect that prevents over-confidence. They also trigger more thinking about the goal,[379] and often result in pursuing the goal with newfound vigor. But perhaps the greatest benefits of setbacks derive from the learning opportunities they present. You can learn what tempts you, what triggers your negative ABC cycles, and what doesn't work in terms of avoiding them. Ask yourself what can be learned from your setback, and consider how you can apply that learning for greater success in the future.

These principles underlying an effective strategy for setbacks may be easy to remember now, but after a setback you may experience "myopia" that focuses you on your immediate disappointment. To stay focused on your strategy, try carrying a *reminder card* to review after a setback. Here's an example from a study of smoking cessation by Alan Marlatt, a pioneer in understanding addiction and relapse; it's a nice combination of snowball prevention via pausing, pre-empting negative emotions, managing attributions, and most importantly, learning. "A slip is not all that unusual. It does not mean that you have failed or that you have lost control over your behavior. You will probably feel guilty about doing what you have done, and will blame yourself for having slipped. This feeling is to be expected; it is part of what we call the Abstinence Violation [snowball] Effect. There is no reason why you have to give in to this feeling and continue to smoke. The feeling will pass in time. Look upon the slip as a learning experience. What were the elements of the high-risk situation which led to the slip? What coping response could you have used to get around the situation? Remember the old saying: One swallow doesn't make a summer. Well, one slip doesn't make a relapse, either. Just because you slipped once does not mean that you are a failure, that you have no willpower, or that you are a hopeless addict. Look upon the slip as a single, independent event, something which can be avoided in the future with an alternative coping response."[380]

Want to learn more about the power of learning? First take a moment to see how Dick and Jane are doing, and then simply turn to the next chapter…

. . .

A Persistence Example:
See Dick and Jane Try To Keep On Keepin' On

Jane's Vision, SCAMPI goals, and blossoming sense of Belief form a strong foundation for Persistence, and those alone greatly increase her chances of rebounding from a setback. But she doesn't stop there – she aggressively uses several additional Persistence tools.

Learning to challenge her destructive automatic negative thoughts was good practice for managing her attributions (Persistence Promoter #2). Although it seems a bit "forced" and artificial at first, she soon finds it both natural and satisfying to make 3P (personal, permanent and pervasive) attributions for positive outcomes, and to avoid those attributions for negative outcomes. When she makes good progress toward her goals, she takes credit for that success and praises herself for her hard work. When she goes several days without exercising on a business trip, she avoids 3P attributions by placing blame on the schedule-imbalancing rigors of the trip. She reminds herself that it only amounts to a few days of weak progress, and she can get back on track as soon as she returns home.

She began re-shaping her physical environment (#4) when she was formulating her Strategy by placing her goals and adventure travel brochures on her coffee table (which also helps focus her attention on her Vision; #8); she continues that process now by doing a cue purge and removing all unhealthy foods from her home. She's always had a supportive family, but now sets herself up for even more social support by forming a Dream Team of three friends (#3). Together they use the deposit-and-refund method to lose weight (#6). Each person deposits $1,000. That may seem like a lot, but they decide the process will be most powerful if they use the money for a group trip to Europe, so it seems worth the investment. The deposit-and-refund technique also ensures that she publicly commits to her goals (#5) in front of her friends. She takes the notion of commitment one step further and uses pre-commitment when she hires a personal trainer before she feels ready for that kind of personalized, professional advice.

Dick's weak foundation for personal change finally comes back to haunt him. His weak Vision, resolutions and shaky Belief in himself leave him vulnerable to the snowball effect, which hits with full force when he has a single slice of pizza. With his no pizza resolution broken, and year-end weight loss goal too far in the future to be motivating, Dick says "what the hell" and gorges himself on an entire pizza. Because he viewed success in all-or-none terms, he had formulated no strategy for setbacks (#10) – he doesn't surf the urges, or pause when the urge strikes. He then compounds the problem by making a 3P attribution for his slip, blaming it on his own weakness and lack of willpower. He also fails to think like a genius (#1), making no effort to become more optimistic, thinking in inflexible terms, and not looking to mentors or role models in his efforts to change his life.

He tries to get "back on the wagon" and uses a self-punishment (#7) technique to strengthen his resolve. He's had a lot of practice punishing himself, given his tendency to deny himself things he enjoys and beat himself up over minor setbacks, but that doesn't make it an effective strategy. He writes a check for $100 to a political party he hates, and gives it to a friend, asking her to send it if he has another pizza. Unfortunately, that amount of money is too small to motivate his behavior. He compounds his weak self-punishment strategy by drinking alcohol to lessen his focus on his negative ABC cycles, but that also focuses him on immediate stimuli rather than his goals and ambitions (#8), further setting himself up for failure.

Chapter Eight

Step Five: Learning –
The Science of Making
"Course Corrections" in Life

*"I have lived my life as an adventurer, and my goal was to taste things
as fully and as deeply as I could and to learn from every
experience because there is not a single experience that you
can't learn something from." Eleanor Roosevelt*

You've probably heard the story of Sisyphus, the mythological figure cursed to spend eternity trying to push a massive boulder to the
top of a steep hill. Each time he neared his goal, the rock rolled back
down the hill. Sisyphus had each of the first four steps in abundance: Vision (get the rock up the hill), Strategy (push it), Belief (he
was strong and confident), and Persistence (he tried *forever*). He was
weak only on the final step: Learning. He never recognized that his
Strategy wasn't working. He didn't pay attention to the feedback from
his environment about whether his action plan was taking him closer
to his Vision. He could have revised his Strategy, perhaps seeking
the help of Hercules, or trying to pull the rock up the hill with a team
of horses. Admittedly, he had limited options, having been cursed
by Zeus and imprisoned in the lowest region of the underworld, but,
hey, you get the idea.

Despite a highly measurable goal, Sisyphus never undertook a
course correction. As modern ships, planes and even space shuttles

travel to their destinations, they are "off course" as much as 90% of the time. The shortest distance between two points may be a straight line in geometry, but in life it is more often the path of least resistance. Ships take advantage of ocean currents, planes use the jet stream, and spacecraft leverage gravitational fields to propel them toward their objectives faster and more easily than straight-line navigation. They only arrive at their destinations because of frequent course corrections. Life is similar. When clinically depressed people become frozen with inaction, believing they need more information before acting, they are getting hung up on trying to plot straight-line courses of perfect action toward their life destinations. Successful people take action, and rely on course corrections to navigate successive approximations to success. Psychologist Abraham Maslow: "Let us think of life as a process of choices, one after another. At each point there is a progression choice and a regression choice.... To make the growth choice instead of the fear choice a dozen times a day... is a movement toward self-actualization."

Persistence is good. Progress is better. Persistence can be misguided. Persistence can be achieved by effort alone, but progress requires Persistence and Learning. You must learn whether you are persisting in the right direction, and whether course corrections are necessary. And as we all know, successful people learn from every experience, even negative ones...

· · ·

COMMON KNOWLEDGE:
SUCCESSFUL PEOPLE LEARN FROM EVERY EXPERIENCE, EVEN NEGATIVE ONES

I keep a list "lame excuses for not being highly successful," and I've found many of them can be traced to failures in learning. Here are a few of the most common...

"But I don't have a degree..." Perhaps Mark Twain said it best: "I have never let schooling interfere with my education." Albert Einstein

was a notoriously poor student, and Bill Gates was a college dropout; neither made the mistake of equating a degree with true learning. Financially successful people have learned the same lesson. *The Millionaire Mind* documents that the average college GPA of millionaires is just 2.92 (slightly below a B average), and they rank "graduating at or near top of their class" dead last when making attributions for their personal success, but they value learning the kind of "success skills" covered in this book. When asked what they learned in school, for example, about three-fourths cited the lesson that "hard work is more important than genetic high intellect in achieving." And that leads to the next lame excuse for not being highly successful...

"But I'm not smart enough..." This excuse is just as weak as not having a degree, as we've just seen that highly successful people aren't necessarily brainiacs with advanced degrees. But it's even more insidious because so many people erroneously believe their level of "smarts" can't be changed. There are many kinds of intelligence, and some are more easily improved than others. Fortunately, success skills are easily learned, and offer a very practical way of "getting smarter." Of course, you won't get smarter if you don't believe you can get smarter. Believing in the "improvability" of smarts becomes a self-fulfilling prophecy, and is the key to overcoming this lame excuse. Business school students told that a difficult managerial decision-making task is a learnable skill enhanced by practice perform much better than those told it reflects their basic cognitive ability and was thus difficult to change; they exhibit greater confidence, set more challenging goals, and bring about a higher level of employee performance.[381] Your own personal "theory of intelligence" influences your goals and level of achievement in many ways,[382] as shown in the table on the next page.

Your personal "theory of intelligence"	Intelligence is a fixed entity that can't be changed	Intelligence is a skill that can be improved
Mental focus	Proving your ability	Improving your ability
Attitude toward "effort"	Putting forth a lot of effort to achieve a goal implies that you have to overcome low natural ability	More effort leads to greater rewards
Attitude toward people who struggle in life or perform poorly	Blame them; distance yourself; growth of prejudice and stereotyping	Feel empathy, compassion, and a desire to help
Types of goals chosen	Challenging goals when confidence is strong; will avoid challenges and learning opportunities if they might convey appearance of weak performance	Challenging, learning-oriented goals, regardless of confidence level
ABC cycles	Positive if confidence and progress are strong, but otherwise negative	Positive regardless of confidence because of attainable learning goals

"But I've had such a hard life..." Everyone suffers personal failures, and everyone has tragic injustices thrust upon them. After negative experiences, everyone asks "why" and searches for some kind of meaning. Some are able to make sense of their negative experiences, but some are not; those who do fare better psychologically and physically than those who don't. It's been said that successful people are characterized by "inverse paranoia" – they think the universe is conspiring to open up positive opportunities for them. They believe the old cliché that "Everything happens for a reason," and today's more hip, colloquial version, "It's all good." Or, as Winston Churchill put it, "An optimist sees an opportunity in every calamity; a pessimist sees a calamity in every opportunity." Consider these remarkable examples of people who not only learn from setbacks, but thrive despite them...

- Over half of breast cancer sufferers report that the disease triggered positive changes in their lives.[383] Some feel a stronger sense of priorities, refocusing on important goals and intimate relationships. Others feel a newfound pride about the personal strength they didn't know they had. Many find they are better able to put life's minor nuisances in perspective. As one woman put it, "I have much more enjoyment of each day, each moment. I am not so worried about what is or isn't or what I wish I had. All those things you get entangled with don't seem to be part of my life right now."[384]
- Incest victims who derive some sense of meaning from their abuse, who learn from it in some way, fare better than those unable to do so. They have less psychological distress, better social relationships, and higher self esteem, whereas those still searching for meaning often find themselves "stuck" in negative ABC cycles triggered by intrusive and disruptive memories. Interestingly, the ability to make sense of such horrific treatment is not predicted by the age at which the abuse began or ended, the length or intensity of the abuse, or having sought professional assistance. It is not even predicted by the length of time since the incest occurred. Instead,

one of the very few factors that makes a difference is whether or not the victim confides in someone about the abuse, reflecting the combination of two success factors discussed earlier: social support, and the ability to express emotions about negative events.[385]

• Eminent figures in history – including political leaders, scientists, writers, and artists – are more likely than their less famous colleagues to have lost a parent at a young age.[386] In fact, their rates of early parental loss rival that of juvenile delinquents and clinically depressed people. This is particularly true for those in creative fields; those who won a Nobel Prize for literature are eight times more likely to have been orphans than those who won the Nobel Prize for physics. "The bereavement reaction can be an impetus for creative effort, a force for good, or it can have the effect of stunting personality growth and producing the concomitant antisocial acts, destruction of social relationships, and even the taking of one's own life."[387] Of course, I'm not saying that parental loss is a good thing, but simply that people who have convinced themselves they can't be successful because of early trauma have done themselves a disservice.

• The lessons learned from personal setbacks can reverberate across generations. The Great Depression affected people of all social classes, but in its aftermath middle class girls were far more likely than lower class girls to live psychologically healthy and well-adjusted lives. Middle class girls came from families that, for the most part, recovered financially as the economy improved; they learned that bad times pass, and they learned not to make permanent or pervasive attributions for negative events. Lower class girls came from families that, for the most part, never recovered financially; they learned that bad times are permanent, and that people are helpless to alter the course of their lives. As those girls aged and had children of their own, they passed their attributional styles on to their daughters. Those who learned that bad times are temporary instilled that sense of optimism in their kids, whereas those who learned helplessness passed on that sense of futility.[388]

"I've tried. I just can't do it. I'm a failure." This is the excuse Sisyphus would have used, and more often than not, it is uttered by someone who has doggedly pursued an ineffective Strategy. It signals a lack of Learning, and a failure to recognize the need for course corrections. The key to countering this excuse is paying attention to the feedback your environment provides. Goals only enhance performance if you get feedback about whether your efforts are taking you closer to your objectives.[389] One study, typical of those addressing this issue, found that the combination of goals and feedback led to performance improvements of nearly 60%; goals without feedback didn't impact performance, and neither did feedback without goals.[390] This is why the M in SCAMPI is so important – measurable goals enable feedback. As we saw in the Strategy chapter, people given the specific challenging goal of reducing their electricity use by 20% are only successful in conserving if they are able to measure their progress. Those given reports of kilowatt usage reduce consumption, but those who don't get feedback fail to reduce their consumption.[391] Feedback kicks off a potent cycle: feedback → Strategy refinement → better progress → enhanced Belief and Persistence → new and more challenging goals → more feedback, and so on. True success requires careful attention to what works and what doesn't in your life. After all, successful people learn what truly drives their success and happiness...

. . .

UNCOMMON KNOWLEDGE:
SUCCESSFUL PEOPLE LEARN
WHAT DRIVES THEIR SUCCESS AND HAPPINESS

One of my favorite psychology experiments was conducted by famed Harvard psychologist B. F. Skinner.[392] He placed hungry pigeons into cages and fed them at completely random intervals. The results were startling – the pigeons responded with bizarre, seemingly pointless patterns of behavior. One twirled in counter-clockwise circles. Two others rocked back and forth like pendulums. Another twitched repeatedly as if using its head to lift an invisible bar. Seemingly "obsessive" patterns of pecking were common as well – one pecked at, but stopped just short of, the floor, while another pecked at the air in an upper corner of the cage.

What's going on? Did something as straightforward as random feeding times create "neurotic" pigeons? The answer is simple. The birds were reinforced for whatever behavior they happened to be engaging in when fed. A pigeon that happened to pecking at the floor when the food appeared, in a sense, came to "believe" that its pecking *caused* the food to appear. The pigeons developed "theories" that their odd behavior led to the appearance of the food, and those theories led them to engage in what Skinner called "superstitious" behavior.

Skinner, of course, would spin in his grave if he heard me talking about pigeons "holding beliefs" and "developing theories." An adamant behaviorist, Skinner believed that psychology should concern itself only with observable actions, not internal cognitive processes or ABC cycles (leading to an old behaviorist joke that I heard Skinner tell when I was in graduate school: Two behaviorists make love. Afterward, one says to the other: "That was good for you – how was it for me?"). But you get the idea – random reinforcement can lead to superstitious behavior because incorrect theories about why things happen sometimes lead us astray. In other words, superstitious behavior occurs when we don't understand the true causes of our actions and our outcomes.

It doesn't just happen to pigeons. Skinner himself pointed out that the odd behavior of the pigeons was analogous to the rituals and superstitions that abound in casinos. Superstition is most likely when rewards happen randomly, as in casinos, but it happens elsewhere as well. In fact, people are often unaware of the factors that drive success and happiness in their daily lives. Many people dramatically overestimate the impact of how much sleep they get on their overall mood, or subscribe to the popular but erroneous theory that overeating provides long-lasting relief from bad moods.[393] Inaccurate theories like these lead to wasted effort and counter-productive actions, whereas more accurate theories, such as recognizing that exercise is a better mood booster than overeating, lead to much more efficient and effective actions.[394]

Highly successful people understand the true drivers of their success and happiness. They avoid the unproductive, superstitious behavior that results from inaccurate theories; they avoid being the human equivalents of misguided pigeons turning endlessly in circles. Professional athletes, for example, routinely keep performance logs to identify the factors that contribute to their best performances, and this practice can indeed enhance performance.[395] Here, as elsewhere, it is important to have approach goals and focus on the positive; competitive bowlers who keep records of their bowling performance with an eye toward what they did well improve their scores, whereas those who make records of their errors do not.[396]

. . .

TOOLS: ANALYZING THE PATTERNS OF SUCCESS AND HAPPINESS IN YOUR LIFE

This chapter is the shortest of the five steps, and this Tools section is the most straightforward, not because this step is the easiest, but because we have laid the foundation for it so effectively. Learning should flow almost naturally from the success framework created by the first four steps. If you have a clear Vision, SCAMPI goals, true Belief, and Persist over time, it will be difficult not to notice when you are making strong progress, and what contributes to that progress.

Plato wrote, "The unexamined life is not worth living," and the primary tool you'll use for Learning is based on examining your life in a very simple but systematic way. All that's required is recording your progress toward each goal, and periodically reviewing your records. Analyzing the patterns of progress and happiness in your life is the key to making the course corrections crucial for success. In her famous diary, Anne Frank wistfully wrote, "How noble and good everyone could be if, at the end of each day, they were to review their own behavior and weigh up their rights and wrongs. They would automatically try to do better at the start of each new day and, after a while, would certainly accomplish a great deal." She was right. Regularly recording behavior – a process psychologists call *self-monitoring* – enhances success in making a variety of life changes, and is routinely used as a first step in therapy. Simply recording behavior has been shown to lead to reductions in hallucinations, facial tics, nail biting, excessive scratching, disruptive classroom behavior, alcohol consumption, smoking and obesity; on the positive side, it has been shown to lead to more effective parenting and improved academic performance.[397] Of course, simply recording behavior itself tends to have modest effects that diminish over time.[398] The real power of the process comes from combining self-monitoring with Vision, Strategy, Belief and Persistence. One weight loss clinic had their patients make daily records of what they ate – these records, and the feedback they enabled, only contributed to weight loss among those who had set very specific (SCAMPI) weight loss goals, even though all the patients were overweight and in a weight loss clinic.[399]

Recording behavior enhances performance for three main reasons…

- *Self-monitoring is a self-reward.* Making records of your actions serves as a small reward when you are doing well, and a gentle but thought-provoking punishment if you are doing poorly. If you're recording progress toward each goal on a zero to ten scale, then it's very gratifying to write down a ten each evening; on the other hand, writing down a zero is very dissatisfying, and you'll find yourself highly motivated to avoid repeating that experience. Recording progress encourages you to celebrate success and counteracts the natural tendency to overlook progress, as when dieters focus on when they broke their diet, overlooking all their successes.[400]
- *Self-monitoring is self-focusing.* Recording your progress focuses your attention internally in much the same way as posting your goals or looking in a mirror. It makes you more aware of your actions and how you spend your time, highlighting aspects of your

day of which you might not normally be conscious, such as how much time you spend watching TV or your calorie intake. It will make clear the obstacles you must overcome, the factors that facilitate strong progress, and the triggers of your negative ABC cycles. It helps keep your "eyes on the prize," sharpening your Vision and clarifying whether your strategy is being effective, as it did for this salesperson: "At the beginning of the fiscal year I put a graph on the wall over my desk and tracked out twelve months, with dollar increments going up the side, to one million dollars. That picture of where I was going helped guide me in making day-to-day decisions. Every month I would plot out my results and where I was going on the graph, and it kept me focused on the overall goal."[401]

- *Self-monitoring enhances accountability.* Without self-monitoring, it is easy to rationalize weak progress or ignore repeated setbacks. Recording progress forces you to be honest with yourself, as it did for this student: "When I was keeping records of my eating, some days I wouldn't record. After this had happened several times, I had to admit to myself that I wasn't keeping the records because I wanted to pig out. So I had to face my true feelings. Did I want to stop overeating or not? I decided I did, so I forced myself to record the reasons why I wasn't keeping a record. That worked well, and pretty soon I went back to keeping records all the time."[402]

Some people consider self-monitoring, well, a little weird. As far as I'm concerned, that's a good thing because, as we saw in the Vision chapter, successful people are, in fact, a little crazy. Frankly, I've never really understood why some people consider such a proven technique for success odd. If you tried to run a business without measuring progress toward corporate goals, you'd be fired. The fact is that successful people have been hearing, and ignoring, this criticism for years. Consider the perspective of Anthony Trollope, a 19th century English author of more than 50 novels: "I have entered, day by day, the number of pages that I have written, so that if at any time I have slipped into idleness for a day or two, the record of that idleness has been there, staring me in the face, and demanding of me increased labor.... I have been told that such appliances [record keeping journals] are beneath the notice of a man of genius. I have never fancied myself to be a man of genius, but had I been so I think I might well have subjected myself to [this process].... It has the force of the water-drop that hollows the stone. A small daily task, if it be really daily, will beat the labours of a spasmodic Hercules."[403] Hemingway also measured his output, in his own unique style. He recorded "his daily progress – 'so as not to kid myself' – on a large chart made out of the side of a cardboard packing case and set up against the wall under the nose of a mounted gazelle head. The numbers on the chart showing the daily output of words differ from 450, 575, 462, 1250, back to 512, the higher figures on days Hemingway puts in extra work so he won't feel guilty spending the following day fishing..."[404]

. . .

How Do You Record Progress?

Exactly how you record your progress isn't as important as doing it regularly. Keep it simple, and you'll be more likely to stick with it. Businesses have a long history of recording, and publicizing, very simple measures of progress to motivate employee behavior. Years ago, steel magnate Charles M. Schwab visited an underachieving mill and asked how many heats (slabs) of steel the day shift made. When told six, Schwab wrote a big "6" on the floor in chalk. The next morning, Schwab returned to the plant and found that the night shift had rubbed out the "6" and written "7," staking their claim to superiority. That night, he found the day shift had struck back with a "10." Soon this competition, created simply by measurement and without changing goals or incentives, turned this mill into one of his most productive.[405] In the 1970s, Emery Air Freight used a similar procedure. Group performance goals were set for customer service and shipping dock personnel. When progress was posted publicly and each individual kept personal records of his or her actions, performance improved significantly. When this feedback was removed, performance dropped back to baseline levels.[406] Sports teams often get a similar boost in performance when they post practice results so that all team members can see them.[407]

Benjamin Franklin used a slightly more complex process for tracking progress toward the 13 personal goals he had set for himself:[408]

- Temperance (eating and drinking in moderation)
- Humility (in his words, "Imitate Jesus and Socrates")
- Resolution (setting and accomplishing goals)
- Industry (working hard and being productive)
- Silence (avoiding unnecessary "small talk")
- Justice (treating others fairly)
- Tranquility (staying calm)
- Order (being organized)
- Frugality
- Sincerity
- Moderation
- Cleanliness
- Chastity

Franklin tried to act in accordance with these "virtues," saying he wanted to "acquire the habitude" (yes, that's the phrase he used, even though "acquire the habitude" sounds like a line from *Fast Times at Ridgemont High*, or perhaps *Dude, Where's My Car?*). To aid his efforts, he kept detailed progress grids in his personal journals. He worked on one goal each week, making marks for each failure; his progress could be seen "by clearing successively my lines of their spots." The following week, he would move to the next goal, cycling through his 13 week "virtue course" four times a year. He was pleased with the success of his technique: "I was surprised to find myself so much fuller of faults than I had imagined, but I had the satisfaction of seeing them diminish.... Perhaps the most important part of [my] journal is the plan found in it ... for the regulating of my future conduct in life." He even thought it could play a key role in the development of a virtuous world society. He intended to write a book about this practical technique for success, and planned to distinguish it from the motivational pump-ups found in most success books of the day. He never wrote the book, which he intended to call *The Art of Virtue* – apparently he never committed to that goal and recorded his progress toward it.

· · ·

Recording Progress, the 21st Century Way

Benjamin Franklin obviously didn't have a computer, so he wasn't able to use today's user-friendly software programs for setting goals and tracking progress. Of course, I'm biased, preferring the ViSTA software made by my company, and I'll focus on its capabilities because it is obviously the package I know best. I named it ViSTA for its four key functions: Visualizing your ideal future, Setting goals, Tracking progress, and Analyzing success. The final two concern us here. For each goal, you track your progress each day by simply rating your progress on a zero to ten scale, with zero reflecting no progress at all, and ten denoting very strong progress (in addition, you record a few other elements of your day, including time spent exercising, amount of sleep, overall happiness, etc.). It takes about five minutes. After doing this for just a few days, you are ready to analyze your success. There are four major kinds of analyses, each of which requires just the click of a mouse and no understanding of math or statistics other than the ability to count to ten:

• *Summarize my success...* displays simple bar charts reflecting your overall level of progress toward each goal.
• *Track my success over time...* reveals line charts displaying the ups and downs of your progress toward each goal over time.
• *Happiness drivers...* identifies which of your goals has the greatest impact on your happiness.

• *Success drivers...* pinpoints which elements of your daily life, such as amount of exercise or sleep, have the greatest impact on your overall level of success.

For more about how to use these analyses for greater success and insight, take the self-monitoring challenge...

• • •

A Self-Monitoring Challenge

If recording your behavior still seems odd to you, then simply take this challenge: try recording your progress each day for two weeks. Just five minutes a day for two weeks. If you don't like it, then don't continue doing it. But you'll probably find that it provides many of the success-enhancing benefits described above. Why two weeks? That's long enough for it to start feeling like a habit, and you'll need at least 14 days of "progress data" to reliably identify your happiness and success drivers. There are four elements of this self-monitoring challenge...

First, record your progress daily. Using software makes it easy and provides powerful analytic tools, but if software isn't for you, commit to recording your progress in some other way. Use a simple rating scale like the zero to ten scale used in software packages.

Second, focus on the positive. In addition to your progress ratings, write a paragraph or two about your daily successes. Learn from your setbacks, but don't dwell on them. People with low self-esteem or clinical depression too often focus only on the negative things that happen to them; recording positive events, or using other techniques that focus their thoughts and attention on the positive, helps alleviate their problems.[409]

Third, analyze your progress at least every three days. Do the four key analyses described above. Although you may feel the motivating power of self-monitoring very quickly, remember that you will need a week or two to reliably ascertain the drivers and patterns of your success.

- *Summarize your success:* Overall, how are you doing? Toward which goals are you making strong progress? Weak progress? How can you address areas of weakness?
- *Track your progress over time:* What can be learned from your patterns of success over time? Do your graphs show consistent upward progress? Are there "volatility patches" – dramatic ups and downs? What causes them? How can you even them out with more consistent progress? Do you suffer from "weekend snowballs" – strong progress during the week, but major setbacks on weekends? This pattern is common for eating and weight loss goals – how can you minimize setbacks on weekends?
- *Happiness drivers:* On what days are you happiest? Which of your goals has the greatest impact on your happiness? How can you restructure your life so that you can focus on the goals that bring you joy?
- *Success drivers:* Which factors in your life contribute to success? To weak progress? How can you reshape your physical and social environment to contribute to even greater success?

The fourth and final step, which is more than a two-week obligation, is to commit to enhancing the skills that you need to achieve your goals. We saw in the Strategy chapter that the effect of goals unfolds over time because it takes time to Learn which action plans are effective and which are not. Training can accelerate the beneficial effects of goals. Commit to investing 3-5% of your income, and at least five hours per week, in training, seminars, books or other vehicles for personal growth. In other words, commit to investing your time and money in Learning – you will find it a worthwhile investment.

. . .

A Learning Example:
See Dick and Jane Make Course Corrections (or Not)

Learning is almost ridiculously easy for Jane. With a clear Vision,

SCAMPI goals, Belief and Persistence, it becomes almost impossible for her not to notice when she is making progress and when she needs a course correction. She started keeping a journal soon after setting goals, and now begins using software for more sophisticated analyses and insights.

- Reviewing her overall progress data reveals that she's made more progress toward her eating goals than toward her exercise goals. Course correction: she decides to meet with her personal trainer twice a week until exercise becomes a more ingrained habit.
- Tracking her progress over time reveals that she regularly suffers eating and exercise setbacks on weekends. Course correction: she begins cooking on weekends, and therefore avoids the temptations of her old weekend restaurant habit.
- Analyzing her success drivers reveals that she makes the most progress toward her goals on days when she wakes up early. Course correction: instead of getting up at different times on different days, she decides to wake up at 6:30 every day, and exercise before going to work.
- Examining her happiness drivers reveals that she is happiest on days that she progresses strongly toward her identity goal of being an athlete. Course correction: she steps up her efforts to get back into competitive sports, joining a soccer team as well as coaching one.

Dick's lack of Learning is all too familiar. He doesn't keep records of his progress, and therefore gains little insight into the factors that drive his successes and trigger his setbacks. He prefers to stay in denial about his failures, and as a result never recognizes the inadequacy of his Strategy or the need for a course correction. Having pigged out on pizza, and temporarily abandoned his resolution of losing 40 pounds, he then climbs "back on the wagon" and begins the whole dysfunctional cycle all over again.

Chapter Nine

The Power of Putting It All Together: A Formula for Success and Well-Being

ULTIMATELY, SUCCESS REQUIRES two things. The first is desire. Change comes to those who truly want to change. People who don't yet see the need for change – who are in the "pre-contemplation" stage – turn their own inertia into a self-fulfilling prophecy of stability.[410] Hence the old psychologists' joke: How many psychologists does it take to change a light bulb? Just one, but the light bulb has to really want to change. Change starts with the decision to begin trying, and that decision that must ultimately come from within.

The second necessity for success is the right tools. Recall our bottom line on success: *True success is not rare because people are weak or lazy or lack willpower. True success is rare because too often people use flawed strategies for success.* Even the best strategies don't guarantee success – they just greatly increase the odds. It's like cigarette smoking and cancer – not everyone who smokes gets cancer, and not everyone who gets cancer smoked, but it is clear that smoking greatly increases the odds of getting cancer. Therapy, like the five steps, is a tool that helps many people, but not everyone – I've met people who have been in therapy for years, and who can give witty and thoughtful lectures on their problems, but they are still plagued by them.

Failure in life typically results, not from mysterious or unknowable causes, but rather from more practical failures to apply the five very straightforward steps detailed in this book. Consider weight loss, the most commonly set goal, yet the least commonly accomplished. The failure of most people to lose weight and keep it off derives from the fact that, in attempting to lose weight, most people don't use any of the five steps effectively.

- *Poor Vision.* Most overweight people have extremely unrealistic expectations about how much weight they can lose, and how quickly.[411] Unfortunately, not every man can look like Tom Cruise, not every woman can have the body of a supermodel, and no one can safely lose 50 pounds in a month, yet these and other unrealistic expectations about weight loss and personal appearance abound.
- *Poor Strategy.* People gravitate toward quick-fix fad diets, rather than more sensible and sustainable strategies. And even those who do eat rationally typically underestimate the importance of frequent, vigorous exercise.
- *Poor Belief.* Most people lack confidence that they can lose weight. In fact, low self-efficacy concerning weight loss often triggers bingeing.
- *Poor Persistence.* Dieters are highly susceptible to the snowball effect, telling themselves "what the hell" and bingeing after a single, minor setback.
- *Poor Learning.* As if the spectacular failures on each of the first four steps weren't bad enough, most dieters then repeat the entire process, going back to their unrealistic Vision and re-implementing the same ineffective Strategies they didn't really Believe in initially. Besides further undermining their confidence, yo-yo dieting and repeatedly cycling through these negative ABC spirals can alter metabolism and make weight even more difficult to lose.[412]

Recall from Chapter Three the rather dismal conclusion about weight loss reached by the National Institute of Health: "Weight loss at the end of relatively short-term programs can exceed 10% of individual body weight: however, there is a strong tendency to regain weight, with as much as two-thirds of the weight loss regained within 1 year of completing the program and almost all by 5 years."[413] But there was one additional conclusion from their report: "Importantly, however, a small percentage of participants do maintain their weight loss over more extended periods." Who are these people? What is the secret to their success? It should be clear by now that success lies not in secrets but rather in the consistent application of our five steps, as indicated by the National Weight Control Registry,[414] which tracks people who have kept off 30 pounds for at least a year. These individuals have effective Strategies, eating sensible diets low in "bad" fats and, importantly, regularly eating breakfast (i.e., they don't starve themselves or set themselves up for eating binges). They also exhibit Persistence, exercising about an hour a day, significantly more than the 20-minutes-a-day three-times-a-week typical of people who say, "I can't understand why I'm not losing weight even though I'm exercising." And perhaps most importantly, they Learn what drives success in their lives by recording aspects of their own behavior. They weigh themselves regularly, keep track of what they eat, and thereby Learn when they need to make course corrections or alter their weight loss strategies.

Weight loss isn't the only kind of success dependent on the five steps. As we've seen throughout this book, wealthy individuals intuitively use each step in the financial aspects of their lives (*resource recommendation*: read *The Millionaire Mind* by Thomas Stanley, a well-documented and inspiring look at the myths and realities of wealth in America). Excellent physical health depends on the five steps as well. In *Spontaneous Healing*, Andrew Weil identifies the key characteristics of people who heal and thrive despite major illnesses. The typical "spontaneous healer" has a clear Vision of herself as healthy or pain-free. Besides adhering to medical regimens, she makes significant and often permanent lifestyle changes, even if they are difficult at first (Strategy, Persistence). She continues to have faith in her optimistic Vision, and her ability to bring it about, despite discouraging prognoses (Belief). She doesn't hesitate to make additional life changes or find new health care providers if her current strategies aren't working, and she comes to appreciate that there are beneficial aspects to even the most serious health problems (Learning).

Organizational success has its roots in the five steps as well. Successful groups of all types have a clear Vision of the future and their desired role in it, often honed through off-site meetings and other corporate Vision Quest equivalents. They have effective strategies, based on SCAMPI goals, for achieving that Vision. They inspire Belief, which in organizations manifests itself as morale – do the rank-and-file really believe the organization can succeed? Successful companies Persist in their efforts, and avoid being sidetracked by shifting Visions and "Strategy du jour" fads. Finally, they are committed to Learning, not only in terms of training and developing staff, but also in terms of measuring progress toward goals and making course corrections when necessary. From the political dynasties of the Kennedys and the Rockefellers to the business dynasties of GE and Microsoft to the sports dynasties of Vince Lombardi and John Wooden, empires are built by leaders who understand each step, and who know themselves well enough to delegate a step if others are more proficient at it. How do they identify peak performers when they recruit and hire? They ask interview questions that tap whether candidates have used the five steps in their personal and professional lives.

· · ·

The Formula For Success and Well-Being

Spectacular success comes when all five steps align. Spectacular failures result when people "bat 0-for-5" as in typical weight loss efforts. In both cases, these success dynamics arise because of how the five steps interact. The true "formula" for success and well-being, metaphorically speaking, is NOT additive…

Success ≠ Vision + Strategy + Belief + Persistence + Learning

Instead, the formula for success and well-being is multiplicative, like this...

Success = Vision x *Strategy* x *Belief* x *Persistence* x *Learning*

The difference is subtle but crucial. When numbers are multiplied, if any of them are zero, then whole equation becomes zero. Think about the intelligent, well-intentioned people you know who have under-achieved in life, and about the times you have under-achieved in your own life. Quite often, problem is falling short on a single step. Strength on the remaining four steps still leads to less than satisfying results. Think of the otherwise intelligent person who lacks Vision and drifts in life. The dreamer with an inspiring Vision but no Strategy for making it happen. The individual who knows what he wants but lacks the confidence to even attempt it, or begins pursuing it only to give up because he lacks Persistence. The modern-day Sisyphus who persists in the same failed strategy without Learning that a course correction is needed.

The multiplicative nature of the five steps helps explain the enduring mystery of why some people are "wrecked" by initial successes in their lives. George Bernard Shaw wrote, "There are two tragedies in life. One is not getting your heart's desire. The other is to get it." Henry Miller put it more bluntly (and neatly summarized every episode of VH-1's *Behind the Music*) when he said, "The surest way to kill an artist is to give him everything he wants." Freud called it "surprising, indeed bewildering ... that people occasionally fall ill precisely because a deeply-rooted and long cherished wish has come to fulfillment. It seems then as though they were not able to tolerate their happiness..."[415] Success brings many challenges: isolation, jealousy, heightened expectations. But being wrecked by success can most often be traced to the lack of an inspiring new Vision. Without new challenges and new ambitions, they suffer from what German philosopher Friedrich Nietzsche called "the melancholia of everything completed." The sudden shortcoming on just a single step leads to under-achievement on the heels of massive success. Serial achievers understand the need for a new Vision, and recognize that happiness is more about the process than about accomplishing goals per se. They revel in their success for a bit, and then find a new Vision, often one that involves rediscovering an interest or hobby which they had "set aside" while striving toward their initial success.[416] Fortunately, success skills are like muscles. Setting and accomplishing goals strengthens your success skills, even though they deplete your strength in the short-term.[417] Armed with a new Vision, people who have achieved great success are more likely to achieve it again.

The fact the success formula is multiplicative is a classic "good news/bad news" situation. The bad news: Just as a group of mountain-climbers roped together move at the pace of their slowest member, you will tend to perform "down" to the level of your weakest step. If your performance on that step is zero, your under-achievement will be significant. Success, then, requires something of a fanatical devotion to the process. As one psychologist put it, successfully making long-term life changes requires "obsessive-compulsive self-regulation."[418] Little wonder then that the most successful athletes are often those most "obsessed" with their sports – they dream about it the most, they talk about it the most in "everyday situations," and they talk about it the most to themselves.[419] They also make the most sacrifices. Whether it is sports or daily life, true success only comes from going "five-for-five," and that is not easy. The good news: While it's true that a zero on any step will reduce overall success to zero, it also means that small changes – raising that single under-performing step to anything above zero – can lead to massive change and "non-linear" improvements in the trajectory of your life.

Chapter Ten

Thank You, and an Invitation

TIME IS A PRECIOUS COMMODITY, now more than ever. I appreciate the time you invested in this book, and I have tried to treat your time with respect. I hope you use the ideas in this book to improve not only the trajectory of your life, but those of your friends, family, co-workers, and even your children. By about the age of three, children can grasp the essence of the five steps[420] (of course I don't mean they could read this book! – just that they can grasp the basic principles). During the "terrible twos," kids develop a sense of independent self-hood. Having successfully navigated that transition, children by the age of three can focus on setting goals, and delaying gratification to produce results in the future, as opposed to focusing solely in the moment on actions themselves. They can monitor their own actions, change strategies based on that monitoring, and experience a sense of happiness about both the process and the results. By teaching them the five steps, you can help children quickly learn the success basics that most must pick up slowly by trial-and-error.

I invite your feedback. You can contact me at my web site, *www.NextLevelSciences.com*. Live long and prosper, my friends…

Footnotes

[1]Myers, 2000. In addition, articles focusing on negative emotions outnumber those focusing on the more positive aspects of life by 14 to 1, and treatment exceeds prevention as a topic by 7 to 1. The fact is that we know much more about dysfunction and delinquency and retardation than we do about creativity and contribution and genius. This focus, I believe, has fueled the growing popularity of personal coaches. Increasingly, "normal" people are seeking tools to help them achieve more, but mainstream psychology and therapy, in their focus on psychological deficits, have not provided them (of course, there are drawbacks to the "personal coach" concept as well, particularly the fact that "coach" is an unregulated profession, meaning that absolutely anyone can call themselves a "coach"). Fortunately, "positive psychology" – the study of healthy, well-adjusted people – is a growing topic of interest among scientific psychologists and therapists alike.

[2]OK, "Show me the money" wasn't technically Jerry McGuire's catch phrase – it was primarily used by the athlete McGuire represented. But you get the idea.

[3]The most accessible article on subliminal snake oil is *The Cargo-Cult Science of Subliminal Persuasion* by Anthony Pratkanis, a professor at the University of California at Santa Barbara. The studies and statistics described over the next four pages are documented more fully there. Published in the Spring 1992 issue of the *Skeptical Inquirer*, it can be found at www.csicop.org/si/9204/subliminal-persuasion.html. It documents the studies demonstrating the ineffectiveness of subliminal tapes, and also offers a fascinating review of subliminal phenomena in American popular culture. Interested readers may also want to check out *Subliminal Perception: Facts and Fallacies* by Timothy Moore (www.csicop.org/si/9204/subliminal-perception.html).

It should also be pointed out that there is an important distinction between subliminal perception and subliminal persuasion. Subliminal success products are built on the assumption that subliminal persuasion is possible – that broad patterns of thought and behavior can be substantially influenced by subliminal messages. As outlined, there is no compelling evidence for subliminal persuasion. There is, however, considerable evidence for subliminal perception. Under highly controlled laboratory conditions, it has been shown fairly conclusively that individuals can perceive images which are flashed very briefly, even though the individual may not even be consciously aware of having seen the image. Marketers of subliminal success products are adept at blurring the lines between these two phenomena; they often deceptively use studies demonstrating subliminal perception as evidence that their products are effective.

[4]For example, it can be found on page 200 of Anthony Robbins' (1986) best-seller *Unlimited Power*, and on page 26 of Bill Phillips' (1999) *Body for Life* (which even gets the legend wrong, describing it as being conducted at Harvard).

[5]See page 38 of their December, 1996 issue, or read it on the Internet at www.fastcompany.com/online/06/cdu.html. The quote from the Yale spokesperson in the following paragraph comes from that article as well.

[6]National Institute of Health Technology Assessment Conference Panel, 1993. For a more recent review that reaches similar conclusions, see Wadden, Brownell & Foster, 2002.

[7]"As Many Opinions as Treatments in Tobacco Fight" by Dan Vergano, *USA Today*, June 19, 2001

[8]Cohen et al., 1989; see also Marlatt, Goldstein & Gordon, 1984, cited in Brownell, Marlatt, Lichtenstein & Wilson, 1986. Relapse rates are similar across major addictions like alcohol, smoking and heroin, ranging from 50-90% (Brownell, Marlatt, Lichtenstein & Wilson, 1986).

[9]For example, Hunt & Bespalec, 1974; Vergano, 2001. It should be kept in mind that this figure may underestimate the effectiveness of formal treatment programs. It reflects "one-shot" success rates, whereas most people who kick addictions do so after several repeated attempts; also, treatment programs attract the most heavily addicted people who have been unable to quit on their own (Brownell, Marlatt, Lichtenstein & Wilson, 1986; Schachter, 1982).

[10]Prochaska, Norcross & DiClimente, 1992; Schacter, 1982

[11]Small Business Administration (http://www.sba.gov/advo/stats/sbfaq.pdf). The four year survival rate in the next sentence is from the SBA as well.

[12]Glasgow, Klesges, Mizes & Pechacek, 1985. The prevalence of willpower-based strategies for change is also illustrated in George Ainslie's study of impulse control (1987). Strategies based on willpower (which Ainslie described as making "private rules" and "promises to the self") were consistently rated as being more useful in controlling impulses than other strategies. Strong inferences cannot be drawn from this study alone, as it was not specifically designed to assess the effectiveness or prevalence of techniques for change; still, when combined with the results of other studies, it contributes to the overall conclusion that willpower is a commonly-used if marginally-effective strategy for change

[13]"New Year's Resolutions in a More Serious Vein" by Jodi Wilgoren, *New York Times*, December 31, 2001

[14]Note that each study was conducted in the final three months of the year, but at slightly different times and with questions phrased in slightly different ways.

- 1998: 38% "very/somewhat likely to make a New Year's resolution". Source: Marist College Institute for Public Opinion
- 1995: 42% "will make a New Year's resolution". Source: ABC News for Money Magazine
- 1940: 17% "going to make a New Year's resolution". Source: Gallup Organization
- 1939: 28% "planning to make a New Year's resolution". Source: Gallup Organization

  Data from these four studies are courtesy of the Roper Center at the University of Connecticut.

[15]In fact, it is difficult to determine precisely how effective New Year's resolutions are as a process for change because few studies have compared a group of "resolution-makers" to a comparable control group of "non-resolution-makers." One exception, Marlatt and Kaplan, 1972, found that resolution-makers were no more successful in losing weight than a control group, but that study didn't examine other types of resolutions. So we have to make due with self-reported success rates, which are likely overstated by interviewees motivated to appear successful, and who tend to remember successes while forgetting failures. In addition, participants in these studies are often asked about whether they kept their primary resolution, and it seems likely that success rates for secondary or lower-priority resolutions would likely be lower. Finally, resolutions are often about less quantifiable elements of one's life such as "being a nicer person" or "getting in shape" – these leave "wiggle room" for people to give themselves credit for success which may not be deserved.

[16]Norcross & Vangarelli, 1989

[17]Opinion Research Corporation poll, 1998, conducted for Take Off Pounds Sensibly. Data courtesy of the Roper Center at the University of Connecticut.

[18]Pechacek & Danaher, 1979. Also, more recent (and generally effective) "substitution treatments" such as nicotine gum or patches are based on gradual reduction strategies. Admittedly, cold turkey may be a preferable strategy after a major health setback such as a heart attack.

[19]Perri, 1985; Perri & Richards, 1977; Perri, Richards & Schultheis, 1977; Heffernan & Richards, 1981; Perri et al., 1984

[20]Seligman, 1993, p. 241

[21]Fast Company poll, March 2001, p. 120

[22]Collins, 2001. Incompatible Visions often underlie failed business mergers and creative collaborations. When family values purveyor Walt Disney teamed with eccentric surrealist artist Salvador Dali to create a movie, a shared vision would be crucial to the success of their odd-couple venture. But while Disney described the plot as "Just a simple story about a young girl in search of true love," Dali's vision was somewhat more grandiose, calling it "A magical exposition of the problem of life in the labyrinth of time." Needless to say, the movie never got

off the ground. (Quotes from *When Disney Met Dali* by Christopher Jones, published in the Boston Globe Magazine and available at http://www.boston.com/globe/magazine/1-30/featurestory2.shtml).

[23]For Sculley's version of this conversation, see Sculley, 1987, p. 90

[24]This study is described by Markus & Nurius, 1986

[25]The statistical issues involved in arriving at this conclusion can be complex, and are thoroughly discussed in Markus and Nurius, 1986. Even after controlling for other elements of the self (e.g., past selves, current selves, and probable selves), ever-considered selves significantly contribute to self-esteem, personal control, and general views of the future. This importance of future selves also highlights just how complex and dynamic the self-concept can be. Studies conducted over the course of decades show basic personality traits such as extraversion or agreeableness tend to be fairly stable over time, but our dreams, goals, and visions of ourselves in the future are dynamic and evolve significantly.

[26]Ruvolo & Markus, 1992

[27]Markus & Nurius, 1986, p. 960

[28]Porter, Markus & Nurius, 1984

[29]Frankl, 1959

[30]Robins et al., 1984; Klerman et al., 1985; Lewinsohn et al., 1993

[31]Reich et al., 1987

[32]Twenge, 2000

[33]Emmons, 1986; Emmons & King, 1988; Palys & Little, 1983; Van Hook & Higgins, 1988

[34]For the most part, the psychological effects of goal ambivalence and goal conflict are similar, but there may be some subtle differences. Some evidence suggests that ambivalence is associated with negative emotions such as depression and anxiety – uncertainty about what we really want appears to lead to a kind of existential angst and worry. Conflicting goals, on the other hand, are more strongly associated with symptoms of physical illness.

[35]Heatherton & Nichols, 1994. The quotes in the following two sentences are from this study as well.

[36]Miller and Rollnick, 1991, p. 37

[37]The best review of the delay of gratification research can be found in Mischel, Shoda, & Rodriguez, 1989. See also Funder & Block, 1989; Rodriguez, Mischel & Shoda, 1989; Mischel, Shoda & Peake, 1989; Funder, Block & Block, 1983. These studies document the conclusions about delay of gratification summarized in the next two paragraphs.

[38]Specifically, within various disciplines, success is often associated with higher scores on psychological measures of "Psychoticism" or "Psychopathic Deviation." For a review, see Simonton, 1994, Chapter 10; see also Simonton, 2000

[39]Ludwig, 1995

[40]Simonton, 1994, p. 294

[41]Quoted in Simonton, 1994, p. 93

[42]Stanley, 2000

[43]Taylor, 1989. These types of biases can contribute to better physical health as well (Taylor, 2000). In recent years, the issue of how beneficial these illusions are has become contentious, with some evidence suggesting that overly positive views of oneself can lead to aggression and other negative outcomes. On the whole, however, I believe the cognitive biases I've discussed, if modest, are more beneficial than harmful.

[44]Greenwald, 1980

[45]Alloy & Abramson, 1988

[46]Schwartz, 1986

[47]Simonton, 1988

[48]Rothenberg, 1979

[49]Janis, 1982

[50]Daly & Burton, 1983

[51]Freeman & Zaken-Greenburg, 1989

[52]Ellis and his colleagues have written numerous books, both for laypeople and for therapists. A good starting point is *A Guide To Rational Living* by Albert Ellis and Robert A. Harper, first published in 1961 and updated in 1997.

[53]Simonton, 1994, p. 378. Also, Earley & Kanfer (1985) found that people exposed to high-performing role models achieve more than those exposed to low-achieving ones.

[54]Zuckerman, 1977

[55]Linville, 1985, 1987; Thoits, 1983

[56]One down side of self-complexity is that it can make decision-making more complex. If faced with the choice of a long but productive day at the office versus a day at home with the kids, a person who views herself both a great businessperson and a great mom will have a difficult decision. Those with less complex self-concepts may make faster and less stressful (but not necessarily "better") decisions (e.g., Halberstadt, Miedenthal & Setterlund, 1996).

[57]Halberstadt, Miedenthal & Setterlund, 1996

[58]Stanley, 2000

[59]Collins, 2001, p. 75

[60]Pennebaker, 1990, p. 64

[61]Tiechman, 1966

[62]Emmons, 1991

[63]Isen, Daubman & Nowicki, 1987

[64]Wright & Mischel, 1982

[65]Goodhart, 1985

[66]Williams & Dritschel, 1988

[67]Singer & Salovey, 1996

[68]Pennebaker, 1990

[69]Ludwig, 1990

[70]Quoted in Tart, 1969, pp. 367-369

[71]Research confirms that Twain was right – as people look back over their lives, they are far more likely to regret things they didn't do rather than mistakes they made. The top five "inaction" regrets are missed educational opportunities (not taking school seriously enough), not "seizing the moment," not spending enough time with friends or family, missed romantic opportunities, and not pursuing an interest in a particular field/hobby/career. Gilovich & Medvec, 1994

[72]Quoted in Simonton, 1994, p. 93

[73]Collins, 2000, p. 110

[74]This question comes from Dr. Robert Schuller

[75]Koestner et al., 2002

[76]Tetlock, 1981

[77]Suefield and Rank, 1976

[78]Pennebaker, 1990, p. 63

[79]Consider the results of a study examining the impact of motivation and strategy on attendance at Alcoholics Anonymous meetings. One group of alcoholics got a motivational pump-up – they were taught the importance of attending, told where and when they could attend, and strongly encouraged to attend. But another group was given help in devising a specific strategy for attending. They were paired up with AA members who offered to accompany them to their first meeting, and who placed reminder calls the night before the meeting. The results? Everyone in the specific strategy group attended, whereas nobody in the pump-up group attended the first meeting. Sisson & Mallams, 1981

[80]Pomerantz, Saxon & Oishi, 1998 (unpublished, cited in Diener et al. 1999)

[81]Snyder, 1994, p. 116

[82]Locke, Frederick, Lee & Bobko, 1984; Latham & Locke, 1991

[83]Latham & Locke, 1991

[84]Brunstein, 1993; Zaleski, 1987

[85]Rehm, 1977; Schlenker & Leary, 1982

[86]This formula is at the heart of what psychologists call "value-expectancy theory." This theory has many variants that are well supported by research. For a specific application of this theory to goal commitment, see Klinger, Barta and Maxeiner (1980).

[87]Tubbs, 1986; Latham and Locke, 1991; Mento, Steel, & Karren, 1987

[88]Locke, Shaw, Saari & Latham, 1981

[89]This finding is important in ruling out the possibility that specific, challenging goals are spuriously, or coincidentally, correlated with stronger performance. For example, it is possible that more talented people set higher goals because they have been successful in the past, and perform better in the future simply because of their talent, not because of their goals. Numerous studies have "controlled for ability" by assigning goals or by other methods, clearly indicating

that specific, challenging goals cause higher performance, regardless of ability level.

[90]Earley, Wojnaroski & Prest, 1987

[91]The study of air traffic controllers was conducted by Tziner & Kopelman, 1988. The quotes are taken from actual performance reviews.

[92]Emmons & King, 1994; Elliott, Sheldon & Church, 1997. See also a study by Elizabeth Miller and Alan Marlatt at University of Washington, available online at http://more.abcnews.go.com/sections/science/dyehard/dye36.html.

[93]Emmons and King, 1994; Elliot & Sheldon, 1997; Elliot & Sheldon, 1998; Elliott, Sheldon & Church, 1997

[94]Singer & Salovey, 1996

[95]Becker, 1978

[96]Wallace & Pear, 1977

[97]Marlatt, 1985

[98]Herman & Mack, 1975. Interestingly, it is dieter's perceptions about the fattening nature of the milkshakes that drives the binge, not the actual caloric content. Dieters binge if they believe the milkshake is fattening, even if it is not; similarly, they will not binge if they believe milkshake is not fattening, even if it is actually quite high in calories.

[99]Steinberg & Yalch, 1978

[100]Tom, 1983

[101]Baumeister, Heatherton & Tice, 1994, pp. 24-25

[102]Buehler, Griffin & Ross, 1994

[103]Klinger, Barta and Maxeiner, 1980

[104]Miller, 1944

[105]Bandura & Schunk, 1981

[106]Bandura & Simon, 1977; see also Stock & Cervone, 1990

[107]Palys & Little, 1983

[108]May & Veach, 1987

[109]Kirschenbaum, Humphrey & Malett, 1981; Kirschenbaum, Malett, Humphrey & Tomarken, 1982; Kirschenbaum, Tomarken & Ordman, 1982

[110]Quote from Ryan & Deci, 2000. See also Sheldon & Elliott, 1998, 1999; Sheldon & Houser-Marko, 2001

[111]Nuttin, 1984; Markus & Ruvolo, 1989; Reither, 1981; Reither & Staudel, 1985

[112]Buckingham & Coffman, 1999

[113]Wood, Mento & Locke, 1987; Locke, Feren, McCaleb, Shaw & Denny, 1980

[114]Locke, Feren, McCaleb, Shaw & Denny, 1980

[115]Kahneman & Tversky, 1979

[116]Buehler, Griffin & Ross, 1994

[117]Buehler, Griffin & Ross, 1994

[118]Buehler, Griffin & Ross, 1994

[119]Buehler, Griffin & Ross, 1994

[120]Barron & Harackiewicz, 2001

[121]Dweck & Legett, 1988

[122]Emmons, 1991; Kasser & Ryan, 1993

[123]Stall & Biernacki, 1986

[124]Goleman, 1995, pp. 170-171

[125]Matthews, Helmreich, Beane & Lucker, 1980

[126]Kasser & Ryan, 1993

[127]Quoted in Lewis, 2000

[128]Emmons, 1991

[129]Emmons, 1991

[130]Cervone, Kopp, Schaumann & Scott, 1994

[131]Rehm, 1977; Schlenker & Leary, 1982

[132]Baumeister, Heatherton & Tice, 1993

[133]The findings in this paragraph are documented in Oettingen et al., 2001

[134]Griffin & Watson, 1978

[135]Cameron & Nicholls, 1998; King, 2001

[136]General Social Survey, 1996

[137]Sheldon & Emmons, 1995

[138]Emmons & King, 1989

[139]Klinger, Barta and Maxeiner, 1980

[140]Wood, Mento & Locke, 1987; Latham & Locke, 1991

[141]Koestner et al., 2002; Brandstatter, Lengfelder & Grassman, 2001

[142]Locke, Frederick, Lee & Bobko, 1984

[143]Brown, Adler & Bifulco, 1988

[144]Rosenthal & Rubin, 1978; Harris & Rosenthal, 1985

[145]Blittner, Goldberg & Merbaum, 1978

[146]Kluckhohn & Strodbeck, 1961. Karniol & Ross, 1996, humorously contrasted this world-view with the pro-active, future-oriented approach more common in Western cultures: "In contrast, many individuals in Western cultures adopt long-term educational, financial and health goals, engaging in activities that are nearly masochistic: attending graduate school, saving for retirement, and jogging."

[147]Doerfler & Richards, 1981

[148]Bandura, 1991; Kelly, Zyzanski, & Alemagno, 1991; Brownell, Marlatt, Lichtenstein, & Wilson, 1986; Candiotte & Lichtenstein, 1981; Locke, Frederick, Lee & Bobko, 1984; Stock & Cervone, 1990; Norcross, Ratzin & Payne, 1989

[149]Lefcourt, 1976; Hollenbeck, Williams & Klein, 1989; Strickland, 1978

[150]Strickland, 1978

[151]The classic study on this point is Glass, Singer & Friedman, 1969. They subjected two groups of people to loud random noises. One group was forced to listen. The second group was told a button would turn off the noise; they were asked not to use the button, but were told they could if they really wanted to (in fact, none did). Having perceived control, even if they didn't exercise that con-

trol, had significant effects. Even though both groups heard the same amount of noise, those with perceived control found the noise less irritating and distracting; they also performed better and persisted longer on difficult tasks. For a more complete discussion of control and reactions to negative events, see Thompson, 1981.

[152]Taylor, 1983; Taylor, Lichtman & Wood, 1984

[153]Taylor, 1983; Taylor, Lichtman & Wood, 1984; Strickland, 1978

[154]Durand & Shea, 1974

[155]Anderson, 1977

[156]General Social Survey, 1988-1991, conducted by the National Opinion Research Center. Available at http://www.norc.uchicago.edu/projects/gensoc.asp

[157]Pew Research Center, 1994

[158]Langer, 1983

[159]For people who inherently don't want control, or prefer to have decisions made for them, having control thrust upon them can be stressful (e.g., Folkman, 1984). And there's no particular benefit to thinking you can control the weather or any other inherently uncontrollable event. People who lived near the nuclear accident at Three Mile Island (a situation largely out of their control) and who used the problem-solving coping strategies associated with an internal locus of control had more physical problems and psychological distress. But these are extreme examples. By and large, a sense of control is a very positive, adaptive way of thinking (Collins et al., 1983).

[160]Snyder, 1994. In many cases, hope is associated with these benefits even after controlling for dimensions like optimism and intelligence.

[161]Seligman, 1998, presents a very personal account of this research, including his perspective on the ethical issues involved.

[162]The classic study on self-handicapping is Jones and Berglas, 1978. See also Berglas, 1986, Chapter 9.

[163]Goleman, 1994, p. 52 presents an interesting case study of this disorder. See also pp. 27-28. Even without brain damage, research shows that the emotional centers of the brain often react before the "thinking" centers of the brain fully register the situation. The result is what Goleman calls an "emotional hijacking" – an intense emotional response that may not be terribly precise or self-understood.

[164]Bower, 1981. This phenomenon is also responsible for the fact things learned in one state (e.g., happy, drunk, or even underwater) are best remembered in that same state.

[165]Heatherton & Nichols, 1994

[166]Lesieur, 1992; Volberg & Steadman, 1989

[167]Detailed descriptions of problem gambling patterns can be found in Dickerson, 1991, and Peck, 1986

[168]In many circumstances, past events are very good predictors of future events. But not in casinos. At the craps table, for example, gamblers often believe that if

recent throws of the dice haven't produced a seven, then a seven is "due." But in fact, each throw of dice is independent of every other throw.

[169]Known generically as "attribution therapy," the use of this technique for panic attack patients was first pioneered by David Clarke. It has since been used successfully by many others, and has impressive success rates as high as 90%. It is more effective than drug therapies, with a lower rate of relapse after treatment, and without the side effects of drugs. For a review, and references for the major outcome studies, see Seligman, 1993, chapter 5.

[170]Shiffman, 1984; Grilo, Shiffman & Wing, 1989. Admittedly, not every study has found this effect (e.g., Bliss et al., 1989).

[171]Shiffman, 1984; Norcross, Ratzin & Payne, 1989

[172]Three principles from physics explain why, under the proper conditions, virtually anyone can walk on fire without seriously hurting themselves. First, the *Leidenfrost effect* refers to the fact that a thin, insulating layer of steam develops between wet feet and the coals. This is why damp grass is often placed before the coals – to maximize the amount of moisture on the feet (although the adrenaline of the event creates plenty of sweat as well). The Leidenfrost effect is seen in everyday life as well, as when a droplet of water moves about on a hot pan without immediately boiling off.

The second and third physical principles – differences in *heat capacity* and *thermal conductivity* – can also be demonstrated by an example from the kitchen. Suppose you are baking a cake, and the oven is heated to 350 degrees. The cake, the oven, and the air in the oven are all 350 degrees. If you open the oven and stick your hand in, the air does not burn your hand. Touching the cake doesn't burn your hand either. But touching the inside of the oven will burn your hand immediately. Even though all three are the same temperature, they differ in their ability to store and transfer heat – principles that physicists refer to as heat capacity and thermal conductivity. The coals used in firewalking are indeed hot, but are very low in heat capacity and thermal conductivity. Wherever firewalking rituals are found throughout the world, they are invariably done across surfaces with these two physical characteristics.

Sources: The physics behind firewalking have been known for decades, and are summarized by Bernard Leikand and William McCarthy in the Fall 1985 issue of Skeptical Inquirer (pages 23-34). Interested readers might also want to check out "The Physics Instructor Who Walks on Fire" by Matt Nisbet (www.csicop.org/genx/firewalk) and "The Physics Behind Four Amazing Demonstrations" by David Willey (www.csicop.org/si/9911/willey.html). The latter explores the physics behind walking on broken glass, lying on a bed of nails, and dipping fingers into molten lead.

[173]One such incident garnered national attention and was documented in the St. Petersburg Times, October 7, 2001

[174]This statistic, and the other findings concerning Outward Bound, are documented

by Hattie, Marsh, Neill & Richards, 1997

[175]Heatherton & Nichols, 1994

[176]Miller & C'deBaca, 1994

[177]Stall & Biernacki, 1986

[178]Seligman, 1993, pp. 212-213. It should be pointed out that those with mild cases of alcoholism have the highest recovery rates.

[179]For a more complete discussion, see Chapter 12 of Baumeister's (1991) *Meanings of Life*.

[180]Jacobs, 1984

[181]Pennebaker, 1990. Not only do individuals repress negative events that happened to them personally, but groups of people can collectively repress events. After John F. Kennedy's assassination, Dallas residents avoided discussing it. Unlike nearby cities, Dallas did not engage in community-based "group therapy" efforts like naming schools after Kennedy or building memorials. Perhaps fueled by this collective denial, suicide and murder rates in Dallas surged over 20% in the months after the assassination, compared to just 1% nationally. Similarly, deaths due to heart disease increased in Dallas while decreasing elsewhere. A similar pattern of collective denial and adverse health impacts occurred in Memphis in the wake of Martin Luther King Jr.'s assassination. Source: Pennebaker, 1990, pp. 162-167

[182]Lindemann, 1944

[183]Silver, Boon & Stones, 1983

[184]Alexander & French, 1946

[185]Brewer, 1975

[186]People who attend *est* or the Landmark Forum generally report positive benefits from the experience, but a study that compared attendees with a control group of non-attendees suggests that the seminar produces only a short-term boost in locus of control, and no measurable long-term effects (Fisher et al., 1989; see also Finkelstein, Wenegrat & Yalom, 1982). But perhaps the most compelling critique of *est* came from psychologist Irvin Yalom, who pointed out an inherent inconsistency in *est*. It preached taking total responsibility for every aspect of one's life, yet it imposed rigorous and heavily-enforced rules that undermined personal freedom: no watches, no moving your chair, no snacks or bathroom breaks except at designated times, etc. Yalom's reasoning can be found in his book *Existential Psychotherapy*, which is excerpted at http://perso.wanadoo.fr/eldon.braun/awareness/est-yalom.htm.

[187]Bandura & Cervone, 1983

[188]Research conducted with therapy patients suggests that even people with conditions much milder than schizophrenia can expect the same fate: they can learn to cope more effectively, but must ultimately "learn to live with" deep-seated conditions or emotional responses (Luborksy & Crits-Christoph, 1990).

[189]Aaron Beck, the founder of cognitive therapy, was the first to label these reflex-

ive, deep-seated assumptions about oneself "automatic thoughts."

[190]Lochman, 1994. See also Goleman, 1994, pp. 234-239.

[191]If used excessively, comparing yourself to less successful people will lead you to set lower goals and accomplish less. But in the short-term, comparing yourself to others who are worse off can help you deal with the stress of negative events. For example, among breast cancer victims, those with a lump removed compare themselves with those who have a breast removed; those who lose one breast compare themselves with those who lose two; those with the most advanced cases compare themselves to those suffering more or dying; older women compare themselves with younger ones. As one woman put it, "The people I really feel sorry for are these young gals. To lose a breast when you're so young must be awful. I'm 73; what do I need a breast for?" (Taylor, 1983)

[192]Smyth, 1998

[193]Pennebaker, 1990, pp. 38-40; Pennebaker, 1997

[194]Pennebaker, 1990, p. 102

[195]Smyth, 1998

[196]Cameron & Nicholls, 1998; King, 2001

[197]Pennebaker, 1997

[198]Pennebaker, 1990, pp. 85-86

[199]Watson & Tharp, 1993, p. 191. Italics in original.

[200]Coyne, Aldwin, & Lazarus, 1981

[201]Stall and Biernacki, 1986; Klingemann, 1991

[202]Darwin, 1872/1965, p. 365

[203]Strack, Martin & Stepper, 1988

[204]Izard, 1990

[205]Carroll, 1978; Gregory, Cialdini & Carpenter, 1982. This latter study also documents how marketers leverage visualization by comparing the effectiveness of two sales pitches for cable TV (in the early 80s, cable was still a new innovation). Some were simply told of the benefits of cable (e.g., "cable will provide you with many entertainment options"), whereas others were asked to visualize the benefits of cable (e.g., "take a moment and imagine how cable will provide you with many entertainment options"). Only 20% of those provided with information subsequently subscribed to cable, whereas 47% of those asked to imagine the effects subscribed to cable.

[206]Schultheiss & Brunstein, 1999

[207]Suinn, 1983

[208]Suinn, 1987

[209]Cautela & Samdperil, 1989

[210]Stanley, 2000

[211]These basic principles are based on the work of Suinn, 1983, 1987; Watson & Tharp, 1993; Mahoney & Avener, 1977

[212]Pham & Taylor, 1999

[213]Dempster, 1988

[214]Cautela & Samdperil, 1989

[215]Hollon & Back, 1979; Fuchs & Rehm, 1977

[216]Psychologists refer to this as "narrowing antecedent control." For a brief review of the findings summarized in the next two paragraphs, and the specific citations, see Watson & Tharp, 1993, p. 139

[217]Marlatt & Marques, 1977; Ost, 1987; Burnete, Koehn, Kenyon-Jump, Hutton & Stark, 1991; Throll, 1981

[218]Eppley, Abrams & Shear, 1989

[219]Lyubomirsky & Nolen-Hoeksema, 1993

[220]For a review of the research, see Tavris, 1989

[221]Nolen-Hoeksema, 1987

[222]Dubbert, Martin, Raczynski & Smith, 1982

[223]Erber, 1996; Thayer, 1987

[224]Steele & Josephs, 1990

[225]Baumeister, Heatherton & Tice, 1994

[226]Wegner, Shortt, Blake & Page, 1990

[227]Polivy & Herman, 1985

[228]Davidson, Denney & Elliott, 1980

[229]Davidson, Denney & Elliott, 1980

[230]Watson & Tharp, 1993, p. 167

[231]Vaillant, 1983; Stall & Biernacki, 1986; Perri, 1985; Brown, Stetson & Beatty, 1989

[232]Brown, 1978

[233]Kobasa, 1979. It should be pointed out that although Kobasa framed her hypothesis using these terms, her measures reflected slightly different concepts. Still, I think the hypothesis is correct.

[234]Lamott, 1994

[235]Vaughn, 1986. See also Baumeister, 1991, pp. 308-312.

[236]Cohen et al., 1989

[237]Collins, 2001, pp. 165, 169

[238]Collins, 2001, p. 92

[239]General Social Survey, 1993, conducted by the National Opinion Research Center. In contrast, 53% believe "such things are decided by God," 52% believe "society gives some people a head start and holds others back," 38% point to genetics, and 20% believe "it's just a matter of chance."

[240]General Social Survey, conducted by the National Opinion Research Center. Available at http://www.norc.uchicago.edu/projects/gensoc.asp

[241]Pew Research Center for the People and the Press Values Update, November 1997. Available at www.people-press.org/valuetop.htm

[242]Harris Interactive poll, cited in *Spirit Magazine*, January 2000. Jesus Christ, Martin Luther King and Colin Powell topped the list of most popular heroes.

[243]Baumeister & Wotman, 1992

[244]Norcross & Vangarelli, 1989

[245]"Devotion: The Secret to Academic Success" Psychology Today, March/April 2001

[246]"You Are What You Eat," Psychology Today, March/April 2001. Original study published in New England Journal of Medicine.

[247]Dennis, 1955; Price, 1963; Simonton, 1994. "Price's law" states that, if there are "x" number of people in a given scientific or artistic field, then about half of all the contributions to that field will be made by "square root of x" number of people. For example, if there are 144 psychologists researching peak performance, then 12 of them will make about half the contributions to that field.

[248]Simonton, 1994; Lubinski & Benbow, 2000

[249]The scientific literature on happiness is massive. The conclusions I draw over the next two paragraphs about what doesn't contribute to happiness are detailed more fully in Lane, 2000; Myers, 2000, 1993; Diener, Suh, Lucas, & Smith, 1999; Baumeister, 1991; Argyle, 1987; Campbell, 1981; Campbell et al., 1976.

[250]General Social Survey, cited in Myers, 2000

[251]Campbell, 1981, p. 41

[252]Popular success books have historically underestimated American happiness. Books like Dennis Wholey's (1986) *Are You Happy?* and John Powell's (1989) *Happiness is an Inside Job* provide estimates that only about 10-20% of Americans are happy.

[253]General Social Survey, conducted by the National Opinion Research Center. Available at http://www.norc.uchicago.edu/projects/gensoc.asp

[254]This quote is taken from Myers, 2000. I also recommend his book on this subject, *The American Paradox: Spiritual Hunger in a Time of Plenty*.

[255]Lykken & Tellegen, 1996

[256]Brickman, Coates, & Janoff-Bulman, 1978. Similarly, paralyzed accident victims experience an initial surge of negative emotions, and gradually get happier, coming close to but not quite reaching their previous level of happiness, at least within the first year after their accidents. As a general rule, negative experiences have more powerful and lasting emotional impacts than positive ones, in the same way that people will typically do more to avoid pain than they will to gain pleasure (e.g., Freitas et al., 2002).

[257]Quoted in U. S. News and World Report, September 3, 2001

[258]Baumeister, 1991, p. 221. Similarly, overall happiness is more about how often you feel positive emotions, rather than how intense those positive emotions are (Diener, Sandvik, & Pavot, 1990), and Persistence is the best strategy for feeling positive emotions regularly.

[259]Ekman, 1989. Of course, the human emotional landscape consists of more than just these basic emotions. The English language has over 500 words describing emotional experiences, most of which convey one of the fundamental emotional states, coupled with information about its intensity or cause (Johnson-Laird & Oatley, 1989). Embarrassment, for example, is a variety of fear inspired by be-

ing the center of unwanted attention. In addition, people often experience several emotions, such as anger and sadness, simultaneously (Oatley & Johnson-Laird, 1996); this also fuels the perception that there are more than a handful of emotional experiences.

[260]This table is based in part on the work of Oatley & Johnson-Laird, 1996. Combining insights from evolution and cognitive science, they postulate that goals have been of fundamental importance throughout evolution and even drove the development of basic human emotions. As individuals strive toward goals, success or failure create emotional reactions, which in turn drive new orientations toward the goal. In a sense, they argue, emotions evolved because they help individuals (and species) manage goals.

[261]Little, 1989; Brunstein, 1993; Brunstein, Schultheiss & Grassmann, 1998; Sheldon & Kasser, 1998; Oishi, Diener, Suh & Lucas, 1999; Sheldon & Elliott, 1999; Sheldon & Kasser, 1998

[262]Hsee & Abelson, 1991

[263]Carver, Lawrence & Scheier, 1996

[264]Sheldon & Houser-Marko, 2001

[265]Diener & Fujita, 1995

[266]Diener & Diener, 1993

[267]Myers, 2000

[268]Levinson, 1978

[269]Baumeister, 1991, pp. 71-72

[270]Zaleski, 1987; Sheldon & Elliott, 1999; Latham & Locke, 1991; Bandura, 1997; Brunstein & Gollwitzer, 1996

[271]Epstein & Cluss, 1982

[272]Epstein & Cluss, 1982. Beyond the obvious benefits of continuing to take medication, Persistence in and of itself is beneficial. People who adhere to their regimens are healthier than those who don't, even if they are just taking placebos. Persistence boosts confidence, encourages pro-activity, and builds positive ABC cycles.

[273]Perri, 1985; Perri & Richards, 1977; Perri, Richards & Schultheis, 1977; Heffernan & Richards, 1981; Perri et al., 1984; Graham et al., 1983

[274]Schwartz, 1990

[275]Peterson, 2000, p. 44

[276]Author Jim Collins (2001) has called it the "Stockdale paradox": "You must never confuse faith that you will prevail in the end – which you can never afford to lose – with the need for discipline to confront the most brutal facts of your current reality."

[277]Gollwitzer & Kinney, 1989

[278]*Fast Company*, December 1998, p. 196

[279]The Metropolitan Life example comes from Seligman, 1998, pp. 97-107

[280]Goodhart, 1985

[281] Lau & Russell, 1980

[282] Kingdon, 1967

[283] Metalsky et al., 1982

[284] An interesting historical example: Analyses of President Lyndon Johnson's press conferences reveal that when he explained events optimistically, he then took bold action (in the eyes of history, perhaps sometimes too bold). When his attributions were more negative, as they increasingly were toward the end of his term, he tended toward a sense of helplessness and passivity, culminating in his decision not to run for re-election (Zullow, Oettingen, Peterson & Seligman, 1988).

[285] Harackiewicz, Sansone, Blair, Epstein & Manderlink, 1987; Kanfer & Goldstein, 1986

[286] I owe this concept to my good friend and colleague Greg Crabb

[287] Goldstein, Gordon & Marlatt, 1984; O'Connell & Martin, 1987; Oatley & Perring, 1991

[288] Oatley & Perring, 1991

[289] Cowen et al., 1973

[290] This finding, and others detailed in this paragraph, are documented in House, Landis, & Umberson, 1988, and Kaprio, Koskenvou, & Rita, 1987

[291] Brownell, Marlatt, Lichtenstein & Wilson, 1986; Stall & Biernacki, 1986; Clifford, Tan & Gorsuch, 1991; Brownell, Heckerman, Westlake, Hayes, & Monti, 1978; Heatherton & Nichols, 1994; Perri, 1985; Cohen & Lichtenstein, 1990

[292] For reviews, see Rosenthal & Rubin, 1978; Harris & Rosenthal, 1985

[293] Emmons & Kaiser, 1996

[294] Prochaska & DiClemente, 1985

[295] Cohen & Lichtenstein, 1990; Wood, Hardin & Wong, 1984

[296] Palys & Little, 1983

[297] Brownell et al., 1978

[298] Sisson & Azrin, 1986

[299] Simonton, 1984; 1992. One might argue that people gravitate to achievers because of their obvious talents, and that undoubtedly happens, but it is also apparent that the stimulation provided by professional contacts spurs greater achievement.

[300] Rohde, Lewinsohn, Tilson & Seeley, 1990

[301] Repetti, 1989

[302] Coyne, Kessler, Tal, Turnbull, Wortman & Greden, 1987

[303] Perri, 1985

[304] Prochaska & DiClemente, 1985

[305] Renner & Rosenzweig, 1987

[306] Niaura, Rohsenow, Binkoff, Monti, Pedraza & Abrams, 1988

[307] In contrast, Christian theologians such as St. Paul, St. Augustine and Thomas Aquinas – all of whom knew a thing or two about temptation – advocated avoiding sin by avoiding the temptations and likely occasions of sin.

[308]Perri, 1985

[309]Robins, Helzer & Davis, 1975

[310]Grilo, Shiffman & Wing, 1989

[311]Heatherton & Nichols, 1994; Stall & Biernacki, 1986; Doerfler & Richards, 1981

[312]Prue, Keane, Cornell & Foy, 1979

[313]Hollenbeck, Williams & Klein, 1989; Heatherton & Nichols, 1994; Hayes et al., 1985

[314]Kiesler, 1971; Brehm, 1976

[315]Wallace & Pear, 1977

[316]Prochaska & DiClemente, 1985

[317]Schunk, 1984

[318]Heffernan & Richards, 1981; Perri & Richards, 1977; Perri, Richards & Schultheis, 1977; Heatherton & Nichols, 1994; Perri, 1985; Kirschebaum, 1987

[319]Heiby, 1981; Epstein & Cluss, 1982; Chapman & Jeffrey, 1979; Stall & Biernacki, 1986; Boice, 1982; Brownell, Marlatt, Lichtenstein & Wilson, 1986; Schunk, 1984

[320]Receiving modest rewards "along the way" to a larger reward facilitates persistence, even among animals. Chimps perform better at pushing buttons on a demanding schedule if a conditioned reinforcement (light flash) is presented more frequently (e.g., on a less demanding schedule) than a larger reward like food (Findley & Brady, 1965). This flash of light becomes, in a sense, a form of "encouragement" – it's the chimp equivalent of your boss saying "good job" to keep your performance strong until it is time for a more substantial reward like a monetary raise.

[321]Kazdin, 1982

[322]Epstein & Cluss, 1982

[323]Jeffery et al., 1983. Jeffery, Hellerstedt & Schmid, 1990, examined weight loss and smoking cessation. Some people were offered six-month programs that cost $5. Others were offered programs that were identical in every way except that they required a $60 deposit that would be refunded based on success. The $5 program was five times more popular, but the deposit-and-refund program was twice as effective.

[324]Becker, 1960

[325]Jeffery et al., 1983 found that long-term weight loss was the same regardless of whether the deposit was $30 or $300.

[326]Quoted in Watson & Tharp, 1993, p. 216

[327]Jeffery et al., 1983. This finding also emphasizes that rewards don't necessarily undermine intrinsic motivation. Motivation and interest in a task can be undermined if you reward people regardless of performance (e.g., you bribe your kids to practice playing the piano, regardless of how long or how well they practice). Rewards given for strong performance and competence, however, tend to maintain motivation and enhance interest (Bandura & Schunk, 1981).

[328]Jeffery et al., 1983; see also Seidman, Sevelius, & Ewald, 1984

[329]Stuart and Davis, 1972

[330]Shiffman, 1984

[331]Kirschebaum, 1987

[332]Rehm, 1982

[333]Lehman & Rodin, 1989

[334]Worthington, 1979

[335]Kazdin, 1973

[336]Rachlin, 1974

[337]Haley, 1984

[338]Hollenbeck & Williams, 1987

[339]Strack et al., 1985

[340]Wine, 1971

[341]From the Pitney Bowes "Messaging for Innovation" study, July 2000, cited in *Fast Company*, November 2000, p. 104

[342]Diener & Wallbom, 1976. Mirrors were present for both groups of students; 70% cheated when the mirror was to their side, so that participants couldn't easily see themselves, and 7% cheated when mirrors were placed in front of them so that they could easily see themselves. The presence of mirrors in both cases rules out the possibility that the decline in cheating is due to students believing they were being observed through a two-way mirror. Dozens of additional studies have confirmed the self-focusing effect of mirrors.

[343]Hull, 1981

[344]Hull, 1981

[345]People often say that alcohol "picks them up" and makes them feel better. In fact, alcohol has a sedative effect, but by minimizing awareness of internal states, it can minimize awareness of negative ABC cycles, self-critical thoughts, negative emotions, etc.

[346]Wood et al., 1990

[347]Greenberg & Pyszcznski, 1986; Nolen-Hoeksema, 1987; Wood et al., 1990

[348]Okwumabua, Meyers, Schleser & Cooke, 1983

[349]Pennebaker & Lightner, 1980

[350]Brown, Stetson & Beatty, 1989

[351]Johnson & Rusbult, 1989

[352]Ravizza, 1977. The four quotes that follow come from this study as well.

[353]Privette & Landsman, 1983

[354]Csikszentmihalyi, 1985, p. 494

[355]Sarason, 1981

[356]Mahoney & Avener, 1977

[357]Lewis & Linder, 1997; Baumeister & Showers, 1984; Baumeister & Steinhilber, 1984; but see also Schlenker et al., 1995

[358]Koplan et al., 1982; see also Brownell, Marlatt, Lichtenstein & Wilson, 1986

[359]Murphy, Pagano & Marlatt, 1986; Brownell, Marlatt, Lichtenstein & Wilson, 1986

[360]Depression: Many studies have documented this effect; for example, McCann & Holmes, 1984. Stress on health: Brown, 1991. Cope with chronic illnesses: Taylor, Lichtman & Wood, 1984. Anxiety and self-efficacy: Long & Haney, 1988

[361]Neck & Cooper, 2000; Frew & Brunning, 1988

[362]Stanley, 2000

[363]For example, Curry, 1994, cited in Snyder, 1994, p. 188; Stephens, 1988. Also, as Jones (2002) documents, many top women executives are avid athletes, and believe the lessons they learned from competitive sports contribute to their corporate success. The lessons they most frequently cite include the importance of Persistence and Believing in themselves.

[364]Thayer, 1987

[365]The fire drill analogy comes from Marlatt & Gordon, 1985

[366]Prochaska, Norcross & DiClemente, 1994

[367]Prochaska, Norcross & DiClimente, 1992; Schacter, 1982

[368]Candiotte & Lichtenstein, 1981

[369]O'Connell & Martin, 1987; Mermelstein & Lichtenstein, 1983, quoted in Brownell, Marlatt, Lichtenstein & Wilson, 1986, p. 769

[370]Marlatt, 1985; Shiffman, 1982; O'Connell & Martin, 1987; Brownell, Marlatt, Lichtenstein & Wilson, 1986

[371]Niaura et al., 1988

[372]Glynn & Ruderman, 1986

[373]Gormally & Rardin, 1981

[374]George & Marlatt, 1986

[375]Newman & Bloom, 1981a, 1981b

[376]Sandifer & Buchanan, 1983

[377]Curry, Marlatt & Gordon, 1987

[378]Wadden, Stunkard & Brownell, 1983

[379]Klinger, Barta & Maxeiner, 1980

[380]Marlatt, 1982, 359-360

[381]Wood & Bandura, 1989

[382]The table below is based on research by Dweck & Legett, 1988

[383]Taylor, 1983. The quote at the end of the paragraph is from Taylor, Lichtman & Wood, 1984.

[384]Research shows that some of the perceived personal growth that occurs after negative life experiences is illusory (McFarland & Alvaro, 2000). For example, some people who believe they learned to "live in the moment" because of a serious illness are actually mis-remembering and under-estimating the extent to which they "lived in the moment" before getting ill. However, I believe this effect is modest, and much of the personal growth triggered by traumatic events is quite real.

[385]Findings in this paragraph are documented by Silver, Boon & Stones, 1983

[386]Findings in this paragraph are summarized by Simonton, 1994, pp. 153-155

[387]Samuel Butler, cited in Simonton 1994, p. 155

[388]Seligman & Elder, 1985

[389]Tubbs, 1986; Latham & Locke, 1991; Erez, 1977; Locke & Bryan, 1968; Cummings, Schwab & Rosen, 1971; Mento, Steel, & Karren, 1987. Of course, feedback only boosts performance among achievement-oriented people who want to improve their performance; if the feedback isn't used as the basis for strategy refinement and more challenging goals, then it has little impact (Matsui et al., 1982; Latham & Locke, 1991).

[390]Bandura & Cervone, 1983

[391]Becker, 1978

[392]Skinner, 1948

[393]Impact of sleep: Wilson, Laser & Stone, 1982. Overeating and mood: Thayer, 1987

[394]Thayer, 1987; Tice et al., 2001

[395]Kirschenbaum et al., 1982

[396]Kirschenbaum et al., 1982

[397]Kazdin, 1974; Kirschenbaum, 1987

[398]Kazdin, 1974

[399]Bandura & Simon, 1997

[400]Ferguson, 1975

[401]Quoted in Garfield, 1986, p. 42

[402]Quoted in Watson & Tharp, 1993, p. 288

[403]Quoted in Wallace & Pear, 1977, p. 518

[404]*The Paris Review*, quoted in Plimpton, 1965

[405]Hessen, 1975

[406]At Emery Air Freight, 1973

[407]For example, McKenzie & Rushall, 1974

[408]See Franklin's *Autobiography*, as well as Knapp & Shodahl, 1974

[409]Rehm, 1982; Layden, 1982; Kirschenbaum, 1987; Fisher et al., 1976

[410]Prochaska, Norcross & DiClemente, 1994

[411]For example, obese people typically set goals of losing a third of their body weight or more, despite the fact that lasting weight loss of more than 10-15% is relatively rare. On average, they set weight loss goals three times greater than their average weight loss from previous diets. When asked to identify their "dream weight," "happy weight," "acceptable weight," and "disappointed weight," only 9% achieved their "happy weight," and 47% did not even achieve their "disappointed weight," despite nearly a year in a formal treatment program (Foster, Wadden, Vogt, & Brewer, 1997).

[412]For example, animals put on a diet for a second time lose weight at half the rate of their first diet, and regain it three times as fast (Brownell, Greenwood, Schrager & Stellar, 1986, cited in Brownell, Marlatt, Lichtenstein & Wilson, 1986).

[413]National Institute of Health Technology Assessment Conference Panel, 1993

[414]Their web site, http://www.uchsc.edu/nutrition/nwcr.htm, includes references to several published studies based on their data. For more about the registry, check out http://www.lifespan.org/services/bmed/wt_loss/nwcr/

[415]Sigmund Freud, *Complete Psychological Works, Vol. xiv: Those Wrecked by Success*, 1915

[416]This process is often seen not just in serial achievers, but in people who must abandon their goals without having achieved them, as Daniel Levinson found in his 1978 book *The Seasons of a Man's Life*. Many young men focus on ambitious career goals. But Levinson learned that by around age 40, many recognize they will never accomplish them. Others accomplished their goals only to suffer from a "is that all there is?" letdown. The result in both cases is a "mid-life crisis" or sense of disillusionment, which triggers men to set new goals and find new passions. Some refocus on family life, others find new romantic partners, and still others strike out on new careers. But many respond by rekindling a past interest or hobby that had been neglected or dormant.

[417]For example, people who quit drinking alcohol are later more successful at quitting smoking. Carefully controlled laboratory studies arrive at the same conclusion: practicing self-control and self-restraint lead to increased self-control on unrelated tasks (Baumeister, 2001; Zimmerman, Warheit, Ulbrich & Auth, 1990; Muraven, Baumeister & Tice, 1999).

[418]Kirschenbaum, 1987

[419]Mahoney & Avener, 1977; Meyers et al., 1979; Kirschenbaum, 1987

[420]Bullock & Lutkenhaus, 1988

Bibliography

Abraham, S. F., & Beumont, P. J. V. (1982). How patients describe bulimia or binge eating. Psychological Medicine, 12, 625-635.

Ainslie, G. (1975). Specious reward: A behavioral theory of impulsiveness and impulse control. Psychological Bulletin, 82, 463-495.

Ainslie, G. (1987). Self-reported tactics of impulse control. International Journal of the Addictions, 22, 167-179.

Alexander, F. & French, T. M. (1946). Psychoanalytic therapy: Principles and applications. New York: Ronald Press.

Alloy, L. B., & Abramson, L. Y. (1988). Depressive realism: Four theoretical perspectives. In L. B. Alloy (Ed.), Cognitive Processes in Depression (pp. 233-265). New York: Guilford.

Anderson, C. R. (1977). Locus of control, coping behaviors, and performance in a stress setting: A longitudinal study. Journal of Applied Psychology, 62, 446-451.

Argyle, M. (1987). The psychology of happiness. London: Methuen.

Atkinson, J. W. (1964). An introduction to motivation. Princeton, NJ: Van Nostrand.

Banaji, M. R., & Steele, C. M. (1989). Alcohol and self-evaluation: Is a social cognition approach beneficial? Social Cognition, 7, 137-151.

Bandura, A. (1981). In search of pure unidirectional determinants. Behavior Therapy, 12, 30-40.

Bandura, A. (1997). Self-efficacy: The exercise of control. New York: W. H. Freeman.

Bandura, A., & Cervone, D. (1983). Self-evaluative and self-efficacy mechanisms governing the motivational effects of goal systems. Journal of Personality and Social Psychology, 45, 1017-1028.

Bandura, A., & Schunk, D. H. (1981). Cultivating competence, self-efficacy, and intrinsic interest through proximal self-motivation. Journal of Personality and Social Psychology, 41, 586-598.

Bandura, A., & Simon, K. (1977). The role of proximal intentions in self-regulation of refractory behavior. Cognitive Therapy and Research, 1, 177-193.

Barron, K. E., & Harackiewicz, J. M. (2001). Achievement goals and optimal motivation: Testing multiple goal models. Journal of Personality and Social Psychology, 80, 706-722.

Baumeister, R. F. (1991). Meanings of life. New York: Guilford.

Baumeister, R. F. (1994). The crystallization of discontent in the process of major life change. In T. F. Heatherton & J. L. Weinberger (Eds.) Can Personality Change? Washington, DC: American Psychological Association.

Baumeister, R. F. (2001). Ego depletion, the executive function, and self-control: An energy model of the self in personality. In B. W. Roberts & R. Hogan (Eds.) Psychology in the Workplace (pp. 299-316). Washington, D. C.: American Psychological Assocation.

Baumeister, R. F., Bratslavsky, E., Muraven, M., & Tice, D. M. (1998). Ego depletion: Is the active self a limited resource? Journal of Personality and Social Psychology, 74, 1252-1265.

Baumeister, R. F., Heatherton, T. F., & Tice, D. M. (1993). When ego threats lead to self-regulation failure: Negative consequences of high self-esteem. Journal of Personality and Social Psychology, 64, 141-156.

Baumeister, R. F., Heatherton, T. F., & Tice, D. M. (1994). Losing control. San Diego: Academic Press.

Baumeister, R. F., & Jones, E. E. (1978). When self-presentation is constrained by the target's knowledge: Consistency and compensation. Journal of Personality and Social Psyhology, 36, 608-618.

Baumeister, R. F., & Showers, C. J. (1986). A review of paradoxical performance effects: Choking under pressure in sports and mental tests. European Journal of Social Psychology, 16, 361-383.

Baumeister, R. F., & Steinhilber, A. (1984). Paradoxical effects of supportive audiences on performance under pressure: The home field disadvantage in sports championships. Journal of Personality and Social Psychology, 47, 85-93.

Baumeister, R. F., & Tice, D. M. (1985). Self-esteem and responses to success and failure: Subsequent performance and intrinsic motivation. Journal of Personality, 53, 450-457.

Baumeister, R. F., & Wotman, S. R. (1992). Breaking hearts: The two sides of unrequited love. New York: Guildford.

Becker, H. S. (1960). Notes on the concept of commitment. American Journal of Sociology, 66, 32-40.

Becker, L. J. (1978). Joint effect of feedback and goal setting on performance: A field study of residential energy conservation. Journal of Applied Psychology, 63, 428-433.

Berglass, S. C. (1986). The success syndrome. New York: Plenum.

Bliss, R. E., Garvey, A. J., Heinold, J. W., & Hitchcock, J. L. (1989). The influence of situation and coping on relapse crisis outcomes after smoking cessation. Journal of Consulting and Clinical Psychology, 57, 443-449.

Blittner, M., Goldberg, J., & Merbaum, M. (1978). Cognitive self-control factors in the reduction of smoking behavior. Behavior Therapy, 9, 553-561.

Boice, R. (1982). Increasing the writing productivity of "blocked" academicians. Behavior Research and Therapy, 20, 197-207.

Bower, G. H. (1981). Mood and memory. American Psychologist, 36, 129-148.

Brandstatter, V., Lengfelder, A., & Gollwitzer, P. M. (2001). Implementation intentions and efficient action initiation. Journal of Personality and Social Psychology, 81, 946-960.

Brehm, S. S. (1976). The application of social psychology to clinical practice. Washington, DC: Hemisphere.

Brewer, M. (1975). We're gonna tear you down and put you back together. Psychology Today, 1975. Available at http://www.rickross.com/reference/est/estpt8.html

Brickman, P. & Campbell, D. T. (1971). Hedonic relativism and planning the good society. In M. H. Appley (Ed.), Adaptation level theory: A symposium (pp.. 287-302). New York: Academic Press.

Brickman, P., Coates, D., & Janoff-Bulman, R. (1978). Lottery winners and accident victims: Is happiness relative? Journal of Personality and Social Psychology, 36, 917-927.

Brim, O. G. (1988, September). Losing and winning. Psychology Today, 22 (9), 48-52.

Brown, G. (1978). Self-administered desensitization of a cemetery phobia using sexual arousal to inhibit anxiety. Journal of Behavior Therapy and Experimental Psychiatry, 9, 73-74.

Brown, G., Adler, Z., & Bifulco, A. (1988). Life events, difficulties and recovery from chronic depression. British Journal of Psychiatry, 152, 487-498.

Brown, J. D. (1991). Staying fit and staying well: Physical fitness as a moderator of life stress. Journal of Personality and Social Psychology, 60, 555-561.

Brown, S. A., Stetson, B. A., & Beatty, P. A. (1989). Cognitive and behavioral features of adolescent coping in high-risk drinking situations. Addictive Behaviors, 14, 43-52.

Brownell, K. D., Heckerman, C. L., Westlake, R. J., Hayes, S. C., & Monti, P. M. (1978). The effect of couples training and partner cooperativeness in the behavior treatment of obesity. Behaviour Research and Therapy, 16, 323-333.

Brownell, K. D., Marlatt, G. A., Lichtenstein, E., & Wilson, G. T. (1986). Understanding and preventing relapse. American Psychologist, 41, 765-782.

Brownell, K. D., & Wadden, T. A. (1986). Behavior therapy for obesity: Modern approaches and better results. In K. D. Brownell & J. P. Foreyt (Eds.), Handbook of eating disorders: Physiology, psychology, and treatment of obesity, anorexia, and bulemia (pp. 180-197). New York: Basic Books.

Brunstein, J. (1993). Personal goals and subjective well-being: A longitudinal study. Journal of Personality and Social Psychology, 65, 1061-1070.

Brunstein, J., & Gollwitzer, P. M. (1996). Effects of failure on subsequent performance: The importance of self-defining goals. Journal of Personality and Social Psychology, 70, 395-407.

Brunstein, J. C., Schultheiss, O. C., & Graessman, R. (1998). Personal goals and emotional well-being: The moderating role of motive dispositions. Journal of Personality and Social Psychology, 75, 494-508.

Buckingham, M., & Coffman, C. (1999). First, break all the rules: What the world's best managers do differently. Simon & Schuster: New York.

Buehler, R., Griffin, D., & Ross, M. (1994). Exploring the "planning fallacy": Why people underestimate their task completion times. Journal of Personality and Social Psychology, 67, 366-381.

Bullock, M., & Lutkenhaus, P. (1988). The development of volitional behavior in the toddler years. Child Development, 59, 664-674.

Bulman,R. J., & Wortman, C. B. (1977). Attributions of blame and coping in the real world: Severe accident victims react to their lot. Journal of Personality and Social Psychology, 35, 351-363.

Burnette, M. M., Koehn, K. A., Kenyon-Jump, R., Hutton, K., & Stark, C. (1991). Control of genital herpes recurrences using progressive muscle relaxation. Behavior Therapy, 22, 237-247.

Cameron, L. D., & Nicholls, G. (1998). Expression of stressful experiences through writing: Effects of a self regulation manipulation for pessimists and optimists. Health Psychology, 17, 84-92.

Campbell, A. (1981). The sense of well-being in America. New York: McGraw Hill.

Campbell, A., Converse, P. E., & Rodgers, W. L. (1976). The quality of American life: Perceptions, evaluations, and satisfactions. New York: Russell Sage.

Candiotte, M. M., & Lichtenstein, E. (1981). Self-efficacy and relapse in smoking cessation programs. Journal of Consulting and Clinical Psychology, 49, 648-658.

Carver, C. S., Lawrence, J. W., & Michael, M. F. (1996). A control-process pespective on the origins of affect. In Martin, L. L. & Tesser, A. (Eds.) Striving and feeling: Interactions among goals, affect and self-regulation (pp. 11-52). Mahwah, NJ: Lawrence Erlbaum Associates.

Cautela, J. R., & Samdperil, L. (1989). Imagaletics: The application of covert conditioning to athletic performance. Applied Sport Psychology, 1, 82-97.

Cervone, D., Kopp, D. A., Schaumann, L., & Scott, W. D. (1994). Mood, self-efficacy, and performance standards: Lower moods induce higher standards for performance. Journal of Personality and Social Psychology, 67, 499-512.

Chapman, S. L., & Jeffrey, D. B. (1979). Processes in the maintenance of weight loss with behavior therapy. Behavior Therapy, 10, 566-570.

Clifford, P. A., Tan, S. Y., & Gorsuch, R. L. (1991). Efficacy of a self-directed behavioral health change program: Weight, body composition, cardiovascular fitness, blood pressure, health risk, and psychosocial mediating variables. Journal of Behavior Medicine, 14, 303-323.

Cohen, S., & Lichtenstein, E. (1990). Partner behaviors that support quitting smoking. Journal of Consulting and Clinical Psychology, 58, 304-309.

Cohen, S., et al. (1989). Debunking myths about self-quitting: Evidence from 10 prospective studies of persons who attempted to quit smoking by themselves. American Psychologist, 44, 1355-1365.

Collins, J. (2001). Good to great: Why some companies make the leap...and others don't. New York: Harper Business.

Collins, D. L., Baum, A., & Singer, J. E. (1983). Coping with chronic stress at Three Mile Island: Psychological and biochemical evidence. Health Psychology, 2, 149-166.

Cools, J., Schotte, D. E., & McNally, R. J. (1992). Emotional arousal and overeating in restrained eaters. Journal of Abnormal Psychology, 101, 348-351.

Cowen, E., et al. (1973). Long-term follow-up of early detected vulnerable children. Journal of Consulting and Clinical Psychology, 41, 438-446.

Coyne, J. C., Aldwin, C., & Lazarus, R. S. (1981). Depression and coping in stressful episodes. Journal of Abnormal Psychology, 90, 439-447.

Coyne, J. C., Kessler, R. C., Tal, M., Turnbull, J., Wortman, C. B., & Greden, J. F. (1987). Living with a depressed person. Journal of Consulting and Clinical Psychology, 55, 347-352.

Csikszentmihaly, M. (1975). Beyond boredom and anxiety. San Francisco: Jossey-Bass.

Csikszentmihaly, M. (1985). Reflections on enjoyment. Perspectives in Biology and Medicine, 28, 489-497.

Curry, S., Marlatt, A., & Gordon, J. R. (1987). Abstinence violation effect: Validation of an attributional construct with smoking cessation. Journal of Consulting and Clinical Psychology, 55, 145-149.

Daly, M. J., & Burton, R. L. (1983). Self-esteem and irrational beliefs: An exploratory investigation with implications for counseling. Journal of Counseling Psychology, 30, 361-366.

Darwin, C. R. (1872/1965). The expression of emotions in animals and man. Chicago: University of Chicago Press.

Davidson, A., Denney, D. R., & Elliott, C. H. (1980). Suppression and substitution in the treatment of nailbiting. Behavior Research and Therapy, 18, 1-9.

Dempster, F. N. (1988). The spacing effect: A case study in the failure to apply to results of psychological research. American Psychologist, 43, 627-634.

Dickerson, M. (1991). Internal and external determinants of persistent gambling: Implications for treatment. In. N. Heather, W. R. Miller, & J. Greeley (Eds.), Self-control and the addictive behaviors (pp. 317-338). Botany, Australia: Maxwell Macmillan.

DiClemente, C. C. (1994). If behaviors change, can personality be far behind? In T. F. Heatherton & J. L. Weinberger (Eds.) Can Personality Change? Washington, DC: American Psychological Association.

Diener, E. (1984). Subjective well-being. Psychological Bulletin, 95, 542-575.

Diener, E., Colvin, C. R., Pavor, W. G., & Allman, A. (1991). The psychic cost of intense positive affect. Journal of Personality and Social Psychology, 61, 492-503.

Diener, E., & Fujita, F. (1995). Resources, personal strivings and subjective well-being: A nomothetic and idiographic approach. Journal of Personality and Social Psychology, 68, 926-935.

Diener, E., Suh, E. M., Lucas, R. E., & Smith, H. L. (1999). Subjective well-being: Three decades of progress. Psychological Bulletin, 125, 276-302.

Diener, E., & Sandvik, E., & Pavot, W. G. (1990). Happiness is the frequency, not the intensity, of positive versus negative affect. In F. Strack, M. Argyle, & N. Schwarz, (Eds.), Subjective well-being (pp. 119-139). Elmsford, NY: Pergamon.

Diener, E., & Wallbom, M. (1976). Effects of self-awareness on antinormative behavior. Journal of Research in Personality, 10, 107-111.

Doerfler, L. A., & Richards, C. S. (1981). Self-initiated attempts to cope with depression. Cognitive Therapy and Research, 5, 367-371.

Dohrenwend, B., et al. (1982). Report on stress and life events. In G. R. Eliott & C. Eisdorfer (Eds.), Stress and human health: Analysis of implications of research. New York: Springer.

Dweck, C. S., & Leggett, E. L. (1988). A social-cognitive approach to motivation and personality. Psychological Review, 95, 256-273.

Dubbert, P. M., Martin, J. E., Raczynski, J., & Smith, P. O. (1982). The effects of cognitive-behavioral strategies in the maintenance of exercise. Paper presented at the third annual meeting of the Society of Behavior Medicine, Chicago.

Durand, D. E., & Shea, D. (1974). Entrepreneurial activity as a function of achievement motivation and reinforcement control. The Journal of Psychology, 88, 57-63.

Earley, P. C., & Kanfer, R. (1985). The influence of component participation and role models on goal acceptance, goal satisfaction and performance. Organizational Behavior and Human Decision Processes, 36, 378-390.

Earley, P. C., Wojnaroski, P., & Prest, W. (1987). Task planning and energy expended: Exploration of how goals influence performance. Journal of Applied Psychology, 72, 107-114.

Ekman, P. (1989). The argument and evidence about universals in facial expressions of emotion. In H. Wagner & A. Manstead (Eds.), Handbook of social psychophysiology (pp. 143-164). Chichester: Wiley.

Elliott, E. S., & Dweck, E. L. (1988). Goals: An approach to motivation and achievement. Journal of Personality and Social Psychology, 54, 5-12.

Elliot, A., & Sheldon, K. (1997). Avoidance achievement motivation: A personal goals analysis. Journal of Personality and Social Psychology, 73, 171-185.

Elliot, A. J., & Sheldon, K. M. (1998). Avoidance personal goals and the personality-illness relationship. Journal of Personality and Social Psychology, 75, 1282-1299.

Elliot, A. J., Sheldon, K. M., & Church, M. (1997). Avoidance personal goals and subjective well-being. Personality and Social Psychology Bulletin, 23, 915-927.

Emmons, R. A. (1986). Personal strivings: An approach to personality and subjective well-being. Journal of Personality and Social Psychology, 51, 1058-1068.

Emmons, R. A., & Kaiser, H. A. (1996). Goal orientation and emotional well-being: Linking goals and affect through the self. In Martin, L. L. & Tesser, A. (Eds.) Striving and feeling: Interactions among goals, affect and self-regulation (pp. 79-98). Mahwah, NJ: Lawrence Erlbaum Associates.

Emmons, R. A., & King, L. A. (1988). Conflict among personal strivings: Immediate and long-term implications for psychological and physical well-being. Journal of Personality and Social Psychology, 54, 1040-1048.

Eppley, K., Abrams, A., & Shear, J. (1989). Differential effects of relaxation techniques on trait anxiety: A meta-analysis. Journal of Clinical Psychology, 45, 957-974.

Epstein, L. H., & Cluss, P. A. (1982). A behavioral medicine perspective on adherence to long-term medical regimens. Journal of Consulting and Clinical Psychology, 50, 950-971.

Erber, R. (1996). The self-regulation of moods. In Martin, L. L. & Tesser, A. (Eds.) Striving and feeling: Interactions among goals, affect and self-regulation (pp. 251-275). Mahwah, NJ: Lawrence Erlbaum Associates.

Erez, M. (1977). Feedback: A necessary condition for the goal setting-performance relationship. Journal of Applied Psychology, 62, 624-627.

Ferguson, J. M. (1975). Learning to eat. Palo Alto, CA: Bell.

Findley, J. D. & Brady, J. V. (1965). Facilitation of large ratio performance by use of conditional reinforcement. Journal of the Experimental Analysis of Behavior, 8, 125-129.

Finkelstein, P., Wenegrat, B., & Yalom, L. (1982). Large group awareness training. Annual Review of Psychology, 33, 515-539.

Fisher, E. B., Jr., Green, L., Friedling, C., Levenkron, J. C., & Porter, F. L. (1976). Self-monitoring of progress in weight reduction: A preliminary report. Journal of Behavior Therapy and Experimental Psychiatry, 7, 363-365.

Fisher, J. D., et al. (1989). Psychological effects of participation in a large group awareness training. Journal of Consulting and Clinical Psychology, 57, 747-755.

Folkman, S. (1984). Personal control and stress and coping process: A theoretical analysis. Journal of Personality and Social Psychology, 46, 839-852.

Foster, G. D., Wadden, T. A., Vogt, R. A., & Brewer, G. (1997). What is reasonable weight loss? Patients' expectations and evaluations of obesity treatment outcomes. Journal of Consulting and Clinical Psychology, 65, 79-85.

Frankl, V. E. (1959). Man's search for meaning. New York: Pocket.

Freeman, A., & Zaken-Greenberg, F. (1989). Cognitive family therapy. In C. Figley (Ed.) Psychological stress. New York: Brunner/Mazel.

Freitas, A. L., Liberman, N., Salovey, P., & Higgins, E. T. (2002). When to begin? Regulatory focus and initiating goal pursuit. Personality and Social Psychology Bulletin, 28, 121-130.

Frew, D. R., & Brunning, N. S. (1988). Improved productivity and job satisfaction through employee exercise programs. Hospital Material Management Quarterly, 9, 62-69.

Funder, D. C., & Block, J. (1989). The role of ego-control, ego-resiliency, and IQ in delay of gratification in adolescence. Journal of Personality and Social Psychology, 57, 1041-1050.

Funder, D. C., Block, J. H., & Block, J. (1983). Delay of gratification: Some longitudinal personality correlates. Journal of Personality and Social Psychology, 44,
1198-1213.

Garfield, C. (1986). Peak performers: The new heroes of American business. New
York: Avon.

George, W. H., & Marlatt, G. A. (1986). Problem drinking. In K. A. Holroyd & T. L.
Creer (Eds.), Self-management of chronic disease (pp. 59-98). New York: Academic Press.

Gilovich, T., & Medvec, V. H. (1994). The temporal pattern to the experience of
regret. Journal of Personality and Social Psychology, 67, 357-365.

Glasgow, R. E., Klesges, R. C., Mizes, J. S., & Pechacek, T. F. (1985). Quitting
smoking: Strategies used and variables associated with success in a stop-smok-
ing contest. Journal of Consulting and Clinical Psychology, 53, 905-912.

Glass, D. C., Singer, J. E., & Friedman, L. N. (1969). Psychic cost of adaptation to
an environmental stressor. Journal of Personality and Social Psychology, 12,
200-210.

Glynn, S. M., & Ruderman, A. J. (1986). The development and validation of an
eating self-efficacy scale. Cognitive Therapy and Research, 10, 403-420.

Goldstein, S., Gordon, J. R., & Marlatt, G. A. (1984, August). Attributional processes and relapse following smoking cessation. Paper presented at the American Psychological Association Convention, Toronto, Ontario, Canada.

Gollwitzer, P. M., & Kinney, R. F. (1989). Effects of deliberative and implemental
mind-sets on illusion of control. Journal of Personality and Social Psychology,
56, 531-542.

Goodhart, D. E. (1985). Some psychological effects associated with positive and
negative thinking about stressful event outcomes: Was Pollyanna right? Journal
of Personality and Social Psychology, 48, 216-232.

Gormally, J., Black, S., Daston, S., & Rardin, D. (1982). The assessment of binge
eating severity among obese persons. Addictive Behaviors, 7, 47-55.

Gormally, J., & Rardin, D. (1981). Weight loss maintenance and changes in diet
and exercise for behavioral counseling and nutrition education. Journal of Counseling Psychology, 28, 295-304.

Graham, L. E., Taylor, C. B., Hovell, M. F., & Siegel, W. Five-year follow-up to a
behavioral weight loss program. Journal of Consulting and Clinical Psychology,
51, 322-323.

Greenberg, J., & Pyszczysnki, T. (1985). Compensatory self-inflation. A response to
threat to self-regard of public failure. Journal of Personality and Social Psychology, 49, 273-280.

Greenberg, J., & Pyszczysnki, T. (1986). Persistent high self-focus after failure and
low self-focus after success: The depressive self-focusing style. Journal of Personality and Social Psychology, 50, 1039-1044.

Gregory, W. L., Cialdini, R. B., Carpenter, K. M. (1982). Self-relevant scenarios as mediators of likelihood estimates and compliance: Does imagining it make it so? Journal of Personality and Social Psychology, 43, 89-99.

Griffin, D. E., & Watson, D. L. (1978). A written, personal commitment from the student encourages better course work. Teaching of Psychology, 5, 155.

Grilo, C. M., Shiffman, S., & Wing, R. R. (1989). Relapse crises and coping among dieters. Journal of Consulting and Clinical Psychology, 57, 488-495.

Haaga, D. A., & Davison, G. C. (1986). Cognitive change methods. In F. H. Kanfer & A. P. Goldstein (Eds.) Helping people change: A textbook of methods. New York: Pergamon.

Halberstadt, J. B., Niedenthal, P. M., & Setterlund, M. B. (1996). Cognitive organization of different tenses of the self mediates affect and decision making. In Martin, L. L. & Tesser, A. (Eds.) Striving and feeling: Interactions among goals, affect and self-regulation (pp. 123-150). Mahwah, NJ: Lawrence Erlbaum Associates.

Haley, J. (1984). Ordeal therapy: Unusual ways to change behavior. Jossey-Bass: San Francisco.

Hall, S. M., Rugg, D., Tunstall, C., & Jones, R. T. (1984). Preventing relapse to cigarette smoking by behavioral skill training. Journal of Consulting and Clinical Psychology, 52, 372-382.

Harackiewicz, J. M. & Sansone, C. (1991). Goals and intrinsic motivation: You can get there from here. In M. L. Maehr and P. R. Pintrich (Eds.), Advances in motivation and achievement (Vol. 7, pp. 21-49). Greenwich CT: JAI Press.

Harackiewicz, J. M., Sansone, C., Blair, L. W., Epstein, J. A., & Manderlink, G. (1987). Attributional processes in behavior change and maintenance: Smoking cessation and continued abstinence. Journal of Consulting and Clinical Psychology, 55, 372-378.

Harris, G. M., & Johnson, S. B. (1980). Comparison of individualized covert modeling, self-control desensitization, and study-skills training for alleviation of test anxiety. Journal of Consulting and Clinical Psychology, 48, 186-194.

Harris, M. J., & Rosenthal, R. (1985). Mediation of interpersonal expectancy effects: 31 meta-analyses. Psychological Bulletin, 97, 363-386.

Hattie, J., March, H. W., Neill, J. T., & Richards, G. E. (1997). Adventure education and Outward Bound: Out of class experiences that make a lasting difference. Review of Educational Research, 67, 43-87.

Hayes, S. C., Rosenfarb, I., Wulfert, E. D., Korn, Z., & Zettle, R. D. (1985). Self-reinforcement effects: An artifact of social standard setting? Journal of Applied Behavior Analysis, 18, 201-214.

Heatherton, T. F., & Nichols, P. A. (1994). Personal accounts of successful versus failed attempts at life change. Personality and Social Psychology Bulletin, 20, 664-675.

Heatherton, T. F., & Polivy, J. (1992). Chronic dieting and eating disorders: A spiral model. In J. Crowther, S. Hobfall, M. Stephens, & D. Tennenbaum (Eds.), The etiology of bulimia: The individual and familial context. Washington, D. C.: Hemisphere.

Heffernan, T., & Richards, C. S. (1981). Self-control of study behaviors: Identification and evaluation of natural methods. Journal of Counseling Psychology, 28, 361-364.

Heiby, E. M. (1981). Depression and the frequency of self-reinforcement. Behavior Therapy, 12, 549-555.

Herman, C. P., & Mack, D. (1975). Restrained and unrestrained eating. Journal of Personality, 43, 647-660.

Hessen, R. (1975). Steel Titan: The life of Charles M. Schwab. New York: Oxford.

Hollenbeck, J. R., & Williams, C. R. (1987). Goal importance, self-focus, and the goal-setting process. Journal of Applied Psychology, 72, 204-211.

Hollenbeck, F. R., Williams, C. R., & Klein, H. J. (1989). An empirical examination of the antecedents of commitment to difficult goals. Journal of Applied Psychology, 74, 18-23.

Hollon, S. D., & Beck, A. T. (1979). Cognitive therapy and depression. In P. C. Kendall & S. D. Hollon (Eds.), Cognitive-behavioral interventions: Theory, research, and procedures (pp. 153-203). New York: Academic Press.

House, J. S., Landis, K. R., & Umberson, D. (1988). Social relationships and health. Science, 241, 540-545.

Huber, R. M. (1987). The American idea of success. Yew York: McGraw Hill.

Hull, J. G. (1981). A self-awareness model of the causes and effects of alcohol consumption. Journal of Abnormal Psychology, 90, 586-900.

Hunt, W. A., & Bespalec, D. A. (1974). An evaluation of current methods of modifying smoking behavior. Journal of Consulting and Clinical Psychology, 30, 431-438.

Isen, A. M., Daubman, K. A., & Nowicki, G. P. (1987). Positive affect facilitates creative problem solving. Journal of Personality and Social Psychology, 52, 1122-1131.

Izard, C. E. (1990). Facial expression and the regulation of emotions. Journal of Personality and Social Psychology, 58, 487-498.

Janis, I. L. (1982). Groupthink: Psychological studies of policy decisions and fiascoes (2nd ed.). Boston: Houghton Mifflin.

Jeffery, R. W., Gerber, W. M., Rosenthal, B. S., & Lindquist, R. A. (1983). Monetary contracts in weight control: Effectiveness of group and individual contracts of varying size. Journal of Consulting and Clinical Psychology, 51, 242-248.

Jeffery, R. W., Hellerstedt, W. L., & Schmid, T. L. (1990). Correspondence programs for smoking cessation and weight control: A comparison of two strategies in the Minnesota Heart Health Program. Health Psychology, 9, 585-598.

Jeffrey, R. W., & Wing, R. R. (1983). Recidivism and self-cure of smoking and obesity: Data from population studies. American Psychologist, 38, 852.

Johnson, D. J., & Rusbult, C. E. (1989). Resisting temptation: Devaluation of alternative partners as a means of maintaining commitment in close relationships. Journal of Personality and Social Psychology, 57, 967-980.

Johnson-Laird, P. N., & Oatley, K. (1989). The language of emotions: An analysis of the semantic field. Cognition and Emotion, 3, 81-123.

Jones, D. (2002). Many successful women also athletic. USA Today, March 26, 2002. Available at http://www.usatoday.com/money/covers/2002-03-26-women-sports.htm

Jones, E. E., & Berglas, S. C. (1978). Control of attributions about the self through self-handicapping strategies: The appeal of alcohol and the role of underachievement. Personality and Social Psychology Bullein, 4, 200-206.

Kahneman, D. & Tversky, A. (1979). Intuitive prediction: Biases and corrective procedures. TIMS Studies in Management Science, 12, 313-327.

Kanfer, F. H., & Gaelick, L. (1986). Self-management methods. In F. H. Kanfer & A. P. Goldstein (Eds.) Helping people change: A textbook of methods. New York: Pergamon.

Kaprio, J., Koskenvou, M., & Rita, H. (1987). Mortality after bereavement: A prospective study of 95,647 widowed persons. American Journal of Public Health, 77, 283-287.

Karniol, R., & Ross, M. (1996). The motivational impact of temporal focus: Thinking about the future and the past. Annual Review of Psychology, 47, 593-620.

Kasser, T., & Ryan, R. M. (1993). A dark side of the American Dream: Correlates of financial success as a central life aspiration. Journal of Personality and Social Psychology, 65, 410-422.

Kazdin, A. E. (1973). The effect of response cost and aversive stimulation in suppressing punished and non-punished speech disfluencies. Behavior Therapy, 4, 73-82

Kazdin, A. E. (1974). Reactive self-monitoring: The effects of response desirability, goal setting, and feedback. Journal of consulting and Clinical Psychology, 42, 704-716.

Kazdin, A. E. (1982). The token economy: Ten years later. Journal of Applied Behavior Analysis, 15, 431-445.

Kelly, E. L., & Conley, J. J. (1987). Personality and compatibility: A prospective analysis of marital stability and marital satisfaction. Journal of Personality and Social Psychology, 52, 27-40.

Kelly, R. B., Zyzanski, S. J., & Alemagno, S. A. (1991). Prediction of motivation and behavior change following health promotion: Role of health beliefs, social support, and self-efficacy. Social Science & Medicine, 32, 311-320.

Kiesler, C. A. (1971). The psychology of commitment. New York: Academic Press.

King, L. A. (2001). The health benefits of writing about life goals. Personality and Social Psychology Bulletin, 27, 798-807.

Kingdon, J. W. (1967). Politicians beliefs about voters. American Political Science Review, 61, 137-143.

Kirschenbaum, D. S. (1987). Self-regulatory failure: A review with clinical implications. Clinical Psychology Review, 7, 77-104.

Kirschenbaum, D. S., Humphrey, L. L., & Malett, S. D. (1981). Specificity of planning in adult self-control: An applied investigation. Journal of Personality and Social Psychology, 40, 941-950.

Kirschenbaum, D. S., Malett, S. D., Humphrey, L. L., & Tomarken, A. J. (1982). Specificity of planning and maintenance of self-control: 1 year follow-up of a study improvement program. Behavior Therapy, 13, 232-240.

Kirschenbaum, D., Ordman, A., Tomarken, A. & Holtzbauer, R. (1982). Effects of differential self-monitoring and level of mastery of sports performance: Brain power bowling. Cognitive Therapy and Research, 6, 335-342.

Kirschenbaum, D. S., Tomarken, A. J., & Ordman, A. M. (1982). Specificity of planning and choice applied to adult self-control. Journal of Personality and Social Psychology, 42, 576-585

Klerman, G., et al. (1985). Birth cohort trends in rates of major depressive disorder among relaties of patients with affective disorder. Archives of General Psychiatry, 42, 689-693.

Klinger, E., Barta, S. G., & Maxeiner, M. E. (1980). Motivational correlates of thought content frequency and commitment. Journal of Personality and Social Psychology, 39, 1222-1237.

Kluckhohn, F. K., & Strodbeck, F. L. (1961). Variations in value orientations. Evanston, IL: Row, Peterson.

Kluznik, N., Speed, N., Van Valkenberg, C., & Magraw, R. (1986). Forty-year follow-up of United States prisoners of war. American Journal of Psychiatry, 143, 1443-1445.

Knapp, T., & Shodahl, S. (1974). Ben Franklin as a behavior modifier: A note. Behavior Therapy, 5, 656-660.

Knight, L., & Boland, F. (1989). Restrained eating: An experimental disentanglement of the disinhibiting variables of calories and food type. Journal of Abnormal Psycholgy, 98, 412-420.

Kobasa, S. C. (1979). Stressful life events, personality and health: An inquiry into hardiness. Journal of Personality and Social Psychology, 37, 1-10.

Koestner, R. L., et al. (2002). Attaining personal goals: Self-concordance plus implementation intentions equals success. Journal of Personality and Social Psychology, 83, 231-244.

Komacki, J., Barwick, K. D., & Scott, L. R. (1978). A behavioral approach to occupational safety: Pinpointing and reinforcing safe performance in a food manufacturing plant. Journal of Applied Psychology, 64, 434-445.

Koplan, J. P., Powell, K. E., Sikes, R. K., Shirley, R. W., & Campbell, C. C. (1982). An epidemiologic study of the benefits and risks of running. Journal of the American Medical Association, 248, 3118-3121.

Lamott, A. (1994). Bird by bird: Some instructions on writing and life. New York:

Anchor Books.

Lane, R. E. (2000). The loss of happiness in market democracies. Yale University Press: New Haven.

Latham, G. P., & Baldes, J. J. (1975). The "practical significance" of Locke's theory of goal setting. Journal of Applied Psychology, 60, 122-124.

Latham, G. P., & Locke, E. A. (1991). Self-regulation through goal setting. Organizational Behavior and Human Decision Processes, 50, 212-247.

Lau, R. R., & Russell, D. (1980). Attributions in the sports pages. Journal of Personality and Social Psychology, 39, 29-38

Layden, M. A. (1982). Attributional style therapy. In C. Antaki & C. Brewin (Eds.), Attributions and psychological change (pp. 53-82). London: Academic Press.

Lees, L. A., & Dygdon, J. A. (1988). The imitation and maintenance of exercise behavior: A learning theory conceptualization. Clinical Psychology Review, 8, 345-353.

Lehman, A. K., & Rodin, J. (1989). Styles of self-nurturance and disordered eating. Journal of Consulting and Clinical Psychology, 57, 117-122.

Leon, G., & Chamberlin, K. (1973). Emotional arousal, eating patterns, and body image as differential factors associated with varying success in maintaining a weight loss. Journal of Consulting and Clinical Psychology, 40, 474.

Lesieur, H. R. (1992). Compulsive gambling. Society, 29, 43-50.

Lewinsohn, P., et al. (1993). Age-cohort changes in the lifetime occurrence of depression and other mental disorders. Journal of Abnormal Psychology, 102, 110-120.

Lewis, M. (2000). The new new thing. New York: Penguin.

Lewis, B. P., & Linder, D. E. (1997). Thinking about choking? Attentional processes and paradoxical performance. Personality and Social Psychology Bulletin, 23, 937-944.

Levinson, D. J. (1978). The seasons of a man's life (with C. Darrow, E. Klein, M. Levinson, & B. Mckee). New York: Ballanine Books.

Lewin, K. (1951). Field theory in social science: Selected theoretical papers (D. Cartwright, Ed.). New York: Harper & Row.

Lindemann, E. (1944). Symptomatology and management of acute grief. American Journal of Psychiatry, 101, 141-148.

Linville, P. W. (1985). Self-complexity and affective extremity: Don't put all your eggs in one basket. Social Cognition, 3, 94-120.

Lochman, J. (1994). Social-cognitive process of severely violent, moderately aggressive and nonaggressive boys. Journal of Consulting and Clinical Psychology, 62, 366-374.

Locke, E. A. (1966). The relationship of intentions to level of performance. Journal of Applied Psychology, 50, 60-66.

Locke, E. A., & Bryan, J. F. (1968). Goal setting as a determinant of the effect of knowledge of score on performance. American Journal of Psychology, 81, 398-406.

Locke, E. A., Feren, D. B., McCaleb, V. M., Shaw, K. N., & Denny, A. T. (1980). The relative effectiveness of four methods of motivating employee performance. In K. Duncan, M. Gruneberg, & D. Wallis (Eds.), Changes in working life (pp. 301-322). New York: Wiley.

Locke, E. A., Frederick, E., Lee, C. & Bobko, P. (1984). Effect of self-efficacy , goals and task strategies on task performance. Journal of Applied Psychology, 69, 241-251.

Locke, E. A., & Shaw, K. N., Saari, L. J., & Latham, G. P. (1981). Goal setting and task performance: 1969-1980. Psychological Bulletin, 90, 125-152.

Long, B. C., & Haney, C. J. (1988). Coping strategies for working women: Aerobic exercise and relaxation interventions. Behavior Therapy, 19, 75-83.

Lubinski, D., & Benbow, C. P. (2000). States of excellence. American Psychologist, 55, 137-150.

Luborsky, L., & Crits-Christoph, P. (1990). Understanding transference: The CCRT method. New York: Basic Books.

Lyubomirsky, S., & Nolen-Hoeksema, S. (1993). Self-perpetuating properties of dysphoric rumination. Journal of Personality and Social Psychology, 65, 339-349.

Ludwig, A. M. (1990). Alcohol input and creative output. British Journal of Addiction, 85, 953-963.

Ludwig, A. M. (1995). The price of greatness: Resolving the creativity and madness controversy. New York: Guilford.

Lykken, D., & Tellegen, A. (1996). Happiness is a stochastic phenomenon. Psychological Science, 7, 186-189.

Mahoney, M., & Avener, N. (1977). Psychology of the elite athlete: An exploratory study. Cognitive Therapy and Research, 1, 135-141.

Manderlink, G., & Harackiewicz, J. M. (1984). Proximal versus distal goal setting and intrinsic motivations. Journal of Personality and Social Psychology, 47, 918-928.

Marks, I. (1986). Epidemiology of anxiety. Social Psychiatry, 21, 167-171.

Markus, H. & Nurius, P. (1986). Possible selves. American Psychologist, 41, 954-969.

Marlatt, G. A. (1983). The controlled-drinking controversy: A commentary. American Psychologist, 36, 1097-1110.

Marlatt, G. A. (1985). Relapse prevention: Theoretical rationale and overview of the model. In G. A. Marlatt & J. R. Gordon (Eds.), Relapse prevention (pp. 3-70). New York: Guilford Press.

Marlatt, G. A, & Gordon, J. R. (Eds.) (1985). Relapse prevention: Maintenance strategies in addictive behavior change. New York: Guilford.

Marlatt, G. A., & Kaplan, B. E. (1972). Self-initiated attempts to change behavior: A study of New Year's resolutions. Psychological Reports, 30, 123-131.

Matsui, T., Okada, A., & Kakuyama, T. (1982). Influence of achievement need on goal setting, performance, and feedback effectiveness. Journal of Applied Psychology, 67, 645-648.

Marlatt, G. A., & Marques, J. K. (1977). Meditation, self-control, and alcohol use. In R. B. Stuart (Eds.), Behavioral self-management: Strategies, techniques, and outcomes (p. 117-153). New York: Brunner/Mazel.

Matthews, K. A., Helmreich, R. l., Beanne, W. E., & Lucker, G. W. (1980). Pattern A, achievement-striving, and scientific merit: Does pattern A help or hinder? Journal of Personality and Social Psychology, 39, 962-967.

May, J. R., & Veach, T. L. (1987). The U. S. alpine ski team psychology program: A proposed consultation model. In J. R. May & M. J. Asken (Eds.), Sport Psychology: The psychological health of the athlete (pp. 13-39). PMA Publishing Corp.: New York.

McCann, I. L., & Holmes, D. S. (1984). Influence of aerobic exercise on depression. Journal of Personality and Social Psychology, 46, 1142-1147.

McClelland, D. C. (1987). Human motivation. Cambridge: Cambridge University Press.

McFarland, C., & Alvaro, C. (2000). The impact of motivation on temporal comparisons: Coping with traumatic events by perceiving personal growth. Journal of Personality and Social Psychology, 79, 327-343.

McFarlin, D. B., & Blascovich, J. (1981). Effects of self-esteem and performance feedback on future affective preferences and cognitive expectations. Journal of Personality and Social Psychology, 40, 521-531.

McKenzie, T., & Rushall, B. (1974). Effects of self-recording contingencies on improving attendance and performance in a competitive swimming training environment. Journal of Applied Behavior Analysis, 7, 199-206.

Mento, A. J., Steel, R. P., & Karren, R. J. (1987). A meta-analytic study of the effects of goal setting on task performance: 1966-1984. Organizational Behavior and Human Decision Processes, 39, 52-83.

Meyer, J. M., & Stunkard, A. J. (1993). Genetics and human obesity. In A. J. Stunkard & T. Wadden (Eds.), Obesity therapy and treatment (pp. 138-149). New York: Raven.

Mikulincer, M. (1989). Cognitive inference and learned helplessness: The effects of off-task cognitions on performance following unsolvable problems. Journal of Personality and Social Psychology, 57, 129-135.

Miller, N. E. (1944). Experimental studies in conflict. In J. McV. Hunt (Ed.) Personality and the behavior disorders (Vol. 1). New York: Roland Press.

Miller, W. R., & C'deBaca, J. (1994). Quantum change: Toward a psychology of transformation. In T. F. Heatherton & J. L. Weinberger (Eds.) Can personality change? (pp. 253-280). Washington, DC: American Psychological Association.

Miller, W. R., & Rollnick, S. (1991). Motivational interviewing. New York: Guilford.

Mischel, W. (1981). Metacognition and the rules of delay. In J. H. Flavell & L. Ross (Eds.), Social cognitive development: Frontiers and possible futures (pp. 240-271). Cambridge: Cambridge University Press.

Mischel, W., Shoda, Y., & Peake, P. K. (1988). The nature of adolescent competencies predicted by preschool delay of gratification. Journal of Personality and Social Psychology, 54, 687-696.

Mischel, W., Shoda, Y., & Rodriguez. M. L. (1989). Delay of gratification in children. Science, 244, 933-937.

Moore, T. E. (1988). The case against subliminal manipulation. Psychology and Marketing, 5, 297-316.

Muraven, M., Baumeister, R. E., & Tice, D. M. (1999). Longitudinal improvement of self-regulation through practice: Building self-control through repeated exercise. Journal of Social Psychology, 139, 446-457.

Murphy, T. J., Pagano, R. R., & Marlatt, G. A. (1986). Lifestyle modification with heavy alcohol drinkers: Effects of aerobic exercise and meditation. Addictive Behaviors, 11, 175-186.

Myers, A. W., Cooke, C. J., Cullen, J., & Liles, J. (1979). Psychological aspects of athletic competitors: A replication across sports. Cognitive Therapy and Research, 3, 361-366.

Myers, D. G. (1993). The pursuit of happiness: Discovering the pathway to fulfillment, well-being and enduring personal joy. Avon: New York.

Myers, D. G. (2000). The funds, friends and faith of happy people. American Psychologist, 55, 56-67.

Neck, C. P., & Cooper, K. H. (May 2000). The fit executive: Exercise and diet guidelines for enhancing performance. Academy of Management Executive, 14, no. 2 special issue on Executive Health, 72-82.

Newman, A., & Bloom, R. (1981a). Self-control of smoking – I. Effects of experience with imposed, increasing, decreasing, and random delays. Behaviour Research and Therapy, 19, 187-192.

Newman, A., & Bloom, R. (1981b). Self-control of smoking – II. Effects of cue salience and source of delay imposition on the effectiveness of training under increasing delay. Behaviour Research and Therapy, 19, 193-200.

Newman, K. S. (1988). Falling from grace: The experience of downward mobility in the American middle class. New York: Free Press.

Niaura, R. S., Rohsenow, D. J., Binkoff, J. A., Monti, P. M., Pedraza, M., & Abrams, D. B. (1988). Relevance of cue reactivity to understanding alcohol and smoking relapse. Journal of Abnormal Psychology, 97, 133-152.

NIH Technology Assessment Conference Panel. (1993). Methods for voluntary weight loss and control. Annals of Internal Medicine, 199, 764-770.

Nolen-Hoeksema, S. (1987). Sex differences in depression: Theory and evidence. Psychological Bulletin, 101, 259-282.

Nolen-Hoeksema, S., & Morrow, J. (1991). A prospective study of depression and posttraumatic stress symptoms after a natural disaster: The 1989 Loma Prieta Earthquake. Journal of Personality and Social Psychology, 61, 115-121.

Norcross, J. C., Ratzin, A. C., & Payne, D. (1989). Ringing in the new year: The change processes and reported outcomes of resolutions. Addictive Behaviors, 14, 205-212.

Nuttin, J. (1984). Motivation, planning and action: A relational theory of behavioral dynamics. Hillsdale, NJ: Erlbaum.

Oatley, K., & Johnson-Laird, P. N. (1987). Towards a cognitive theory of emotions. Cognition and Emotion, 1, 29-50.

Oatley, K., & Johnson-Laird, P. N. (1996). The communicative theory of emotions: Empirical tests, mental models, and implications for social interaction. In L. L. Martin & A. Tesser (Eds.) Striving and feeling: Interactions among goals, affect and self-regulation (pp. 363-393). Mahwah, NJ: Lawrence Erlbaum Associates.

Oatley, K., & Perring, C. (1991). A longitudinal study of the psychological and social factors affecting recovery from psychiatric breakdown. British Journal of Psychiatry, 158, 28-32.

O'Connell, K. A., & Martin, E. J. (1987). Highly tempting situations associated with abstinence, temporary lapse, and relapse among participants in smoking cessation programs. Journal of Consulting and Clinical Psychology, 55, 367-371.

Oettingen, G., Pak, H., & Schnetter, K. (2001). Self-regulation of goal setting: Turning free fantasies about the future into binding goals. Journal of Personality and Social Psychology, 80, 736-753.

Oishi, S., Diener, E., Suh, E., & Lucas, R. E. (1999). Value as a moderator in subjective well-being. Journal of Personality, 67, 157-184.

Okwumabua, T. M., Meyers, A. W., Schleser, R., & Cooke, C. J. (1983). Cognitive strategies and running performance: An exploratory study. Cognitive Therapy and Research, 7, 363-370.

Omodei, M. M., & Wearing, A. J. (1990). Need satisfaction and involvement and personal projects: Toward an integrative model of subjective well-being. Journal of Personality and Social Psychology, 59, 762-769.

Ost, L-G. (1987). Applied relaxation: Description of a coping technique and review of controlled studies. Behaviour Research and Therapy, 25, 397-409.

Palys, T. S., & Little, B. R. (1983). Perceived life satisfaction and the organization of personal project systems. Journal of Personality and Social Psychology, 44, 1221-1230.

Peck, C. P. (1986). Risk-taking behavior and compulsive gambling. American Psychologist, 41, 461-465.

Peele, S. (1989). Diseasing of America: Addiction treatment out of control. Lexington, MA: Lexington Books.

Pennebaker, J. W. (1990). Opening up. New York: Morrow.

Pennebaker, J. W. (1997). Writing about emotional experiences as a therapeutic process. Psychological Science, 8, 162-166

Pennebaker, J. W., & Lightner, J. L. (1980). Competition of internal and external information in an exercise setting. Journal of Personality and Social Psychology, 39, 165-174.

Perri, M. G. (1985). Self-change strategies for the control of smoking, obesity, and problem drinking. In S. Shiffman & T. A. Wills (Eds.), Coping and substance use (pp. 295-317). Orlando: Academic Press.

Perri, M. G., McAdoo, W. G., Spevak, P. A., & Newlin, D. B. (1984). Effect of a multicomponent maintenance program on long-term weight loss. Journal of Consulting and Clinical Psychology, 52, 480-481.

Perri, M. G., & Richards, C. S. (1977). An investigation of naturally occurring episodes of self-controlled behaviors. Journal of Counseling Psychology, 24, 178-183.

Perri, M. G., Richards, C. S., & Schultheis, K. (1977). Behavioral self-control and smoking reduction: A study of self-initiated attempts to reduce smoking. Behavior Therapy, 8, 360-365.

Peterson, C. (2000). The future of optimism. American Psychologist, 55, 44-55.

Pham, L. B., & Taylor, S. E. (1999). From thought to action: Effects of process-versus outcome-based mental simulations on performance. Personality and Social Psychology Bulletin, 25, 250-260.

Plimpton, G. Ernest Hemingway. In G. Plimpton (Ed.), Writers at work: The Paris Review interviews (pp. 215-239). New York: Viking.

Polivy, J., & Herman, C. P. (1985). Dieting and bingeing: A causal analysis. American Psychologist, 40, 193-201.

Porter, C., Markus, H., & Nurius, P. S. (1984). Conceptions of possibility among people in crisis. Unpublished manuscript, University of Michigan, cited in Markus & Nurius, 1986.

Pratkanis, A. R. (1992). The cargo-cult science of subliminal persuasion. Skeptical Inquirer, September 1992.

Privette, G., & Landsman, T. (1983). Factor analysis of peak performance: The full use of potential. Journal of Personality and Social Psychology, 44, 195-200.

Prochaska, J. O., & DiClemente, C. C. (1985). Common process of change in smoking, weight control, and psychological distress. In S. Shiffman & T. Wills (Eds.), Coping and substance abuse (pp. 345-363). San Diego, CA: Academic Press.

Prochaska, J. O., & DiClemente, C. C. (1986). Toward a comprehensive model of change. In W. R. Miller & N. Heather (Eds.), Treating addictive behaviors: Processes of change (pp. 3-27). New York: Plenum Press.

Prochaska, J. O., DiClemente, C. C., Norcross, J. C. (1992). In search of how people change: Applications to addictive behaviors. American Psychologist, 47, 1102-1114.

Prochaska, J. O., Norcross, J. C., & DiClemente, C. C. (1994). Changing for good: A revolutionary six-stage program for overcoming bad habits and moving your life positively forward. New York: Avon.

Propst, L. R. (1980). The comparative efficacy of religious and nonreligious imagery for the treatment of mild depression in religious individuals. Cognitive Therapy and Research, 4, 167-178.

Prue, D.M., Keane, T.M., Cornell, J.E., & Foy, D.W. (1979). An analysis of distance variables that affect aftercare attendance. Community Mental Health Journal, 15, 149-154.

Rachlin, H. (1974). Self-control. Behaviorism, 94-107.

Ravizza, K. (1977). Peak experiences in sport. Journal of Humanistic Psychology, 17, 35-40.

Rehm, L. P. (1977). A self-control model of depression. Behavior Therapy, 8, 787-804.

Rehm, L. P. (1982). Self-management in depression. In P. Karoly & F. H. Kanfer (Eds.), Self-management and behavior change: From theory to practice (pp. 522-567). New York: Pergamon Press.

Reich, T., et al. (1987). The family transmission of primary depressive disorder. Journal of Psychiatric Research, 21, 613-624.

Reither, F. (1981). Thinking and acting in complex situations – a study of experts' behavior. Simulation and Games, 12, 125-140.

Reither, F. & Staudel, T. (1985). Thinking and action. In M. Frese & J. Sabini (Eds.), Goal-directed behavior: The concept of action in psychology. Hillsdale, NJ: Erlbaum.

Renner, M. J., & Rosenzweig, M. R. (1987). Enriched and impoverished environments: Effects on brain and behavior. New York: Springer-Verlag.

Repetti, R. L. (1989). Effects of daily workload on subsequent behavior during marital interaction: The roles of social withdrawal and spouse support. Journal of Personality and Social Psychology, 57, 651-659.

Richards, C. S., Perri, M. G., & Gortney, C. (1976). Increasing the maintenance of self-control treatments through faded counselor contact and high information feedback. Journal of Counseling Psychology, 23, 405-406.

Robbins, A. (1986). Unlimited power. New York: Simon and Schuster.

Robins, L., et al. (1984). Lifetime prevalence of specific psychiatric disorders in three sites. Archives of General Psychiatry, 41, 949-958.

Robins, L. N., Helzer, J. E., & Davis, D. H. (1975). Narcotic use in Southeast Asia and afterward: An interview study of 898 Vietnam veterans. Archives of General Psychiatry, 32, 955-961.

Rodriguez, M. L., Mischel, W., & Shoda, Y. (1989). Cognitive person variables in the delay of gratification of older children at risk. Journal of Personality and Social Psychology, 57, 358-367.

Rosen, L. W. (1981). Self-control program in the treatment of obesity. Journal of Behavior Therapy and Experimental Psychiatry, 12, 163-166.

Rosenthal, R., & Rubin, D. B. (1978). Interpersonal expectancy effects: The first 345 studies. Behavioral and Brain Sciences, 3, 377-386.

Rothenberg, A. (1979). The emerging goddess. Chicago: University of Chicago Press.

Ruvolo, A. P. & Markus, H. R. (1992). Possible selves and performance: The power of self-relevant imagery. Social Cognition, 10, 95-124.

Ryan, R. M., & Deci, E. L. (2000). Self-determination theory and the facilitation of intrinsic motivation, social development, and well-being. American Psychologist, 55, 68-78.

Sandifer, B. A., & Buchanan, W. L. (1983). Relationship between adherence and weight loss in a behavioral weight reduction program. Behavior Therapy, 14, 682-688.

Sarafino, E. P. (1990). Health psychology: Biopsychosocial interactions. New York: Wiley.

Sarason, I. G. (1981). Test anxiety, stress, and social support. Journal of Personality, 49, 101-114.

Schachter, S. (1982). Recidivism and self-cure of smoking and obesity. American Psychologist, 37, 436-444.

Schiff, B. B., & Lamon, M. (1989). Inducing emotion by unilateral contraction of facial muscles: A new look at hemispheric specialization and the experience of emotion. Neuropsychologia, 27, 923-935.

Schlenker, B. R., & Leary, M. R. (1982). Social anxiety and self-presentation: A conceptualization and model. Psychological Bulletin, 92, 641-669.

Schlenker, B. R., Phillips, S. T., Boniecki, K. A., & Schlenker, D. R. Championship pressures: Choking or triumphing in one's own territory? Journal of Personality and Social Psychology, 68, 632-643.

Schultheiss, O. C., & Brunstein, J. C. (1999). Goal imagery: Bridging the gap between implicit motives and explicit goals. Journal of Personality, 67, 1-38.

Schunk, D. H. (1984). Enhancing self-efficacy and achievement through rewards and goals: Motivational and informational effects. Journal of Educational Research, 78, 29-34.

Schwartz, R. M. (1986). The internal dialog: On the asymmetry between positive and negative coping thoughts. Cognitive Therapy and Research, 10, 591-605.

Sculley, J. (1987). Odyssey. New York: Harper & Row.

Seidman, L. S., Sevelius, G. G., & Ewald, P. (1984). A cost-effective weight loss program at the worksite. Journal of Occupational Medicine, 26(10), 725-730.

Seligman, M. E. P. (1994). What you can change and what you can't: The ultimate guide to self-improvement. New York: Knopf.

Seligman, M. E. P. (1998). Learned optimism: How to change your mind and your life (2nd ed.). New York: Pocket Books.

Seligman, M., & Elder, G. (1985). Learned helplessness and life span development. In A. Sorenson, F. Weinert, & L. Sherrod (Eds.), Human development and the life course, pp. 377-427. Hillsdale, NJ: Erlbaum.

Sheldon, K. M., & Elliott, A. J. (1998). Not all personal goals are personal: Comparing autonomous reasons as predictors of effort and attainment. Personality and Social Psychology Bulletin, 24, 546-557.

Sheldon, K. M., & Elliott, A. J. (1999). Goal striving, needs satisfaction and longitudinal well-being: The self-concordance model. Journal of Personality and Social Psychology, 76, 486-497.

Sheldon, K. M., & Houser-Marko, L. (2001). Self-concordance, goal attainment and the pursuit of happiness: Can there be an upward spiral? Journal of Personality and Social Psychology, 80, 152-165.

Sheldon, K. M., & Kasser, T. (1998). Pursuing personal goals: Skills enable progress but not all progress is beneficial. Personality and Social Psychology Bulletin, 24, 1319-1331.

Shiffman, S. (1984). Coping with temptations to smoke. Journal of Consulting and Clinical Psychology, 52, 261-267.

Shoda, Y., Mischel, W., & Peake, P. K. (1990). Predicting adolescent cognitive and self-regulatory competencies from preschool delay of gratification: Identifying diagnostic conditions. Developmental Psychology, 26, 978-986.

Silver, R. L., Boon, C., & Stones, M. H. (1983). Searching for meaning in misfortune: Making sense of incest. Journal of Social Issues, 39, 81-102.

Simonton, D. K. (1984). Artistic creativity and interpersonal relationships across and within generations. Journal of Personality and Social Psychology, 46, 1273-1286.

Simonton, D. K. (1992). The social context of career success and course for 2,026 scientists and inventors. Personality and Social Psychology Bulletin, 18, 452-463.

Simonton, D. K. (1994). Greatness: Who makes history and why. New York: Guilford.

Simonton, D. K. (2000). Creativity: Cognitive, personal, development and social aspects. American Psychologist, 55, 151-158.

Singer, J. A., & Salovey, P. (1996). Motivatved memory: Self-defining memories, goals, and affect regulation. In L. L. Martin & A. Tesser (Eds.), Striving and feeling: Interactions among goals, affect and self-regulation (pp. 229-250). Mahwah, NJ: Lawrence Erlbaum Associates.

Sisson, R.W., & Azrin, N.H. (1986). Family-member involvement to intitiate and promote treatment of problem drinkers. Behavior Therapy and Experimental Psychiatry, 17, 15-21.

Sisson, R.W. & Mallams, J.H. (1981). The use of systematic encouragement and community access procedures to increase attendance at Alcoholics Anonymous and Al-Anon meetings. American Journal of Drug and Alcohol Abuse, 8, 371-376.

Skinner, B. F. (1948). "Superstition" in the pigeon. Journal of Experimental Psychology, 38, 168-172.

Smith, M. L., Glass, G. V., & Miller, T. I. (1980). Benefits of psychotherapy. Baltimore: Johns Hopkins University Press.

Smyth, J. M. (1998). Written emotional expression: Effect sizes, outcome types, and moderating variables. Journal of Consulting and Clinical Psychology, 66, 174-184.

Sobell, L. C., Sobell, M. B., Kozlowski, L. T., & Tonneatto, T. (1990). Alcohol or tobacco research versus alcohol and tobacco research. British Journal of Addiction, 85, 263-269

Spanier, G. B., & Casto, R. F. (1979). Adjustment to separation and divorce: A qualitative analysis. In G. Levinger & O. C. Moles (Eds.), Divorce and separation: Contexts, causes and consequences (pp. 211-227). New York: Basic Books.

Stall, R., & Biernacki, P. (1986). Spontaneous remission from the problematic use of substances: An inductive model derived from a comparative analysis of the alcohol, opiate, tobacco, and food/obesity literatures. International Journal of the Addictions, 21, 1-23.

Stanley, T. J. (2000). The millionaire mind. Kansas City: Andrews McMeel Publishing.

Steele, C. M., & Josephs, R. A. (1990). Alcohol myopia: Its prized and dangerous effects. American Psychologist, 45, 921-933.

Steinberg, S. A., & Yalch, R. F. (1978). When eating begets buying: The effects of food samples on obese and nonobese shoppers. Journal of Consumer Research, 4, 243-246.

Stephens, T. (1988). Physical activity and mental health in the United States and Canada: Evidence from four population surveys. Preventative Medicine, 17, 35-47.

Stock, J., & Cervone, D. (1990). Proximal goal setting and self-regulatory processes. Cognitive Therapy and Research, 14, 483-489.

Stockwell, T. (1985). Stress and alcohol. Stress Medicine, 1, 209-215.

Storms, M. D., & Nisbett, R. E. (1970). Insomnia and the attribution process. Journal of Personality and Social Psychology, 16, 319-328.

Strack, S., Blaney, P. H., Gannellen, R. J., & Coyne, J. C. (1985). Pessimistic self-preoccupation, performance deficits, and depression. Journal of Personality and Social Psychology, 49, 1076-1085.

Strack, F., Martin. L. L., & Stepper, S. (1988). Inhibiting and facilitating conditions of the human smile: A nonobtrusive test of the facial feedback hypothesis. Journal of Personality and Social Psychology, 54, 768-777.

Strickland, B. R. (1978). Internal-external expectancies and health-related behaviors. Journal of Consulting and Clinical Psychology, 46, 1192-1211.

Suefield, P., & Rank, A. D. (1976). Revolutionary leaders: Long-term success of as a function of changes in conceptual complexity. Journal of Personality and Social Psychology, 34, 169-178.

Suinn, R. M. (1983). Imagery and sports. In A. A. Sheikh (Eds.), Imagery: Current theory, research, and application (507-534). New York: Wiley.

Suinn, R. M. (1987). Psychological approaches to performance enhancement. In M. Asken & J. May (Eds.), Sports psychology: The psychological health of the athlete (pp. 41-57). New York: Spectrum.

Tabak, L. (1996). If your goal is success, don't consult these gurus. Fast Company, December 1996, p. 38.

Tart, C. T. (1969). Altered states of consciousness. New York: Wiley.

Tavris, C. (1989). Anger: The misunderstood emotion. New York: Touchstone.

Taylor, S. E. (1983). Adjustment to threatening events: A theory of cognitive adaptation. American Psychologist, 38, 1161-1173.

Taylor, S. E. (1989). Positive illusions: Creative self-deception and the healthy mind. New York: Basic Books.

Taylor, S. E., Lichtman, R. R., & Wood, J. V. (1984). Attributions, beliefs about control, and adjustment to breast cancer. Journal of Personality and Social Psychology, 46, 489-502.

Tetlock, P. E. (1981). Pre- to post-election shifts in presidential rhetoric: Impression management or cognitive adjustment? Journal of Personality and Social Psychology, 41, 207-212.

Thompson, S. C. (1981). Will it hurt less if I can control it? A complex answer to a simple question. Psychological Bulletin, 90, 89-101.

Tice, D. M., Bratlavsky, E., & Baumeister, R. F. (2001). Emotional distress regulation takes precedence over impulse control: If you feel bad, do it! Journal of Personality and Social Psychology, 80, 53-67.

Tiechman, Y. (1966). The stress of coping with the unknown regarding a significant family member. In I. G. Sarason & D. Spielberger (Eds.), Stress and anxiety (Vol. 2, pp. 243-257). New York: Wiley.

Thayer, R. E. (1987). Energy, tiredness, and tension effects of a sugar snack versus moderate exercise. Journal of Personality and Social Psychology, 52, 119-125.

Throll, D. A. (1981). Transcendental meditation and progressive relaxation: Their psychological effects. Journal of Clinical Psychology, 37, 776-781.

Tom, G. (1983). Effect of deprivation on the grocery shopping behavior of obese and non-obese consumers. International Journal of Obesity, 7, 307-311.

Tubbs, M. E. (1986). Goal setting: A meta-analytic examination of the evidence. Journal of Applied Psychology, 71, 474-483.

Tziner, A., & Kopelman, R. (1988). Effects of rating format on goal-setting dimensions: A field experiment. Journal of Applied Psychology, 73, 323-326.

Van Hook. E., & Higgins, E. T. (1988). Self-related problems beyond the self-concept: Motivational consequences of discrepant self-guides. Journal of Personality and Social Psychology, 55, 625-633.

Vaughn, D. (1986). Uncoupling. New York: Oxford University Press.

de Volder, M. L., & Lens, W. (1982). Academic achievement and future time perspective as a cognitive-motivational concept. Journal of Personality and Social Psychology, 42, 566-571.

Vergano, D. (2001). As many opinions as treatments in tobacco fight. USA Today, June 19, 2001. (summarizes government data and scientific research; available at http://www.usatoday.com/news/healthscience/health/2001-06-19-smoking-cessation.htm)

Volberg, R. A., & Steadman, H. J. (1989). Prevalence estimates of pathological gambling in New Jersey and Maryland. American Journal of Psychiatry, 146, 1618-1620.

Wadden, T. A., Brownell, K. D., & Foster, G. D. (2002). Obesity: Responding to the global epidemic. Journal of Consulting and Clinical Psychology, 70, 510-525.

Wadden, T. A., & Litizia, K. A. (1992). Predictors of attrition and weight loss in patients treated by moderate and caloric restriction. In T. A. Wadden & T. B. VanItallie (Eds.), Treatment of the seriously obese patient (pp. 290-330). New York: Guilford.

Wallace, I., & Pear, J. J. (1977). Self-control techniques of famous novelists. Journal of Applied Behavior Analysis, 10, 515-525.

Ward, C. H., & Eisler, R. M. (1987). Type A behavior, achievement striving, and a dysfunctional self-evaluation system. Journal of Personality and Social Psychology, 53, 318-326.

Watson, D. L., & Tharp, R. G. (1993). Self-directed behavior: Self-modification for personal adjustment. Pacific Grove, CA: Brooks/Cole.

Watson, J. B., & Rayner, R. (1920). Conditioned emotional responses. Journal of Experimental Psychology, 3, 1-14.

Wegner, D. M., Shortt, J. W., Blake, A. W., & Page, M. S. (1990). The suppression of exciting thoughts. Journal of Personality and Social Psychology, 53, 5-13.

Weinberger, J. L. (1994). Can personality change? In T. F. Heatherton & J. L. Weinberger (Eds.), Can personality change? Washington, DC: American Psychological Association.

Wenzlaff, R. (1993). The mental control of depression. In D. M. Wagner & J. W. Pennebaker (Eds.), Handbook of mental control. Englewood Cliffs, NJ: Prentice Hall.

Wheeler, R. J., Munz, D. C., & Jain, A. (1990). Life goals and general well-being. Psychological Reports, 66, 307-312.

Wilson, T. D., Laser, P. S, & Stone, J. I. (1982). Judging the predictors of one's own mood: Accuracy and the use of shared theories. Journal of Experimental Social Psychology, 18, 537-556.

Wilson, T. D., & Linville, P. W. (1982). Improving the academic performance of college freshmen: Attribution therapy revisited. Journal of Personality and Social Psychology, 42, 367-376.

Wine, J. (1971). Test anxiety and direction of attention. Psychological Bulletin, 26, 92-104.

Wood, R. & Bandura, A. (1989). Impact of conceptions of ability on self-regulatory mechanisms and complex decision-making. Journal of Personality and Social Psychology, 56, 407-415.

Wood, R. E., Mento, A. J., & Locke, E. A. (1987). Task complexity as a moderator of goal effects: A meta-analysis. Journal of Applied Psychology, 72, 416-425.

Wood, Y. R., Hardin, M., & Wong, E. (1994, January). Social network influences on smoking cessation. Paper presented at the meeting of the Western Psychological Association, Los Angeles.

Worthington, E. L. (1979). Behavioral self-control and the contract problem. Teaching of Psychology, 6, 91-94.

Wortman, C. B., & Silver, R. C. (1989). The myths of coping with loss. Journal of Consulting and Clinical Psychology, 57, 349-357.

Wright, J., & Mischel, W. (1982). Influence of affect on cognitive social learning person variables. Journal of Personality and Social Psychology, 43, 901-914.

Youdin, R., & Hemmes, N. S. (1978). The urge to overeat: The initial link. Journal of Behavior Therapy and Experimental Psychiatry, 9, 339-342.

Zaleski, Z. (1987). Behavioral effects for self-set goals for different time ranges. International Journal of Psychology, 22, 17-38.

Zimmerman, R. S., Warheit, G. J., Ulbrigh, P. M., & Auth, J. B. (1990). The relationship between alcohol use and attempts and success at smoking cessation. Addictive Behaviors, 15, 197-207.

Zuckerman, H. (1977). Scientific elite. New York: Free Press.

Zullow, H. M., Oettingen, G., Peterson, & Seligman, M. E. P. (1988). Pessimistic explanatory style in the historical record: CAVing LBJ, presidential candidates, and East versus West Berlin. American Psychologist, 43, 673-682.

Zullow, H. M., & Seligman, M. E. P. (1990). Pessimistic rumination predicts defeat of presidential candidates, 1900 to 1984. Psychological Inquiry, 1, 52-61.

Notes

Notes

Notes